JN164309

Unintended Consequences in Transitional Justice

Unintended Consequences in Transitional Justice

Social Recovery at the Local Level

Toshihiro Abe

Kyoto University Press

LYNNE RIENNER PUBLISHERS

The publication of this book is funded by the Japan Society for the Promotion of Science (JSPS), Project #18HP5262, as Grant-in-Aid for Publication of Scientific Research Results.

© 2018 by Lynne Rienner Publishers, Inc. All rights reserved

Published in the United States of America in 2018 by
Lynne Rienner Publishers, Inc.
1800 30th Street, Boulder, Colorado 80301
www.rienner.com

and in the United Kingdom by
Lynne Rienner Publishers, Inc.
Gray's Inn House, 127 Clerkenwell Road, London EC1 5DB

ISBN 978-1-62637-744-8 (Lynne Rienner Publishers)

Published in Japan by
Kyoto University Press
Yoshida-South Campus, Kyoto University
69 Yoshida-Konoe-Cho, Sakyo-ku
Kyoto 606-8315
www.kyoto-up.or.jp

ISBN 978-4-8140-0169-9 (Kyoto University Press)

Library of Congress Cataloging-in-Publication Data
Names: Abe, Toshihiro, author.
Title: Unintended consequences in transitional justice : social recovery at the local level / Toshihiro Abe.
Description: Boulder, Colorado : Lynne Rienner Publishers, Inc., [2018] | Includes bibliographical references and index.
Identifiers: LCCN 2018010689 (print) | LCCN 2018026503 (ebook) | ISBN 9781626377448 (e-book) | ISBN 9781626377448 (hardcover : alk. paper)
Subjects: LCSH: Transitional justice. | Truth commissions. | Peace-building. | Reconciliation—Political aspects.
Classification: LCC JC571 (ebook) | LCC JC571 .A1196 2018 (print) | DDC 320.1/1—dc23
LC record available at https://lccn.loc.gov/2018010689

British Cataloguing in Publication Data
A Cataloguing in Publication record for this book
is available from the British Library.

Printed and bound in the United States of America

The paper used in this publication meets the requirements
of the American National Standard for Permanence of
Paper for Printed Library Materials Z39.48-1992.

5 4 3 2 1

*To the memory of my father,
Toshiharu Abe*

Contents

Acknowledgments ix

1 Unintended Consequences in Transitional Justice 1
2 Recognizing a Transitional Society 21
3 Goodwill and Ideals in the Face of Resistance 59
4 Going Beyond Official Mobilization 93
5 Challenging the Official Scenario 133
6 From Nation Building to Achieving a Dynamic Equilibrium 169
7 Planning for Unplanned Social Recovery 193

List of Acronyms 209
Bibliography 211
Index 227
About the Book 241

Acknowledgments

The initial scene in this book opens with the tension I experienced at a public hearing of the South African Truth and Reconciliation Commission in 1997. At the time, I neither recognized what was happening before my eyes nor knew where my experience would take me in the years that followed. A trip without a map can be fraught with anxiety, surprises, and accidents, yet my own journey has also brought about fortunate encounters with people who guided me into a deep intellectual dimension as they informed, instructed, or even challenged and opposed me. I sincerely thank all those individuals who directed my thoughts as I deployed them in this book.

I owe a great debt of gratitude to Matsuda Motoji in the Department of Sociology at Kyoto University for his advice and unfailing encouragement from the outset of my research. Shigeharu Tanabe recruited me for his research team, although I had no knowledge of Indochina issues, opening my eyes to a comparative approach.

In South Africa, thoughts expressed by Charles Villa-Vicencio and Erik Doxtader directed my research toward a paradox of the reconciliation process. Kwesi Kwaa Prah has been my mentor, embodying the way an academic can maintain passion and rhythm over decades. Zenzile Khoisan is my amicable colleague as well as a source of perpetual inspiration.

I particularly wish to convey thanks to the memory of Vong Em Sam An, in addition to other Cambodian colleagues at the Extraordinary Chambers in the Court of Cambodia and local nongovernmental organizations, for insights into the political landscape.

The basis of the empirical description in the book, including official data supplemented by local interpretation, has been shaped by input from many South Africans and Cambodians, some of whom would prefer not to be named publicly. I dare not attempt to mention all the friends who gave me valuable suggestions and feedback, although I acknowledge their enormous contributions.

Otani University allowed me a research sabbatical that made it possible to extend my field experience to Rwanda, Bosnia, and Serbia. A large part of the manuscript was written during my sabbatical at the Department of Sociology at the University of Oxford. Leigh Payne and Federico Varese generously welcomed me into their network and offered me a place to work. In particular, Payne's sharp analysis has deeply influenced my theoretical argument.

My career, including successive field trips, has greatly benefited from the Japan Society for Promotion of Science research grants (JSPS grant numbers 22683012; 26380718; 16H06318; 23221012; 23401050; 17H01648; 18HP5262). Earlier versions of the arguments in Chapters 3, 4, and 6 appeared in "Reconciliation as Process or Catalyst: Understanding the Concept in a Post-Conflict Society," *Comparative Sociology* 11(6); "Perceptions of the Khmer Rouge Tribunal Among Cambodians: Implications of the Proceedings of Public Forums Held by a Local NGO," *South East Asia Research* 21(1); and "Ebb and Flow of Assemblage in Cambodian NGO Movements: Diaspora Returnees' Human Rights Initiatives on the Khmer Rouge Tribunals," in Shigeharu Tanabe, ed., *Communities of Potential: Social Assemblages in Thailand and Beyond* (Chiang Mai, Thailand: Silkworm Books, 2016). I appreciate the publishers' permission to use revised versions of these articles.

Tetsuya Suzuki of Kyoto University Press has consistently helped me with insightful comments regarding this project.

I especially appreciate the guidance of Lynne Rienner in completing the manuscript. Nicole Moore deserves my thanks for her friendly assistance, and I also laud Shena Redmond and Michele Wynn for their editing.

I thank my family for their unwavering support. I have dedicated this book to the memory of my father, Toshiharu Abe, and only wish I could have heard his comments on it.

1

Unintended Consequences in Transitional Justice

The people surrounding me were complaining in angry tones while a man on the stage was desperately refuting the commissioner's interrogation. Interpreters at a microphone booth had abandoned their duty to translate the proceedings into English, escalating the dispute in Zulu. The chairperson was begging the increasingly agitated audience to display order and discipline. I strained forward, making my best attempt to understand this chaos, but it was hopeless.

This was a public hearing by South Africa's Truth and Reconciliation Commission (TRC), held in Duduza, a small suburb of Johannesburg, in February 1997. The hall, the size of a school gymnasium, did not have enough space for everyone. If you were lucky enough to find a seat, you had to stay put for the next few hours. Six large, old fans were stirring the wet and sticky air. Over the din, I shouted to the man sitting next to me, "What are they fighting about?" "The man may have told a lie, or something similar to a lie!" he shouted back. According to the transcript of the proceedings, which I obtained later, the speaker had been interrogated by the commissioners regarding his exaggerated story and had repetitively offered lame excuses.

The hearing went on into the afternoon. The temperature rose so high the six old fans couldn't cope anymore. The beginning of February in Johannesburg is midsummer. My back itched, perhaps because my sweaty shirt was clinging to my skin. The mixed body odors in the close air dimmed my brain while my ears caught the sad, sometimes absurd stories.

The commissioners' cross-examination continued for a while, and then one speaker stopped answering. After a moment, she burst into tears. This mother was telling the story of her son, who had just begun attending meetings of the smallest unit of an anti-apartheid organization. According to her testimony, he had been shot dead. The mother had not been present at the time of the incident and wanted to know the truth about her son's death. She was a victim, too. The hundreds of people in the audience fell silent. The awkward noise of the old fans echoed in the hall. I could hear quiet sniffling in the audience. The chairperson announced a short break.

In October 1998, TRC chairperson Desmond Tutu handed five volumes of official reports to South African president Nelson Mandela amid a blaze of flashbulbs from jostling journalists. Although the TRC activities were still ongoing, the completed reports, containing specific episodes from the lives of victims and official data, were published. The photo image from the event at which the reports were released—comprising one Nobel Peace Prize laureate who had supervised the project and another who had supported the project—was widely circulated, becoming a visual icon of the apparent success of national reconciliation in South Africa.

However, the public event at which this photograph was taken received scant attention from other political actors in South Africa. More precisely, the representatives from all the main political parties boycotted the launch of this publication. Even the African National Congress (ANC), headed by President Mandela, did not send anyone to the venue. Foreign media paid little attention to this backstory. As such, the media's coverage of the public release of the TRC reports actually worked as what Daniel Boorstin (1961) called a *pseudo-event*. When the commission initially embarked on its work, Chairperson Tutu declared, "We, South Africans, will reconcile with each other." But now Tutu had changed his assertive tone to one of suggestion, saying that the TRC would promote reconciliation among the citizenry. In a survey conducted by Market Research Africa in 1998, two-thirds of South African respondents said that the TRC had worsened racial relationships rather than promoting national reconciliation. The ex-president of the apartheid era, P. W. "Crocodile" Botha, had completely refused to cooperate with the commission when summoned, and the court could not execute persuasive justice in this matter. In such an atmosphere, Mandela said the following in his speech at the ceremony: "Many of us will have reservations about aspects of what is contained in these five volumes. All are free to make comment on it and indeed we invite you to do so. . . . The Commission was not required to muster a definitive and comprehensive history of the past three decades."[1]

What does this message mean in essence? How should we accept its meaning? Is it an indirect expression designed to cover or explain away undesirable outcomes? When Mandela passed away at the end of 2014, many media outlets named his main political accomplishment as achieving national reconciliation in post-apartheid South Africa. However, none of the people applauding this purported achievement made any reference to his nuanced speech at the ceremony in October 1998.

In August 2007, almost ten years after the above episode, I was a passenger on a motorbike taxi in Phnom Penh. It was moving fast in the wrong lane. The roads in Phnom Penh at that time still had no median dividing the two directions of traffic, so motorbikes traveled in both traffic lanes. I was so nervous about crashing that I couldn't stop sending eye signals in vain to the drivers coming at us from the opposite direction. I was on my way to the office of a nongovernmental organization (NGO) headed by a Cambodian returnee lawyer from the United States. The NGO had scheduled a public hearing the next day in a town several hours away by car from Phnom Penh. The hearing was obviously related to the Khmer Rouge Tribunal (the Extraordinary Chambers in the Courts of Cambodia or ECCC), which was in its preparatory stage, and some officers such as prosecutors, lawyers, and persons in charge of public relations (PR) at the court had been invited as special guests. The session provided an opportunity for local attendees to question those official figures, raising even such fundamental issues as why the former cadres needed to be tried, at great public expense and while the social infrastructure remained inadequate, and why those foreign actors who had unquestionably served as proponents of the Khmer Rouge (KR) regime were not being dealt with in the court process.

I was surprised to witness these straightforward interactions among participants in a social context where political matters had always been treated in a sensitive manner. The court officials, in my view, answered the questions sincerely. The court had adopted a hybrid system that included both domestic and foreign elements in terms of legal regulations and participants. Many foreign observers expected that this application of an international judiciary would be a model case of the embodiment of the concept of local ownership. Foreign resources had been donated not only to the court body but also to the various local NGOs, which had spontaneously proceeded with their agenda of outreach activities to raise local awareness of this justice event. The staff gathered at those organizations were mostly young people enrolled in university studies. They were attempting to lift the heavy lid off Cambodian history by using their English competence and information technology skills to cooperate with foreign staff, as well as calling on their fieldwork research skills learned through university courses. All these were new elements in the local context as the project sought to generate information about the past. The young people's passion was intermingled with the institutional uniqueness of the court; in combination, the two factors caused observers to expect a new perspective on the transitional justice project. The fact that more than 50 percent of the local population was under age thirty supported such an expectation.

Ten years have passed since my first experience of traveling fast in the wrong lane in Phnom Penh. Medians have recently been mushrooming in towns under the strict eyes of "diligent" police. The urban landscape has been visibly improving, moving away from the memory of the past conflict. But the same level of improvement in the justice field has not been visible. During my successive visits to Phnom Penh, I have realized that the number of local newspaper articles on the court and its activities has decreased. I will never forget the scene that confronted me in the ECCC courtroom one day in August 2016. The afternoon session was scheduled to resume at 1:30 p.m. at the court venue, located in a former army base. I caught a ride on a tuk-tuk (auto rickshaw) on schedule, but I was detoured by the attractive smell of high-quality durian fruit from Kampong Cham, which is found exclusively during this season, and then an unexpectedly escalated traffic jam ended my hopes of reaching the session on time. I stood in front of the court building at 2:15 p.m., with the strong smell of durian still on my moustache. When the security guard stopped me as I tried to enter the courtroom, I regretted my surrender to olfactory temptation, remembering a sticker often witnessed in Southeast Asia that reads "No durian." But the reason for the guard's action was simply that the court proceeding would be adjourning in a few minutes for the next break.

There was seating provided under the tent outside the court building, and many high school students, who must have been brought there by their teachers as part of their social studies or history class, were chatting and idling their time away. After a while, the time came for them to leave and they pleasantly departed the court premises as if birds had fled from a cage.

When the break began, I entered the courtroom—and I was shocked to discover that there were no spectators inside the auditorium. Numerous lights in the ceiling were shining brilliantly, reflected in the bulletproof glass designed to guard against a terrorist attack. The auditorium of 482 seats felt tranquil. I was caught in a momentary illusion that I was the latecomer to the concert hall. It seemed like I must have missed the performance on the stage. Then a dim figure on a corner seat moved and got up from a crouching position. That hippie-like man seemed to have sunk into an unintentional nap, in keeping with the mood in the auditorium. Two guards were watching us intently; they had nothing else to do. When the chimes announced the resumption of the session, one woman who was monitoring the court process for an NGO rushed in. The invited judges filed into their observation room with its bulletproof glass, and the stage became active. I was again shocked in that desolate auditorium because I remembered how the local crowd filled the seats with expectations for, and serious disputes with, the ECCC. I could see those hopes and disputes were already part of the past, just floating around the auditorium as a sort of afterimage, even though the court process was still ongoing.

Destined to Fail?

I have thought back on my memories of watching the transitions in South Africa and Cambodia while seeking to develop a framework or paradigm by which I can arrange the bulk of the data, episodes, and information on past instances of transitional justice (TJ). South Africa adopted a truth commission (TC), whereas Cambodia used international tribunals. The two were quite different in form, yet they shared a common character, especially in relation to the social reactions that they aroused.

What is this commonality? Is it the significance of victim empowerment? Or perhaps the need to create cooperative networks with local NGOs? Is it the perils of scarce resources? The need for substantial local ownership and international support? One could justifiably propose any of these as plausible answers. Without doubt, all these elements compose the main difficulties that any TJ attempt must face.

However, there is still another way of answering the commonality question. Both cases present the cycle of an initial stage of elation and expectation, often amplified by the media, followed by the appearance of unpredictable obstacles, frustration, and fatigue in prolonged programs, and then disappointment and despondency at the final stage, with unfinished business remaining at numerous impasses. Is this answer too pessimistic when reviewing a currently popular area within post-conflict policymaking? It is restricted, mainly, by what I have observed and experienced in South Africa and Cambodia. However, considering that the essence of this answer is the gap between the initial expectation and the perception at the end of the program, transitional justice literatures on other regions suggest that this retrospective picture seems to be shared not only by locals but also by other fieldworkers who have engaged in researching TJ for a substantial length of time. Both the truth commission and the international judiciary have been typical options in the field of post-conflict social rebuilding. If these options from the past are observed retrospectively as illustrated, what assessment then needs to be provided? Should another new option, besides TJ, be invented? Alternatively, can a different understanding of past cases still be submitted? This book adopts the latter standpoint.

TJ is a dynamic process. Each TJ project is unique and contextually different from another TJ program in another region. Factors of both space and time affect how a particular institution is formed. TJ may change its approach over several years of operation in the face of local political challenges. People's reputations and observers' evaluations may change in the course of diverse and unexpected responses by locals. In such unforeseeable circumstances, the greater the expectation of goal attainment, the deeper the resulting despondency when the goal is not attained.

The literature on TJ cases, particularly the studies that most keenly observed locals' reactions, suggests that TJ efforts seem destined to be criticized as failures, regardless of the context in which they are implemented. Critical analyses have not been limited to the South African Truth and Reconciliation Commission and the Cambodian special tribunals.

Reports from Latin America, West Africa, and Southeast Asia have all described incomplete achievements and unexpected obstacles arising in the course of official activities.

As far as adopting an analytical approach to the framework of the success-failure debate, it is easy to reach the conclusion that TJ efforts are destined to fail. Am I too critical of institutional efforts to reconstruct a society in political transition?

I have walked over to a bookshelf to look for past works with which I can compare my experiences. Séverine Autesserre's *Peaceland* is before my eyes.

Autesserre, who worked in Kosovo, the Democratic Republic of Congo, and Afghanistan for fifteen years on various peace-building missions, looked for explanations of ineffective peace building. Peace building is a different field from transitional justice; however, a scheme that enhances local conditions of social order and stability through international intervention may well be compared to transitional justice, particularly in the case of internationally supported TJ projects.

Autesserre raises the thorny question, "Why do peace interventions regularly fail to reach their full potential?" She answers it by examining the standard but counterproductive patterns of international peace builders' initiatives in their "practices, habits, and narratives that shape international efforts on the ground" (Autesserre 2014:3). The vast majority of foreign interventionists "arrive with little to no understanding of their locale of deployment" because they "usually value technical proficiency." When hired, they are selected on the basis of their prior experience or related knowledge in the field of international intervention. However, they need to make the environment for their mission comprehensible, so "they tend to use prevailing but overly simplified narratives as substitutes for more nuanced explanations of dynamics on the ground" (Autesserre 2014:3). Based on such biased and distorted knowledge, the following undesired outcomes are predictable:

> They regularly misunderstand the phenomena they are trying to address, such as the causes of and potential solutions to violence. As a result, although some projects eventually better the lives of local people, others fail to bring about significant improvements, and some even compound the problems that the interveners originally sought to address. (Autesserre 2014:3)

Although Autesserre's field is international peace building, her observations about interventions that have insufficient influence on local conditions or even counterproductive results are logically applicable to any other context characterized by tension and friction between a global, universalistic mode of humanitarian goodwill and local complexities. An international judicial initiative is akin to a peace-building mission in this regard.

Autesserre's insight is highly instructive for related international operations in exploring why interveners perpetuate even those modes of operation that they know to be counterproductive (Autesserre 2014:5), an issue that we will visit in greater detail in Chapter 3. Institutional conditions surrounding and affecting the interveners' modus operandi are pressured by a requirement, basically from donors—the underwriters of such projects, for example, the United Nations (UN) or leading states such as the United States and Germany to demonstrate positive local change in a limited time span. This naturally leads an operation to pursue an efficient blueprint—one that contains the seeds of future confusion and fosters the ebb and flow of expectations as observed in past TJ cases. Autesserre's probe provides a theoretically critical question about how to assess the consequences of such an intervention, which began with a misunderstanding and was directed by requirements made, for the most part, by the international community. Put differently, such recognition tells us that even a seemingly positive outcome in the local context might have resulted from factors other than the intervention itself. A proper analytical orientation in such a context should not be asking how the result relates to the officially appealed objective of the program but, instead, should be focusing on the process of interaction between interventional initiatives and local reactions. Taking this position even allows us to consider ironically positive outcomes, despite the program starting with a misunderstanding of the local situation.

There is another useful guide on my bookshelf. The theme of inevitable failure of an official project at the macro level has been more widely explored by James Scott in *Seeing like a State* (1998). Although Scott makes no reference to any TJ cases, the instances covered in the book all share the basic intention to create a new society or, at least, to restructure the essential meaning of social life at a macro level. In the implementation process of such a state project, the society is placed in a state of political transition. TJ is comparable in that way to the state projects in Scott's book.

In the framework of a "high-modern state project," which aims to sweep out a local context and replace it with a desirable social space, Scott traces urban planning in Brasilia, the Great Leap Forward in China, collectivization in the Soviet Union, and compulsory villagization in Tanzania, Mozambique, and Ethiopia. The progress of these state projects has historically followed the same trajectory, from spectacles of elation at the beginning to unexpected diversion at the end. Scott notes that although all these "great utopian social engineering schemes of the twentieth century" (1998:4) had "quite genuine egalitarian and often socialist impulses" (1998:346) and carried "the banner of progress, emancipation, and reform" (1998:343), they have failed, even qualifying as tragedies.

The sense of tragedy resonated with my mood after my visit to the empty courtroom at the Khmer Rouge Tribunal. Scott chose the term *tragedy* to describe an unfortunate encounter between a "genuine desire to improve the human condition" and "a fatal flaw" (1998:342). The fatal flaw is recognized as embedded in the framing of a utopian picture drawn by a designer of a state project from the beginning, as well as in the steps of implementing a social-engineering project. Valuing the *simplification* and *legibility* of an object (forest, urban space, large-scale farm, or people at large) from a supervising position with faith in scientific and technological solutions, these social-engineering projects have excluded local practical skills, diversity, buffers against uncertain environmental and human change, and, in general, local knowledge. Historically, the end of these projects has always been divergence from the planned goal—in other words, failure.

Just skimming the surface of this argument could give the impression that Scott has merely repeated the general criticisms of modernism, or modernization in general, while prioritizing the people's narrow-sighted contextual needs or their irrational orientation toward their accustomed lives. However, his insight goes much further. He inquires into the complex and mutually dependent relationship between a state project and local responses. He contemplates what will appear after a "tragedy" has occurred. Even though "the planned 'scientific city' in Brasilia was experienced as a social failure, . . . paradoxically, the failure of the designed city was often averted . . . by practical improvisations and illegal acts that were entirely outside the plan" (Scott 1998:309). Scott then adds an abstract observation about the nature of the modern social order: "Formal order, to be explicit, is always and to some considerable degree parasitic on informal processes, which the formal scheme does not recognize, without which it could not exist, and which it alone cannot create or maintain" (1998:310).

As I read, the fog in my memory started to lift. A planned goal may not be achieved, but an unplanned mending could occur through informal initiatives. This possibility implies that one should not be unduly pessimistic about a state project's negative appearance or surface messiness in the public space. Rather, we should embrace a more complicated reality. Despite my critical observations on past institutional TJ cases, I have not been able to abandon an overall sense of the positive influence of TJ on the affected society. The explanation, I believe, is that the formal "failure" of a state-planned social-engineering project has often been compensated by unplanned informal practices that are not officially recognized for their own identity or political legitimacy, but these informal engagements have brought the public arena into an unexpectedly stable status.

Scott makes significant use of the word "often" here. Such a strange harmony cannot be expected or calculated in *any* circumstances where a modern state project has been executed. And the conditions or specific mechanisms that lead to such an unplanned and unexpected cooperation or continuity between a state project—or even a perfect ruin of the project—and the positive work of local actors cannot easily be prescribed.

My contemplation goes on. The passages cited above from *Seeing like a State* remind me of a conversation with a South African journalist who had worked for the TRC in the late 1990s as an investigating officer.

After my visit to Phnom Penh, I flew to Cape Town to meet this journalist, arriving after an eighteen-hour flight, my head blurred with jet lag. Our main reason for meeting was to discuss the racial and ethnic issues in post-apartheid South Africa, especially in the post-TRC period. I have known this journalist since the time of the TRC in the late 1990s and knew him to be a constant critic of the organization, even though he was once a staff member.

I had in mind a question about public engagement with the TRC and was concerned that he would dismiss the question as outdated. Contrary to my concern, he nodded and began describing a series of people's autonomous actions aimed at social rebuilding that had been unexpectedly spotted in the previous few years. He gave the following examples: a civil-society organization had caused the government to open the confidential documents of the TRC; a victim-support group, organized to accompany the work of the TRC, had filed lawsuits on the responsibility of foreign actors in the apartheid era, despite the former Mbeki government's official refusal to support it; a unit of local government had begun exhumations, even though the local branch of the ruling party was opposed to this; and a university archive had proceeded independently with research on the various stakeholders of the TRC and had made the information widely available. These were, in his words, totally unforeseen movements arising from TRC activities. I even caught a slightly positive tone in his voice.

The TRC has been criticized before, during, and after its work. Critics have included South African locals, foreign observers, and even organization insiders such as this journalist. Having aroused great expectations, the TRC would naturally be criticized for not fulfilling its promise. Yet this journalist's comments illustrated an unexpected conversion of the multitude of criticisms of the TRC into a source of ideas for local self-recovery initiatives. Few South African locals express unconditional agreement with the notion that the TRC has promoted national reconciliation. Given such local responses, a critic could possibly add the TRC to Scott's list of state project failures. However, the above examples vividly resonate with the other aspect of his insight: unplanned informal reactions may transform the failures or insufficiencies of social-engineering projects, bringing about a new balance in public order. Still, these local reactions were unplanned by the TRC, so it is not precisely proper to call them effects, outcomes, or consequences of official projects. Yet they are not unconnected to the institutional initiative, so an influence can be recognized, even though they were not planned and have only gradually been recognized in the years after the end of the official program.

Scott's phrase "planning for the unplanned" (1998:142) will be the compass for this book, which raises questions such as the following. Is planning for the unplanned possible? How can we recognize an unplanned result? What is a positive sign of the unplanned? With these tricky questions to guide us, we will move beyond the simple evaluative dichotomy of success or failure when considering the local influences of a TJ project.

What Is Transitional Justice?

The TJ field is expanding. As mentioned above, I have maintained a comparative view of TJ cases, especially with regard to the cyclical ebb and flow of changing expectations and evaluation of official activities through the course of establishing an organization, implementing programs, and reflection after the work is done.

Yet even this flexible approach, which takes into account the dynamic nature of the TJ phenomenon, does not exactly fit the trend in TJ studies, concerning the options the term *TJ* designates. Hence, the use of the term in this volume needs to be clarified.

Like any other term that identifies fields of practice or academic disciplines that are still developing, TJ remains ambiguous in character. For example, if you ask several scholars or practitioners when a transition can be considered complete, you will receive different answers. Therefore, the direct question "What is TJ?" is inevitably changed into the indirect question "How have scholars and practitioners used and defined the term so far?"

It is generally agreed that the epithet "transitional" refers to a state moving away from a nondemocratic, violent political status involving armed conflict or an authoritarian dictatorship, but the direction in which the transition is supposed to be moving remains contentious (Dancy 2010:370–371). Consequently, scholars and practitioners have offered various interpretations of the term *transitional state*.

According to Ruti Teitel's classical definition, TJ is "the conception of justice associated with periods of political change, characterized by legal responses to confront the wrongdoings of repressive predecessor regimes" (Teitel 2003:69). Such a definition excludes the Truth and Reconciliation Commission. On the other hand, a 2004 UN report defined TJ, including the TRC, as the

> full range of processes and mechanisms associated with a society's attempts to come to terms with a legacy of large-scale past abuses in order to ensure accountability, serve justice, and achieve reconcilia-

tion. These may include judicial and non-judicial mechanisms with differing levels of international involvement (or none at all) and individual prosecutions, reparations, truth-seeking, institutional reform, vetting and dismissals, or a combination thereof. (United Nations Security Council 2004)

The International Center for Transitional Justice (ICTJ) in New York City, the leading international NGO in this field, which has been engaging TJ efforts in several countries, endorses this definition.[2]

Between these two poles, there are variations of TJ programs. The narrowest definition of TJ is restricted to the contents of the term within the scope of legal sanction. This strictly legal *retributive* approach holds that TJ is intended to "hold violators responsible for their actions and punish them accordingly, after a rigorous process of determining their guilt before a neutral decision maker" (Ohlin 2007:52).

Broader terminology in line with the UN definition opens up space for several programs combining legal and nonlegal options. Some scholars set the baseline as consisting of trials and truth commissions (Kent 2012:3; Subotić 2009:18; Thoms et al. 2010:330). The middle-range application adopts some essential elements such as commissions of inquiry, trials, vetting, and restitution or reparation (Kritz 1995); truth-seeking, reparations, and institutional reform (Boraine and Valentine 2006:17–27);[3] or trials, truth commissions, vetting, institutional reform, security-sector reform, and reparations (Mani 2007:2).

The list of TJ options can be even longer. David Crocker (1999:60) proposes that a TJ program should incorporate at least some of the following: the official acknowledgment of harm done; official apologies and other official gestures; the promotion of public fact-finding or truth-telling forums, including a platform for victim reparations or restitution; justice in the form of trials or lustrations; the establishment of the rule of law; public gestures of commemoration through the creation of monuments, memorials, and holidays and other educational and cultural activities; institutional reform and long-term development; and public deliberation. Elizabeth Cole (2007:121) adds didactic materials for schools to this list. This trend of enriching the list of TJ options can be extended to include any mechanism that tackles general negative heritages from past conflicts.

Reflecting on this trend, one scholar has looked at the history of TJ as the expansion of the application of the term to various circumstances (Duthie 2011). Adding new elements, in a snowballing manner, is seen as legitimate. According to Duthie, since the 1990s, when the term *transitional justice* emerged, "the measures associated with transitional justice have been increasingly applied both in post-conflict contexts (in addition to post-authoritarian contexts) and in countries that have not undergone significant political transition and those that are still experiencing conflict" (p. 243). In this trend, disarmament, demobilization, and reintegration (DDR) need to be integrated into the TJ framework (Dwyer 2012; Campbell and Connolly 2012). Furthermore, TJ "should address corruption in terms of both theory and practice" (Robinson 2015:33).

Dustin Sharp (2015:154) describes this tendency as dissolving the borders between neighboring fields by "looking at potential linkages between peacebuilding and transitional justice, in particular with respect to specific initiatives like security sector reform (SSR) and disarmament, demobilization and reintegration (DDR)." This contemporary understanding of TJ—expanding the category—has inevitably become interdisciplinary while being viewed as a consequence of "the political project of attempting to decolonize law's hold on the discourse, and even colonize transitional justice within other disciplines. . . . The call for interdisciplinarity is in part a call for transitional justice to cut free from its roots in law" (Bell 2009:21).

This expansion of the field has reached an apex with the field now having its own encyclopedia (Stan and Nedelsky 2013). Yet this expansion in both theory and practice may also lead to reservations, doubts, and even surprises in relation to the criteria for selecting eligible institutions (de Greiff 2013:549–550). Offering too many options may blur the idea of what TJ is and how TJ manages those options: "Transitional justice may tell us that victims want everything—retributive and restorative justice— but it gives us no generic principles for deciding how to prioritize these demands" (van der Merwe and Fletcher 2014:3).

In addition to the decolonization of the TJ field from domination by legal concerns, there is another contentious dichotomy in the effort to categorize options: institutional versus noninstitutional activities. This axis can be translated into another standard: state-level or non-state-level. For instance, an international tribunal is positioned in the former category, whereas a sociopolitical movement of local actors is in the latter. Several important examples of relevant work by local initiatives can be recalled from Latin America: Mothers of the Plaza de Mayo in Argentina; a Brazilian investigation project on torture in the military regime operated by civil society groups, which published the report *Brasil: Nunca Mais*; the Uruguayan NGO Servicio, Paz, y Justicia, which published *Uruguay: Nunca Más*; and the Human Rights Office of the Archbishop of Guatemala, which provided documentation for the use of a future truth commission.

On the other hand, the localization of TJ, or admitting a local initiative as a TJ case, has been among the recent agendas in the field of TJ. From this perspective, any social or political movement that expresses the intention to redress social injustice or to pursue public accountability might be identified as such a TJ initiative. Examples are the Greensboro Truth and Reconciliation Commission, which conducted investigations into the 1979

Greensboro massacre by the Ku Klux Klan and the American Nazi Party, and the Canadian Truth and Reconciliation Commission, which dealt with the forcible assimilation of indigenous children.

However, the TJ programs covered in this volume will not include those types of movements. More precisely, some such movements will be discussed (and favorably evaluated) in the following chapters, but not as a direct example of TJ initiatives. Rather, they will be depicted as local responses to the officially established TJ programs or other related official policies, and as playing a more significant role in a local context than an official program. The TJ cases to be discussed in this book are as follows:

- truth commissions in South Africa, Sierra Leone, Peru, Kenya, and East Timor;[4]
- international tribunals in the former Yugoslavia and Rwanda:
- internationalized (hybrid) tribunals in Cambodia, East Timor, and Sierra Leone;
- some cases and programs in the International Criminal Court (ICC); and
- other truth-seeking official entities such as the gacaca court in Rwanda and the Commission of Truth and Friendship in Indonesia and East Timor.

I call these official initiatives examples of institutional TJ and place them at the center of the empirical description in the following argument. All these cases have been operating since the 1990s and, as I will discuss in detail in the next chapter, can be identified as belonging to the era of "normalized transitional justice" (Teitel 2003:91).

Overview of the Book

This book will explore the institutional TJ cases listed above with particular attention given to local responses to those programs. Bearing in mind the phrase "planning for the unplanned," while describing the patterns of locals' various ways of accepting and digesting an official program and considering whether they appear in an overt or covert manner, I will also search for signs of local self-recovery from a fragmented social and political situation. Sociological thoughts will be incorporated within this entry into what Alexander Hinton calls the "messiness" (Hinton 2010a:15) of local TJ reality.

Chapter 2 draws a theoretical map of this volume, particularly showing the linkage to sociological analysis. I have already established in this introduction that a residual space for unexpected and informal, but occasionally supplemental, local reactions to a TJ program may remain through the course of institutional implementation. The background of that tendency can be attributed to the basic character of a transitional society, in which multi-directional distrust, even toward the justice system, is pervasive. Thus, a TJ project's essential dilemma and inevitable paradox consists in the fact that a justice initiative must be implemented in a context in which justice norms no longer work. In addition to that dilemma, we need to consider that "normalized" contemporary TJ projects have proceeded in circumstances where knowledge and information about TJ have been well arranged and pervasive in international human-rights regimes. Policymakers and donor entities have plenty of documents about past TJ programs, whereas tactically skilled governments have learned that a TJ program could be used as a front for their own political purposes, disguising their unwillingness to change the country's human-rights conditions. In such a normalized or mature context with a flood of information and discourse surrounding TJ, I approach contemporary TJ characteristics by considering external expectations as well as the organizational or internal justifications of a TJ program. I do this rather than scrutinizing the sincerity of a local government's desire to reform human-rights conditions or a local society's degree of democratization through a TJ program. A scenario of current institutional TJ programs might constitute the following series of collective activities or events:

- public announcement and enlightenment;
- mobilization of locals at a symbolic venue;
- providing a spectacle to be shared among locals; and
- arranging a collective identity in the form of social integration, typically expressed as national reconciliation.

Although discourse among practitioners and scholars in past studies has stated repeatedly that a one-size-fits-all manual would not fit all cases, it may actually be difficult to neglect these particular elements when designing and planning a TJ project in a present-day context. All these elements directly reflect the *official expectations* of most external actors—foreign donors—who need to confirm that their resources have been spent effectively to promote democratization, ensure protection of human rights, and establish the rule of law through a proper mechanism reflecting the ideal of local ownership. How could one verify the presence of local influence if a TJ institution has no such elements in its objectives or its activities? Moreover, these elements constitute a means for a local TJ entity or government to justify its activities, first, for the local participants (including dissidents), and second, for the international inspectors who look for evidence of positive influence of the project on the local society.

However, the following chapters will offer empirical data and episodes of past TJ cases that illustrate that such an expected scenario has not necessarily been realized in actual context, just as Autesserre and Scott have shown in other contexts of idealistic (and sometimes international) institutional endeavors. The concept of *unintended consequences* has been used to designate such conditions not only by these two scholars but also by other scholars in TJ studies. Chapter 2 examines the logic of that term by referring to past works of sociological theory, to clarify what local responses can be grasped by the term and to further articulate a subcategory of the concept.

Chapters 3 through 6 address empirical data and episodes from various TJ contexts based on the above understanding of the term *unintended consequences* with additional sociological input. The stages where failures of institutional TJ on the surface have been witnessed are translated into terminology such as the following: politics of discourses, repertoires of mobilization, dramaturgy and performance on the political stage, and nationalism and social cohesion. In this way, these chapters are designed to arrange the concepts and terms around informal local practices to achieve a better understanding of TJ with closer attention on the surrounding circumstances in a transitional society.

An institutional TJ project begins its work in a barren landscape where few people actually know what TJ can be or how it works in society, because it is new and different from other standard and permanent official institutions in a modern society. A society has no established image with which to compare or in which to contextualize a TJ policy. No shared image of an organization exists. Therefore, a TJ entity's first task should be to disseminate an official image of the organization with an explanation of its activities. In this sense, a TJ entity represents itself as a pedagogic mass medium based on goodwill, promoting the ideal of serving a traumatized new nation and facilitating future national integration. In inspiring and stimulating an audience's moral receptors, a TJ entity attempts to elicit spontaneous support from locals. But it faces unexpected responses. Chapter 3 thus deals with the question of why and how these audiences challenge and dismiss the types of formal goodwill and ideals of a new society. The chapter sketches two critical episodes:

- A highly strategic political maneuver that the Serbian government executed in the course of cooperating with the International Criminal Tribunal for the Former Yugoslavia (ICTY).
- Cambodians' perception of justice, which showed a fundamental dissonance with Extraordinary Chambers in the Courts of Cambodia (ECCC) technical and procedural inclinations, requiring a reconsideration of the term *local ownership*.

The context for understanding these issues will be framed by the concept of agenda setting in media studies, Michel Foucault's discourse analysis on knowledge production in the public arena, and arguments on the politics of victimhood.

Chapter 4 focuses on outreach and mobilization. As Chapter 3 shows, a pedagogic mass medium cannot easily earn support from skeptical audiences that stand in pervasive distrust by simply making an official statement of goodwill and ideals at a head office in a capital city. More direct communication is needed. Outreach thus becomes the next obligatory operation for a TJ body. Staff members travel the country, town by town and village by village, with leaflets, pamphlets, booklets, T-shirts, and short movies for screening. They explain what TJ is and how people can participate in the programs, and they invite people to testify before the TJ organization. Following these preparative stages, a TJ entity expects to mobilize nationals to TJ venues, such as court hearings or truth commission forums.

This method would seem to properly address locals' complaints about the lack of a consultation process, which Chapter 3 discusses. But concern about a *too-perfect mobilization* has emerged because it can be perceived as similar to the forced mass mobilizations that occurred during the very conflict with which a TJ entity is dealing. Testimony from Rwanda and East Timor demonstrates societal pressure to attend TJ gatherings and suggestions that absence would be regarded as subversive to a collective value of national integration. Additionally, the chapter challenges TJ entities' claims of seemingly successful mobilizations by referring to C. Wright Mills's (1940) idea of vocabularies of motive, a term that describes the behavior of tailoring expressions so as to acquire or maintain social acceptance. Further, foreign donors have increasingly required mobilization as well, as they want to confirm the actual influence of TJ programs in the society and to assess the objective evidence of a long-term, costly operation. Data showing that *something has been constantly increasing during a certain period* support these foreign donors' assessments. Such data also help a TJ body, particularly a court, to demonstrate "ongoing success" while a few actual judgments are rendered.

On the other hand, after recognizing the limitations of an official body, some local initiatives have diverged from the main body and deployed their activities to supplement insufficient aspects, or the unfinished business, of TJ. Official mobilization has occasionally remained a residual space for diverging mobilization by other local entities. Chapter 4 also introduces some unplanned but continuous divergences from TJ bodies, while offering reservations about the typical assessment of current forms of outreach and mobilization in TJ activities. In doing so, this chapter illustrates the complex linkages that connect social pressure, vocabularies of motive, and alibis among various mobilized people in the global human-rights regime.

Even though locals do not necessarily accept a TJ body's announcements and mobilization in the desired manner, the body's next task is to establish an official theater in the form of a court or truth commission hearing. Chapter 5 explores the official drama that an institutional TJ body stages at this official theater. This rhetoric, which identifies a court as a theater, has been legitimized by a functionalist understanding of the court as a process that provides collective memories and shapes a sense of unity among audiences. The judiciary's efficacy and role are seen as not limited to findings of guilt or innocence. This role is clearly rooted in Emile Durkheim's argument (Durkheim 1960) that society needs evil and punishment for solidarity, or that an authentic gathering secures the renewal of collective identity. The term *expressivism* partly shares this line of understanding, leaving a space for potential victim healing through a series of dramatic performances at a TJ venue. Victim participation and public testimony have thus become standard TJ methods. However, as the previous chapters suggest, a TJ body's official drama is also not immune to challenge, confusion, disorder, divergence, or covert action by participants. A TJ body may have its own script for an official drama, yet different interpretations and meanings appear on the stage. Triggers for the rupture of an official drama include:

- a staff member's neutrality being suspected;
- officials' prioritizing their authority over a victim's dignity;
- a pervasive impression that such drama is a closed game for political elites; and
- the image of a "put-up job."

A TJ body stands at a difficult point that requires a balance between demonstrating authenticity and taking people's needs into consideration. But a TJ body's failure to maintain a front in the public arena might inspire participants to create and perform a different drama on a parallel stage. Such unexpected dramas have occurred in Rwanda, East Timor, Sierra Leone, and Cambodia. Some actors boldly challenge an official script and fail. Others recognize the limitations of an official stage, yet still attempt to utilize the scenario for their own purpose. The cases recorded in Sierra Leone may cause readers to experience vertigo from the actors' complex, highly strategic, and confusing performances. Secrecy, calculation, cautious cooperation, and the misunderstanding of implicit rules of communication in court involved the actors in a strange drama of deciphering, bringing all of them to the point where goodwill and the ideals of justice and reconciliation began to ring hollow.

As Erving Goffman (1959) teaches us, a person performs not only for his or her own benefit but also to maintain order within the public space. Yet at the same time, an actor may commit an error in recognizing the situation or may misunderstand the signs of other actors. Chains of such factors can make participants' experiences on a TJ stage complicated, but they need to be thoroughly considered if we wish to understand the substantial or raw meaning of TJ in a local context. Otherwise, local actors, who covertly perform a parallel scenario on the same stage, and foreign experts who commit to the TJ project with enlightened motivation will not truly encounter each other, *living together separately*.

A main reason that governments have established institutionalized TJ bodies is to build a reconciled nation to prevent the recurrence of abuse. A transitional society cannot presuppose an already constructed, collective identity that indirectly serves as a hidden basis for ordinary justice without the epithet "transitional," because having a sense of "us" implies the existence of a shared set of social norms. Chapter 6 examines the TJ body's main assumption that its activity can lead to national reconciliation. Does a TJ body function as a medium of nation building? Does it promote positive nationalism within the new nation? These questions might face immediate opposition. Those opposed might assert that TJ as a nationalistic policy does not benefit victims, because it forces them to be subject to a nationalistic, totalitarian story that has no sensitivity to personal victimhood. This is a fundamental dilemma. A TJ project needs to remedy a fragmented collectivity, but such an orientation cannot cause various disparate positions to become aligned. Thus, many have criticized the attempt to create a national identity through TJ activities.

However, other discussions of possible social integration through TJ initiatives have opened up a different path from those that start from the assumption that people are unified through shared public memory, symbols, or sense of identity. Incorporating the notion of social cohesion into this issue, to balance continuous conflicting relationships and sustainable communication, leads to a further argument on the collective status of social constituents in a post-conflict or transitional context. Chapter 6 therefore juxtaposes classic works, such as those of Lewis Coser and René Girard, with contemporary political thought on deliberative democracy, along with the latest TJ arguments on this topic, such as Leigh Payne's concept of "contentious coexistence" and Will Kymlicka's "substate nationalism." A shift in viewpoint thus appears in Chapter 6, toward considering the status of social cohesiveness as a model of *dynamic equilibrium in a certain range of interactions*, including interactions of conflict, instead of a collective model of subjects who share the common marker of "us." This chapter offers a preliminary case study on post-TRC South Africa, specifically focusing on the relationship between Colored—or Khoisan—people and black South Africans. Both groups were racially categorized as non-European in the apartheid classification. Yet in a new political landscape, they have been competing for an authentic South African-ness, developing a rivalry rather than peacefully sharing a common identity.

Chapter 6 concludes by returning to the question posed at its beginning: Is planning for the unplanned possible by a TJ project in order to assist social recovery? As Chapters 3 through 6 illustrate, the official justification of TJ as a producer of the rule of law and democracy is questionable. Yet the assessment of TJ as simply a failure in light of official slogans and objectives should also be dismissed. The various episodes related in this volume reveal the *by-products* of TJ: forms of divergence, tactical negotiations, and unintended consequences. If people's reactions have been recognized within a certain range of interactions—keeping or developing interactions of meaning-making—they can be retrospectively assessed as forming a dynamic equilibrium. Continuous meaning-making has significance in two important ways. First, I hypothesize that the recovery of the affected society happens only when local stakeholders engage in the process of meaning-making spontaneously. The term *social recovery* thus connotes the status of managing the process of meaning-making by local constituents. Second, I propose that when such meaning-making occurs in several different contexts during/after the TJ implementation, TJ demonstrates its potential to indirectly elicit active commitment from various actors. A TJ body might function as a catalyst for the realization of such a commitment, although that function is never formally guaranteed.

A remaining question concerns what conditions prepare for and promote such a situation. One relevant factor centers on exactly how the TJ project is perceived as inadequate or improper. A particular type of blank space may induce an external motion to fill it, because nature abhors a vacuum.

An institutional TJ program will likely face increasing pressure to demonstrate its achievements in challenging circumstances. What could result from that demand? The gap between maintaining international standards of justice, or procedural fairness, and reflecting an idea of local ownership in more substantial ways will be a perpetual aporia under the given condition of scarce resources. The approach taken in this volume will offer hints for the consideration of that situation.

Sociological Implications

Although I explain in detail in the next chapter the sociological approach taken in this volume, I want to briefly illustrate here the purpose and motivation of sociological settings. In this volume, a starting point for inquiry is the premise that people cannot completely control their living circumstances, yet people cannot help being involved in their circumstances if they want to improve their situation. Because people invariably have insufficient knowledge of the mechanism and conditions of the surrounding situation, they can deploy their plans only imperfectly, and further unexpected events and errors will follow their involvement. The societal results of people's collective input, in a strict sense, have always been unpredictable. Nonetheless, people destined to be caught in such a contingency have been and will be driven, or obliged, to act in or react to any social setting with their utmost effort.

This nuance can also be observed in TJ experiences. Colleen Duggan described the features of TJ policy based on unavoidable contingencies rather than features of the programs:

> Interviews with those involved in such commissions—commissioners, staff, witnesses, and victims—all attest to the fact that these processes never follow a linear pathway. They elicit unexpected and unanticipated divergences and upheavals, and they involve a high degree of creativity and constant adaptation of general principles from previous truth commissions to fit the new context. (Duggan 2010:327)

In a more abstract sphere, from the micro dimension of our personal communication in everyday settings, which George Herbert Mead depicted as a series of trial-and-error attempts, to a macro dimension such as the state projects that Autesserre and Scott have critically reflected, human actions are always being derailed from the planned scenario, generating derivatives, some of which are perceived to be undesirable, while tackling or coping with these unexpected, unforeseen happenings. Some of those derivatives will turn up in our lives to accommodate the new context; however, we are often not aware of the fact that the present impasse is caused by our own past engagements. Continuous collective responses to such unexpected outcomes have been retrospectively recognized as a form of history or the continuity of a society.

However, sociological arguments have not abandoned such derailments or derivatives as matters of random appearance. Those unexpected outcomes rest on the assumption that the derailment of collective behaviors may be conceived within a certain range, threshold, pattern, or frame. Human collective behaviors and their results may not be linked completely with each other in a cause–effect scheme, but neither are they buried in total randomness and contingency. Incorporating a sociological framework to interpret the complex reality of a transitional society rests on the idea that focusing on unplanned reactions might well contribute to our understanding of a TJ program, including its "failure" on a surface level.

Notes

1. Nelson Mandela's speech can be accessed at www.mandela.gov.za/mandela_speeches/1998/981029_trcreport.htm, accessed on January 12, 2018.

2. See the ICTJ's definition at https://www.ictj.org/about/transitional-justice.

3. Boraine and Valentine (2006:5) posited five factors as part of their "holistic approach": accountability, truth recovery, reconciliation, institutional reforms, and reparations.

4. East Timor's TRC (Comissão de Acolhimento, Verdade e Reconciliação, or CAVR).

2

Recognizing a Transitional Society

Recently, one popular topic in TJ scholarship has been localization. Consistent with the policy emphasis on local ownership, how local stakeholders perceive, react to, and digest the normative program, which reflects a universalistic guise and is supported by international specialists, has been understood to be crucial for long-lasting substantial influence within a specific society.

As to why institutional TJ is adopted, one common explanation is the lack of resources (both human and fiscal) available to implement ordinary criminal justice. Another reason is victim empowerment, aimed indirectly at preventing a future recurrence of conflict. However, a more fundamental and difficult explanation lies in the pervasive presence of distrust across all social spheres. In these societies, the judiciary, politicians, and governmental bodies are often viewed with suspicion, and legal norms tend to be dysfunctional. TJ has been considered necessary in such a situation. This chapter thus begins by examining such crucial factors as the lack of resources, need for victim empowerment, and pervasive distrust in public spaces in transitional societies that choose to employ a TJ approach.

To cope with such factors, the following four steps have been serving as basic requirements for the institutional design of TJ: publicly announcing justice and reconciliation in a moralistic tone; mobilizing as large a group of locals as possible at official events; staging a formal drama to bring national healing and overcome the past; and attempting to establish a shared collective identity among former enemies. However, even such deliberate executions of TJ have usually produced unexpected reactions from local societies. As a result, some scholars have applied the concept of unintended consequences in interpreting impacts on a local society. Yet the prior arguments centered on the unintended consequences of TJ still leave space for further sociological examination of the usage of the term. This chapter describes that perspective and explains how it will be applied to the case studies presented in the subsequent chapters.

Focusing on Local Context

Kieran McEvoy (2008:45) advocates for "the 'from below' perspective . . . to deliver to those who have been most affected by conflict." Yet this perspective is not easily accommodated in a practical context because much TJ discourse has been dominated by self-justifying and self-replicating legalistic tendencies (McEvoy 2008:28). In a collection (Hinton 2010b) that aims to provide a baseline framework "toward an anthropology of transitional justice" (p. 6), the contributors' research interest is "more oriented to the complexities of the encounter between global/transitional mechanisms and the local realities on the ground" (p. 9). The "encounter" is, in the authors' observation, not necessarily peaceful and modest but accompanied by "messiness" and "unintended consequences" (pp. 15, 17). Messiness refers to local reactions such as the intentional maneuvers to co-opt or foil a TJ program by local political actors, competition among victims for better social position and for entitlement to reparations, and negative intensification of local power relations. Although Rosalind Shaw and Lars Waldorf (2010:5, 21) share a similar perspective on the "complex, unpredictable, and unequal encounter among international norms, national agendas, and local practices and priorities through the operations of transitional justice in particular locations," these authors warn of "the current fascination with 'transitional' justice" because it may hide the local patterns of oppression or alienation of certain people under the banner of local ownership.

Conditions That Shape a Transitional Society

In search of feasible social conditions that bring about this unexpected messiness and unintended consequences, other features of a transitional society must be recognized.

Implementing institutional TJ means that the society concerned chooses TJ—or that external players such as the United Nations arrange it—largely because the ordinary criminal justice system has become invalid. Why is the ordinary justice system invalid? Because there are not enough resources and conditions enabling the society to maintain an ordinary functioning criminal justice system, in addition to the generally unstable political situation. A tight governmental budget and the lack of skilled legal experts are common preconditions; these inadequacies may be present because of past conflict or a long-lasting authoritarian regime. Furthermore, the judiciary may not be politically neutral, or the judges may not be able to decide cases and mete out sentences in an impartial and independent manner. Experts who manage legal logic at the level of a stable Western society have sometimes not been welcome in such societies (January 2009; Kent 2012; Payne 2000; Robins 2011). The rule of law is generally not rooted in such a society.[1] A court can be established anywhere, but trials in such situations cannot escape political influence. Judgment is sometimes not based on legal examination inside the courtroom but on the input of a higher political entity, typically the national government or the ruling party. Otherwise, the judicial and democratic system formally exist but are not managed properly.[2] This may be a relatively common phenomenon in a transitional society, even if few on the domestic political scene admit it; therefore, most citizens do not trust court judgments to be impartial and independent (Clark 2010; Hayner 2010; Kelsall 2013; Krog 1998). In such a context, court judgments do not guarantee justice; rather, they demonstrate a political decision.

Therefore, the international community insists on its responsibility of intervening in these spiraling injustices. Nevertheless, the fundamental problem of a transitional society cannot be remedied by the presence of that seemingly legitimate party, the international entity. Locals often distrust not only the domestic courts, local governments, and ministry officials, but also the foreign interventionists. A TJ with international backing needs to be cognizant of that reality.

The Cambodian case is illustrative. The international community, particularly the UN, engaged in the issue of post-conflict justice in Cambodia in the late 1990s after the political menace of the Khmer Rouge subsided. The UN saw itself as a beacon of justice. Yet not only the tactical Cambodian politicians but also the local Cambodians, including the victims, cast a suspicious eye on the UN's actions to secure justice for those who had suffered under the rule of the Khmer Rouge. For many of them, the UN was an untrustworthy entity that had changed its stance on the Khmer Rouge according to changing circumstances. The UN in fact supported the Khmer Rouge as a legitimate representative of Cambodia until the year 1990 and gave it an authorized seat even after its expulsion from the capital by Vietnamese-backed troops in 1979. Many questioned the UN's ability to deliver justice in Cambodia because it had supported the Khmer Rouge during its rule and even after it had ended..

There have also been reports of murky issues and corruption in Cambodia among local court staff since the inception of the special tribunals. Foreign legal experts have entered the court building for their inaugurations, promising to demonstrate that no force could stand above the law. But after a few years of internal conflict with the local Cambodian players (prosecutors and investigating judges) about providing basic direction or setting down the rules of the court—which are not really connected to delivering judgment—these foreign legal experts would depart from the country before any legal sentence was delivered. The more the locals witnessed these smart figures pursuing their careers, the more they lost all expectation of worthwhile outcomes from the internationally backed court or from international society.

After looking at other contexts, Nicola Palmer offers these dry comments from a Rwandan survivor on the ideals of TJ: "Forgiveness, peace, reconciliation, the words are very nice. It is like medication for a headache. . . . They are trying to say good things, but there are no roots to this forgiveness. It is not a bad thing but it is just justice words . . . while for me it is like a headache to just continue to live" (2015:172).

A distrust of official institutions, including the judiciary, is usually prevalent among locals in a transitional society. Elizabeth Drexler indicates the "poisonous legacy of mistrust" in the context of East Timor, which was "generated by the occupying Indonesian state's militarization of society." The poisonous legacy that had formed "in gray zones of collaboration and betrayal, coupled with the total impunity enjoyed by high-level planners and perpetrators" finally led to a situation where "ordinary people knew that no one could be trusted—neither international prosecutors and their staff who were asking for testimony nor the ordinary people, fellow villagers and even intimates with whom people had to deal in their daily lives" (Drexler 2013:76).

A distrust of the judiciary is often rooted in its historical abuse by politicians in power. In a report from Nepal, Simon Robins (2011:86) voiced his reservations regarding the adage that locals distrust the law: "For the most disempowered victims, the law has always either been a tool of power used against them or invisible to them through their lack of access to justice." Distrust might be shown toward political slogans, government, law, political groups, and even neighbors (Duggan 2010; Eriksson 2009). This brings to mind Antjie Krog's (2003) remarks on the challenge that post-apartheid South Africa has been facing: How can the judiciary, which has long been a symbol of injustice, recover its legitimacy through any justice project? Underlying these utterances of distrust of everything is a sense of resignation, which is close to indifference, and this is the invisible but most feasible difficulty that a TJ program needs to address.

Distrust is further amplified in circumstances where mutual fear between perpetrators and victims still lingers in daily lives. Not only victims but also perpetrators experience fear. Phil Clark explained this mutual fear in Rwanda:

> Everyone is still fearful—the prisoners and the survivors. The biggest fear though is among those coming back from the prisons [former perpetrators]. . . . For those coming back, their fears are justified because

the survivors are still angry. It depends how bad [the prisoners'] crimes were. But for the survivors, the genocide is still haunting. (Clark 2010:224)

But there was no opportunity for direct communication between these two parties, and fear on both sides was circulating in a close conduit. A perpetrator expressed his fear of revenge on his release from prison: "I don't know who's waiting for me in the village. People talk about survivors waiting there for us, maybe wanting to hurt us. I hear stories of survivors waiting for us in the market" (Clark 2010:227). On the other hand, a victim said: "I got very scared when I first heard the radio message that the prisoners were going to be released. . . . I think to myself, 'Will they hurt me? Am I safe here? What will happen when I see them at gacaca [the community justice court]?'" (Clark 2010:227).[3]

Pervasive distrust and mutual fear may stem from or promote traumatized subjectivity, which arises from the conflict or the authoritarian context and might lead to distrust or fear of the official entity and legal action, because the notion of traumatized subjectivity connotes a lack of a stable sense of self, which is usually supplied by society. A vulnerable subject with a weak sense of self, in theory, cannot accept social norms unconditionally because a societal anomaly, such as radicalized conflict among nations or rapid transition from a previous political regime, undermines the sense of a perpetual reference point for one's values and judgments. When the sense of society cannot be trusted, this also means that the society cannot secure each person's public role based on various norms. Thus, the foregrounding of the dysfunction of social norms formally appears among many locals as an attitude of skepticism and distancing, as well as a resigned or passive attitude about the capacity of democratic procedures to handle social problems.

A society in which people distrust the judiciary tends to become one where legal norms are dysfunctional. This might result from the combination of a culture of impunity, a lack of education, pervasive political nepotism, the prevalence of firearms and their widespread use in resolving disputes, a shortage of legal experts, and no shared sense of the rule of law. Nepotism and political connections may work overtly and covertly under the surface of legal exercise, thus the sense of a legal norm itself can be used as a front in support of the illicit activities of leaders. Dark clouds of skepticism, indifference, fear, dullness, cynicism, and resignation as well as the more straightforward emotions of anger, sadness, and a sense of injustice cover the social spaces where lies and silences are commonplace.

Although expressions of political objection are not often visible in the public domain of these transitional societies, such distrust toward political interventionists as well as toward neighbors is a typical feature of local behavior. Examples from the field perpetuate the following sorts of assessment: locals have continued to display their indifference to the TJ project through their activities, or there has been no remarkable change in the local context in terms of the rule of law, or justice in general. In other words, these negative assessments might be converging to a view that this is an exclusive game played over a short time span among political and judicial elites.

Furthermore, a TJ program, regardless of which option it chooses, is hampered by two more ambiguities in its implementation. First, it often has to begin its work under political pressure, without having enough time for preparation, and then has to stop its work before accomplishing all the required tasks to achieve the expected outcomes, sometimes because of resource restrictions or lack of local government's support, or because of the withdrawal of foreign donors. (These difficulties are not unique to TJ initiatives but are tendencies widely seen in any policy operation in a developing country.) The nature of TJ programs is defined by these insufficient conditions, making predictions about outcomes difficult. The second ambiguity relates to the local actors' intention or will to implement TJ. It is not always clear whether local actors, such as local authorities, are positive enough to lead or engage in this contentious program, even if on the surface they have agreed to it. We can express their figures with the phrase "getting close but not too close to the past." Various entities in a local context may not be completely opposed to the idea of holding a formal accountability project; however, each of them may push a certain agenda or withdraw its cooperation with the proceedings. Thus, the experiences that are officially dealt with under the name of TJ inevitably demonstrate unique bias, insufficiency, or ambiguity according to the local context in which they are executed (to be discussed at greater length later in the book). Given these features of a transitional society, research on the results of implemented TJ projects should go beyond a simple assessment of success and failure. The term *unintended consequences* is a key to grasping that context.

Elizabeth Drexler analyzed the TJ experience in East Timor, which consisted of a series of institutions such as the Commission for Reception, Truth, and Reconciliation in East Timor (Comissão de Acolhimento, Verdade e Reconciliação de Timor Leste, or CAVR), an Indonesian ad hoc tribunal held in Jakarta; the special panels for serious crimes in Dili (a UN-supported hybrid international tribunal); and a Commission for Truth and Friendship to restore good relations between Indonesia and East Timor. Amid these various inquiries, an essential factor in the conflict—namely, the involvement and direct perpetration of crimes by Indonesian military cadres—was totally omitted from the process. As a result, the process was evaluated as having produced unintended consequences by reinforcing "the idea that the powerful were beyond the law, extending patterns in which the law was corrupt and arbitrary" (Drexler 2010:54). There is no doubt that the term *unintended consequences* is used here to capture a negative outcome of the projects.

Referring to Drexler's argument, Roger Duthie (2011:252–253) maintains that we need to anticipate "some unintended consequences of transitional justice efforts" as "the specific risks they may give rise to in a given context." Based on this perspective, Duthie recommends distinguishing three layers of unintended consequences of TJ, namely, those that may "be foreseen and short-term," those that are more fundamentally problematic and may in fact undermine the long-term goals of justice, and those that are the result of processes that, strictly speaking, may not qualify as transitional justice measures (p. 253). The first layer is associated with local resistance such as competing narratives, disagreements, and dissident understandings of the concept of justice. The second layer is associated with TJ measures that could undermine sustainable peace and democratization or create risks. The view that a TJ process generates an opposite result from its official objectives (the democratization of a local society, victim empowerment, and redress of disparity and injustice rooted in past conflict) has been subsumed under the term *unintended consequences*.

Finding a mechanism for achieving local ownership and victim empowerment without such an "opposite result" has, therefore, been one of the central questions surrounding the subject of localizing TJ. Yet the term *unintended consequences* is not the only one to designate a negative outcome for a specific action. Duthie criticizes unintended consequences arising from the "failed" efforts of a TJ project, but his argument also leaves room for further exploration of this issue in a more nuanced manner. He acknowledges that "if levels of resistance and disagreement remain below a certain threshold, it could be argued that achieving long-term goals—such as reconciliation and sustainable peace and democratization—may be worth taking some short-term risk" (2011:253). Although the term *unintended consequences* is still used in a negative way, it is recognized as being a possible seed for positive influence in the future.

Rethinking Unintended Consequences

Other scholars who also emphasize the need to localize analysis of TJ projects but have deployed their studies from different perspectives have suggested the keywords "kinetic social institution" (Clark), "unanticipated effects" (Orentlicher), and "positive deviants" (Duggan). The arguments of these scholars are significant when considering a different avenue of analysis of TJ from the success-failure debate in using the term *unintended consequences*.

With his rich firsthand data on the Rwandan gacaca, the community justice court, Phil Clark emphasizes the need for a methodological focus on "unpredictable outcomes of popular participation in gacaca, and consequently the dynamic nature of the institution as a whole and its effect on the public's evolving interpretations of, and involvement in, gacaca" (2010:348), which often diverge from the goal-oriented legal documents generated by that court. "The dynamic nature of gacaca" is observed in detail in other expressions such as "a kinetic social institution that is shaped heavily by the population's perceptions and actions" (Clark 2010:7), and "the population's perceptions and actions" are captured in their "proclivity to shape gacaca in its own image, often contrary to the original intentions of gacaca's creators" (p. 27). As the concept of gacaca is applied to a more general category of TJ, Clark's remarks parallel this book's themes.

Rosalind Shaw and Lars Waldorf (2010:3–4) also insisted on the need to analyze how the globalized concepts and processes of TJ may be reshaped in unexpected directions. Referring to Sally Merry's term *vernacularization* (Merry 2006), Lia Kent (2012:43) proposed investigating how "East Timorese survivors have responded to the transitional justice process in a range of complex ways that are beyond simply accepting or rejecting official processes." Colleen Duggan provides an interesting and helpful term, "positive deviants," to this line of thinking.[4] Even scholars conducting mainstream TJ legal studies have expressed an inclination to adopt this line of thought, which pays attention to outcomes outside the official goals: "Future policy decisions about international and hybrid courts would benefit at least as much from research that captures unanticipated effects of these bodies as from studies assessing whether they achieved the goals that supported their creation" (Orentlicher 2013:541).[5]

These unplanned and unexpected aspects of TJ implementation are all unintended consequences but are not negatively perceived in these studies. This viewpoint, which goes beyond a simple success-failure scheme, works well when one needs to acknowledge the influence of TJ in a local context where signs of pervasive distrust have been witnessed. Any short-term official project presupposes that the reactions of designated actors are anticipated and controllable, yet the probability of derailment is amplified by unidentified factors in a transitional context. TJ is not an exception. The term *unintended consequences* will help to display the complexity of such a situation. Although the term *unintended consequences* has been incorporated into many analyses of TJ for its localizing aspect, the use of the term has usually carried a negative meaning. However, the sociological term entails another aspect of unfolding a reality: latent function. I will briefly review the theoretical background of the term to clarify the following argument.

Max Weber's *The Protestant Ethic and the Spirit of Capitalism* provides a basic perspective for this inquiry. Weber argued that the desire of Protestants to acquire personal redemption led collectively to the molding and growth of capitalism in its early stages. This argument does not necessarily explain the negative outcomes of capitalism[6] (although we can well imagine that for a serious pastor, capitalist attitudes were seen as the product of a misconception of Christian teaching and became a source of headaches). Thus, the concept of unintended consequences in Weber's work explains the generation of a new system of logic from another system of logic, which had no intrinsic program by which to generate the successive one.

To clearly understand the range of use of the term *unintended consequences*, Robert Merton's theoretical framework on functionalism should be mentioned. Merton (1957) proposed the scheme of functionalism, which is formed by crossing two axes: *manifest* and *latent* functions, and *eufunction* and *dysfunction*. Eufunction is generally regarded as the positive influence of a certain factor on a society, which can be in a manifest (visible) or latent (invisible or unrealized) form. Dysfunction also takes manifest as well as latent forms.

According to this terminology, the negative reception of TJ norms by locals and the negative influence of TJ activities on a society are examples of manifest dysfunction. On the other hand, TJ's unexpected influence or unplanned outcomes, which have been described by such scholars as Clark, Kent, and Orentlicher, fit the category of latent functions, because they do not directly align with the official objectives of a particular institutional TJ organization and do not worsen the social situation. When recovery of victims' autonomy and dignity, which should be one of the goals of TJ in general, is observed as a by-product of their deviance from the official program, such local reactions can be assessed as the result of the latent eufunction of TJ activity.

Based on this understanding of the terminology of Merton's functionalism, we can elucidate the arguments for TJ's influence on a local society by using the term *unintended consequences* in the following manner: the arguments deployed by Drexler and Duthie exemplify unintended consequences related to the manifest dysfunction of TJ, whereas the arguments deployed by Clark, Kent, and Orentlicher, along with some parts of Duthie's analysis, are unintended consequences that display the latent eufunction of TJ. The former group of scholars uses the term *unintended consequences* to describe an intention that was derailed by the expectations directed toward or held by an institutional TJ. The latter group uses it to illustrate local stakeholders' active engagement in changing their circumstances through the TJ process, although the locals' reaction to or perception of the TJ project does not correspond with the official objective—or, at least, not with the official slogan—of the TJ entity.

Researchers interested in the problems of a local society tend to refer to unintended consequences that exhibit the manifest dysfunction of TJ, whereas those interested in the local actors' self-recovery or any sort of autonomous utilization of the TJ venue are inclined to emphasize unintended consequences that represent the latent eufunction of TJ.

In this book, I will adopt the concept of unintended consequences as an analytical key phrase, with primary focus on the interpretation connected to latent eufunction. Although various types of deviations and derivatives from official TJ programs by local stakeholders can be understood as appearances of the latent eufunction of TJ, whether these deviations and derivatives could be associated with locals' own meaning-making and autonomous self-recovery remains a topic for further inquiry. Locals' own meaning-making and autonomous self-recovery are naturally categorized as an objective or ideal of TJ in general; however, when incorporating the concept of unintended consequences into the following argument, this volume assumes that these impacts might instead be found among the locals' unexpected reactions, which are sometimes called failures of official programs. Scott's indication that unplanned informal "suturation" in urban space could appear in a social flaw, which could resonate with my interest here, as quietly supplementing a flaw in TJ to achieve a formal objective of TJ, which would promote the healing of locals and the recovery of victims' dignity.

This volume thus adopts the logic of unintended consequences, stressing the aspect of latent eufunction. Furthermore, the argument focuses on the locals' reactions, which have often been described as signs of the failure of official TJ programs. The crux of this argument is that those elements of unintended consequences of TJ implementation, which have been viewed negatively at first glance, and those influences in the local context, which could be associated with meaning-making and possibly self-recovery, constitute a paradox. This paradox is recognized as the situation in which a specific form of failure in a certain system of collective meaning would be a trigger to create another system of collective meaning. The fact that the deployment of the latter system is not intentionally embedded in the former system is also designated as an unintended consequence.[7]

When this volume explores various patterns of deviations, derivatives, and unexpected reactions from official TJ programs to search for their unintended consequences, the approach refers to those sociological concepts that serve as a guide to understanding the collective activities.

Emergence of Unintended Consequences

In her essay "Transitional Justice in a New Era," which analyzes the evolution and direction of TJ, Ruti Teitel (2003:894) observes that "in its most contemporary phase, the post-conflict dimension of transitional justice is moving from the exception to the norm, to becoming a paradigm of the rule of law for our time." In the normalized phase[8] of TJ, the process is differentiated from "mid-century post-war justice" with an orientation "to include, rather than exclude, the various political actors involved in the conflict" by being "acceptable to all, so as to offer a basis for a stable transition" (Teitel 2003:898).[9] Teitel's association of the contemporary phase of TJ with the term *normalization* is primarily aligned with the legalist inclination in the related discourse. The trend has been observed "in the form of post-conflict law, the rise of humanitarian law, and the return to international judgment, reflected in the creation of international tribunals, as well as in the spread of universal jurisdiction" (Teitel 2003:902). Teitel's perspective resonates, for instance, with that of a prominent international NGO, Amnesty International, which insists that the world today needs "a legal system that ends impunity to perpetrators of the worst crimes known to humanity," both to prevent the recurrence of such crimes and to empower victims (Subotić 2009:20).

Locating TJ in the movement toward the establishment of an international legal system explains the still-heavy presence of legal experts in many TJ entities, whereas with regard to the issue of normalization, we can take another path. Rather than questioning what the norm is among possible TJ options, we can look at what characterizes or forms the *normalized phase*.

We can answer this question from the paradigmatic viewpoint, which has recently been pervasive worldwide and has been called *global liberalism* or the *global human-rights regime* (Hopgood 2013). In that normalized phase of TJ as paradigm, one of the TJ policy options, the truth commission, has reached a point where Claire Moon (2008:24) could refer to it as "an almost mandatory requirement of any state in transition." A related phenomenon to normalization is the industrialization of TJ. The normalization of a certain value or approach means that it has obtained an authority—political power—and the economic networking entailed by that power. The International Center for Transitional Justice began its work in 2001 with only four permanent staff members at temporary offices (Subotić 2012:117). But in fifteen years, it has become the leading NGO in the TJ field, with more than 120 employees, managing an annual budget of around $20 million at a central headquarters in New York City.[10]

As Jelena Subotić notes, the forming of an "industry" not only provides opportunities to work in international human-rights programs, but it also defines an ideological perspective from which to see and understand reality in a reflective manner. In the process of enlarging their scale, international organizations in this field gain the power to influence international policies through lobbying high-profile actors on the issues, as these organizations want to interpret, understand, and resolve conflicts. This dimension is also critical because these organizations produce "a self-reinforcing cycle that has further institutionalized their professional authority" (Subotić 2009:22–23).

Thus, the normalized phase of TJ introduces new, problematic issues about how to normalize which options by whose hegemony. However, this volume instead puts the focus on the behavioral aspects of stakeholders in relation to a TJ project. Put differently, this question can be represented as follows: What can the persons who are involved in the design and implementation of an official TJ institution do in the course of their work when TJ has already been normalized? Or, alternatively, what practices characterize the normalized phase? This volume assumes that specific behavioral patterns can be commonly observed in the arrangement and implementation phases of any institutional TJ.

Normalized contemporary TJ is primarily understood here as any TJ plan or design by any local government or international agency that can—or must—review and refer to the accumulated information about prior TJ cases. Various examples and case studies of past TJ projects, in addition to the *Encyclopedia of Transitional Justice* (Stan and Nedelsky 2013), have already been prepared, not only for policymakers in a post-conflict society but also for international donor entities that plan to support a TJ initiative. The title of TJ and a public announcement that TJ has been selected as a transitional policy option both serve as signals that a country is stepping onto the democratizing path. Making TJ a norm means acquiring a position as a brand, which involves accompanying advertising and an attractive public image.

Through this process, cases of *fake* TJ have also appeared. They may be entitled to be called TJ, but they cannot be counted alongside remarkable TJ programs of the past, because neither their organizational activity nor their political will share common features with the best examples.

This fake TJ is, on its surface, similar to some TJ projects (or local political reactions to TJ) that could have been assessed as political fronts, such as Serbian politicians' tactics with the International Criminal Tribunal for the Former Yugoslavia (see Jelena Subotić's argument in the next chapter) and the case in East Timor. The Serbian authority used the ICTY to promote a sense of solidarity among the citizenry, inventing the term *voluntary surrender* (which means that a patriot will accept an unjust or unfair political deal) for the high-ranked political figures summoned to The Hague. East Timor, in balancing the political relationship with Indonesia and dealing with the injustices of its past conflict, has systematically sidestepped the issue of the responsibility of former Indonesian military members for the plight of the East Timor victims. This issue of political maneuvering is actually not restricted to the TJ field when we consider politics in a post-conflict or post-authoritarian state.

Yet the term *fake TJ* further exemplifies the phenomenon of states pretending to be implementing a "brand policy" in the international political arena. It differs from political maneuvering or politics, such as in the cases of Serbia and East Timor. A fake TJ process tends to have no official mechanism for mobilizing and sharing experiences among nationals in a public space, even though the effort's name seems to offer truth or reconciliation. Fake TJ bodies serve to strengthen the current government's political foundation and to exclude certain social or political groups rather than to promote national integration among various dissidents. Such cases of pseudo-TJ or fake TJ have been reported from Thailand, Russia, and Sri Lanka. I will briefly introduce each of these cases here.

Many foreigners view Thailand as a Buddhist country, but the southern border provinces of Yala, Nrathiwat, and Pattani have Muslim majorities of up to 80 percent of the population. The historical conflict between Muslims in these provinces and the Thai government has escalated, particularly since 2004, with more than 6,000 casualties reported in the last ten years. To address the conflict, the then prime minister, Thaksin Shinawatra, established a National Reconciliation Commission (NRC) in March 2005. The NRC developed from the idea of a group of academics who were critical of the Thaksin government's managing of the southern Muslim crisis, and the effort was aligned with royalists. The Thaksin government accepted the NRC as a concession following disturbances during the general elections of February 2005 (McCargo 2010:77).

Although the NRC's report referred to preceding TJ projects, such as those in Argentina, Chile, El Salvador, and South Africa, as "similar efforts" (National Reconciliation Commission 2006:132–133), Duncan McCargo indicated that the NRC's practice differed from other TJ cases in its lack of emphasis on witness testimony, a quasi-judicial model of proceedings, and various representations of conflicting stakeholders in the proceeding, of whom "two-thirds . . . were from outside the Southern region," where the core of the conflict zone was located (McCargo 2010:77).[11] Furthermore, the Thaksin government issued an emergency decree on the southern crisis in mid-2005, thus creating the situation of "two parallel policies on the South: the nominal exercise of research, consultation and reconciliation under the NRC and the de facto policy of securitization controlled by Thaksin himself" (McCargo 2010:79). The NRC published its report in June 2006, but a military coup d'état against the Thaksin regime in September 2006 eliminated any potential realization of the commission's recommendations. Thus, the NRC, initially installed by the Thaksin government to manage domestic political tensions, was then used politically by Bangkok elites without any significant input from or involvement of Malay Muslims. This finally led to the dissolution of the body by regime change, and in the end, TJ had no influence on Thai society.

The Russian case more directly reflects political utilization of TJ. President Dmitry Medvedev, in May 2009, announced the creation of a "Historical Truth Commission," officially called the Commission to Counteract Attempts at Falsifying History to Damage the Interests of Russia. It appeared to mirror other countries' earlier truth commissions, but its political aim was to uphold the current government's historical view, and "only [the] form and name" of a TJ project were used, so as to benefit elites' political purposes (Andrieu 2011:213).

Similar political utilization has been observed in Sri Lanka. The Lessons Learnt and Reconciliation Commission (LLRC), established in 2010, was a remarkable exercise of political maneuvering that excluded a certain political group. Many viewed the process as "motivated by political ambitions to slander members of the political opposition at the time" (Anonymous 2011:38). In such a political context, "their work was restricted and compromised and their recommendations for prosecutions and reform were buried; many voices of dissent who engaged with these commissions have been threatened and the justice aspirations of those who gave testimony have been betrayed" (Anonymous 2011:38–39).

These citations illustrate that governments can use the framework of human-rights policy in the name of TJ to pretend to be legitimate, even though their purposes are clearly located in a dimension other than human rights or victim empowerment—sometimes even in opposition to the ideals of TJ. How can observers react to a so-called TJ of this nature? In some cases, governments may apply the title of TJ to any project that professes accountability or responsibility related to the country's past while pursuing their own politics. Should we distinguish between true TJ and false TJ? Is the TJ carried out with goodwill, or is it pretended or disguised TJ? In some cases, a project depicted as TJ may change its character from the initial stage in the course of operation, as a consequence of the effects of domestic politics or other unpredictable social conditions. In such a case, does the TJ program need to be evaluated from several chronological standpoints?

While granting that pseudo-TJ or falsely publicized TJ projects have taken place, in this volume I set aside the question of whether TJ is based on goodwill. The clue to coping with this problem will be presented in the next section, as I examine how to grasp the basic character of contemporary TJ, particularly in an institutionalized form.

Construction of Contemporary Institutionalized TJ

In addition to the basic context of a contemporary TJ program, in which a policymaker or project designer is required to access and learn past TJ data and case studies, there may be model cases available, along with specialists who can provide the proper interpretations of those cases. In other words, an institutionalized TJ on the normalized stage requires the contemplation of various patterns of past cases. This means that if you become an employee of any TJ organization, before planning your TJ program you must study not only past cases but also the authorized assessments of them completed by leading scholars or prominent practitioners. In this situation, where should you start if you are put in charge of designing and mapping out a new TJ program?

Given that a TJ initiative has no preceding reference in the society concerned, you may need to start with a public announcement of the new project. The fact that a TJ undertaking will be an ad hoc organization requires sufficient public relations about what organizations will conduct which activities and with what objectives in mind. This communication is crucial to achieving any positive outcomes in the public space in a limited period of time. This method of kick-starting a project is surely important because reaching as many potential supporters as possible at this point could secure greater local participation in the ensuing process.

Next, you may be required to mobilize many participants to attend public TJ events such as public hearings of international (or internationalized)[12] tribunals, testimony forums of truth commissions, or court tours of the countryside and school visits with official staff if there is no public event at a TJ venue. A statement-taking session of a truth commission and a public-relations forum by an official entity are additional mobilizing strategies.

A TJ then typically plans to have local participants share a specific type of experience at official events. Without a doubt, no participant should return home with a sense of injustice after attending a court examination. A truth commission hearing needs to be organized in a way that does not exacerbate the participants' trauma. An official venue of institutional TJ has a planned but hidden agenda in which the participants are led in a certain direction with regard to experiencing and understanding the past. TJ thus can be viewed as an official drama with a scenario that reflects a positive perception of justice or reconciliation, depending on the local context. As a corollary of this need for positive perceptions, no international court following a long-term armed conflict or civil war will find it strategically desirable to declare all the accused not guilty, although such a result is theoretically possible.

In the course of public announcement, collective mobilization, and staging of the official events, an institutional TJ program is directed to a specific goal, which is often publicized in a slogan or in a speech by a representative of the organization. At the very least, a TJ organization needs to express firmly that it aims to achieve harmonious social integration when asking for external donor support. Victim empowerment and destigmatization of perpetrators might be inevitable subtopics of this goal, features identified by Teitel (2003) as part of TJ normalization. A public project with an official budget is obliged to submit an authorized document at the end of its working period, such as a court's judicial decision or the final report of a truth commission. The fact that a published text with such authorization is shared among social constituents would be interpreted as symbolic proof of social integration, reminding us of Benedict Anderson's (1983) idea of imagined community, in that a specific document is offered as evidence of resolution while animosity often lingers.

Even though the phrase "one size fits all" has been dismissed as a negative cliché in designing a TJ project, any contemporary TJ that lacks the factors described above would be a dubious prospect not only for foreign donors but also for local stakeholders, including dissident actors. These steps are presented by the TJ organization as its self-justification from the planning stage to completion. A TJ organization is also required to be fully accountable. If an organization with no prior reference in the concerned society executes public events related to the past conflict without these steps of legitimatization, it will be open to politically biased maneuvers, approaching a form of pseudo- or fake TJ.

In summary, the actions of public announcement, pervasive mobilization, collectively shared experiences at official events, and publishing an authorized text that embodies a social decision are at the core of institutionalized TJ as a normalized choice.

In terms of these basic requirements, Patrick Vinck and Phuong Pham (2010) summarized the background context of a contemporary institutionalized TJ, focusing on the significance of outreach activity. Among experts in the international judiciary, according to Vinck and Pham, the assumption that victims and local populations will become active participants when sufficiently informed about a TJ project has become "the emerging consensus"; to foster that orientation, consultation processes with locals "are also proposed to ensure that accountability mechanisms better reflect the population's needs and expectations" (p. 422).

An emphasis on public information, public outreach, and consultation and on defining a TJ as an accountability mechanism admirably suits the practices of a truth commission. For instance, the South African TRC carried out its work in accordance with the above principles. It held several public hearings to gather ideas from the society before establishing the TRC, even regarding the choice of commissioners and what activities should be contained in the commission's mandate. As an outcome of such preparatory public consultation, gender-sensitive issues were handled with specific care. Although all the hearing proceedings were recorded by video camera, the public hearing held specifically for women used a partitioning screen beside a testifier. Only female commissioners managed the hearings for women. For more substantial protection of identities, some areas chose "wise women" who represented the female victims from their residential community, and who thus indirectly gave the women's testimony to the TRC.

Once the organization was set up, it asked for cooperation with local NGOs and provided special programs on each local radio station to disseminate information about the coming events. During these preparatory stages, statement takers from the TRC and trained volunteers from the local NGOs began to collect victim testimonies. Followed by these "sowing seeds" practices, the TRC held various public hearings, among them human-rights violation hearings, amnesty hearings, and hearings for specific social actors such as medical experts, correctional service officers, and religious representatives. Such public hearings—365 of them—colored South African society for five years. Each one was accompanied by the commissioner's ritualistic comments on various experiences of victimhood, usually subsumed under a nationalistic understanding of preparing for a changed era and the birth of a new nation, which was also criticized as a "master narrative" (Chidester 1999:135) that turned the focus away from the unique experience of each individual. The activities closed with the publication of an official report, which was introduced at a public national ceremony.

These basic elements of the South African TRC have been adopted by other truth commissions such as those in East Timor, Sierra Leone, and Peru. In addition, this tendency to weigh public relations, emphasize the interaction between a TJ entity and locals, and focus on giving substantial feedback on proceedings to the local society has also been shared by international justice projects.

The International Criminal Court, in an official document published in 2006, described the direction of its judicial mission as "intended, indirectly, to contribute to long-lasting respect for and enforcement of international criminal justice, the prevention of such crimes, and the fight against impunity," and for the realization of that mission, the ICC recognized that "making judicial proceedings public is a central element of a fair trial and therefore necessary" (ICC 2006:3).

Put succinctly, "Justice must be both done and seen to be done" (ICC 2006:3). Referring to the preceding cases of the International Criminal Tribunal for the Former Yugoslavia and the International Criminal Tribunal for Rwanda (ICTR), which have often been criticized as a type of distant justice that has rarely effected change for the concerned society, giving more substantial influence and positive feedback to the local society has been seen as a crucial part of the agenda. To achieve such outcomes, the ICC recognized that

> it must seek to bridge the distance between the Court and these communities by establishing an effective system of two-way communication. This communication should serve first of all to increase the confidence of these communities in the international criminal justice system, since they will be better informed about the Court and its role. (ICC 2006:3)

The document goes on to state that for "ensuring the quality of justice and being a well-recognized and adequately-supported institution," the following are taken into account as practical objectives:

1. To provide accurate and comprehensive information to affected communities regarding the Court's role and activities;
2. To promote greater understanding of the Court's role during the various stages of proceedings with a view to increasing support among the population for their conduct;
3. To foster greater participation of local communities in the activities of the Court;
4. To respond to the concerns and expectations expressed in general by affected communities and by particular groups within these communities;
5. To counter misinformation; and
6. To promote access to and understanding of judicial proceedings among affected communities.

The first of these six objectives matches the step of public announcement in the assumed four basic elements of institutionalized TJ discussed above. A positive outcome for objective 1 may lead to greater understanding (objective 2), which in turn facilitates a smooth mobilization of locals at official events (3). Objectives 4 to 6 are related to obtaining positive local feedback on the court process.

In studying the ICC with attention to the "new justice innovations" in its mechanism, Benjamin Schiff (2008:128–136) named the Victims and Witness Unit, the Victims Participation and Reparations Section, and the Office of the Prosecutor as the responsible ICC bodies for victim participation, witness protection, and outreach activities in general.

One of the ongoing ad hoc tribunals, the Extraordinary Chambers in the Courts of Cambodia, or ECCC, has been following the above principles. Established in 2006, it adopted Internal Rule 23, which states that the court would establish a mechanism to promote victim participation. The Victims Unit was formed in 2007 and started its outreach activities in 2008, but no budget was allocated to it and employee turnover was high (Elander 2012:107–108). Nevertheless, once it was functioning properly, the ECCC began active outreach activities along with implementing other guidelines in the ICC document: making special TV and radio programs, networking with local NGOs, organizing short trips to the court building and related historical sites in Phnom Penh (to create "local educators/recruiters"), visiting local schools, and holding seminars at universities. However, especially in terms of ICC objectives 3 (participation of local communities), 4 (responding to the concerns and expectations expressed by affected communities), and 6 (promoting access to and understanding of judicial proceedings), one surprising official event took place at the ECCC: after the judgment of Case 001, the ECCC held a "ceremony."[13]

Representatives from government ministries and institutions, as well as university students, monks, and members of the military gathered in the public gallery of the ECCC on July 11, 2012, to receive a copy of the final judgment in Case 001, which sentenced Kaing Guek Eav, alias "Duch," former chairman of Security Center S-21, to life imprisonment. The distribution ceremony was led by H. E. Tony Kranh, acting director of the Office of Administration of the ECCC, who delivered the introductory remarks, and was followed by a question-and-answer session.

Why did the ECCC need to hold this ceremony after a fair judicial process had been completed? What were the underlying reasons for holding it? This case eloquently demonstrates how the nature and social role of this court were perceived in Cambodian society, at least by the local government. Merely reading a judgment text does not by itself express any understanding of the court's position in the society. But the ceremony, which officially signaled the completion of the ECCC's first case, was designed to have a clear symbolic impact on locals. It was a public device to promote national reconciliation and social integration, although on the surface, it was also a statement of full-fledged political control.

The conception of the four elements of normalized TJ reflects the idea that *TJ is a series of social events and discourses*. In other words, these items focus particularly on the formal aspects of contemporary TJ in relation to expectations and self-justification. Existing scholarship has tended to frame TJ using political and justice norms such as democratization, redress policy, victim empowerment, and accountability mechanisms. How to approach the reality of TJ is closely linked to how one defines it. But the four steps of institutionalized TJ described above are not proposed here as components of the definition. They might also serve as helpful checkpoints for TJ staffers and proponents in justifying the programs as well as legitimizing the results.

Although the institutional TJ field has developed through the implementation and examination of actual cases, such as performed by the ICTY, ICTR, South African and other truth commissions, and Rwandan gacaca, the formal aspects of TJ programs share common characteristics with concepts in the fields of conflict resolution and social psychology. Put differently, we could infer that the reason such "expectations and self-justification" have been perceived as being legitimate in institutional TJ design is because those related fields have surely affected the context of the current intellectual landscape in the study of large-scale conflict, political regime change, and social recovery.

Scholars, with their approach based primarily on the assumptions of social psychology, conflict resolution, and peace building, have proposed a formula for reaching a settled condition after conflict, with such resolution including mutual understanding, acceptance of former enemies, and social reconciliation. The key terms at the center of their arguments are *moral repair*; *growth of mutual empathy*; *restructuring, redefinition, and transformation of identity*; and *re-categorization of the we/them grouping* (Du Bois and Du Bois-Pedain 2008; Kelman 2008; Kriesberg 2001; Nadler and Shnabel 2008; Rasmussen 2001; Riek et al. 2008; Rigby 2001; Siani-Davies and Katsikas 2009). Settlement of conflict is thus defined as a possible mental or attitudinal status among conflicting parties that could be achieved through certain steps of psychological transformation.

The arguments in this *sequential model* all assume more or less the following sequence: (1) all of the stakeholders should accept the legitimacy of accommodation for dialogue; (2) the self-identification of the participants and the image of their opponents should be transformed through dialogue; and (3) an agreement should be reached, and future promises made, cooperatively, and these should be public.[14] We can compare this sequence to the elements of normalized TJ: (1) this sequential model corresponds to outreach activities and public mobilization of TJ; (2) might happen in the course of interactions among participants in an official stage such as public hearing; and (3) illustrates another aspect of appearance of collectively shared identity based on mutual understanding.[15]

The field of TJ has often been framed by the normative objective of projects, such as democratization and victim empowerment, yet by contrast, the design of programs, and the assessment method of the programs by insider staff or third-party practitioners, rather reflect the expectations or assumptions shared by the fields of conflict resolution, peace building, and social psychology.

These steps are expressed conversely in terms of the expected localization of TJ as follows: enhancing recognition of the activity, forming motivation to participate in the process, experiencing and engaging in public events, and molding a collective identity based on unified memory. As such, a normalized TJ is formed as a product of discursive social construction that constitutes formalized public expectations among both local and foreign actors and a process of self-justification, which reacts to the preceding pattern of expectations.

Criticisms of Past Transitional Justice Programs

In reviewing past case studies of TJ, I found few that escaped these criticisms. The only "analyses" in which such criticisms do not appear are the self-justifications by internal TJ staff and stereotypical (foreign) media articles that say, for example, in an optimistic tone, "Nelson Mandela has promoted national reconciliation through the TRC."

Official TJ staffers never say that their work was a failure, because an honest confession would also require them to explain how they spent the official resources that were provided to them in exchange for their positive predictions. Therefore, staff assessments cannot be fully genuine reports and are not always useful for the purpose of evaluation of actual outcomes. However, they provide data by which researchers can understand how the official TJ body attempted to justify the ongoing process.

Just how do the formal expectations of an institutional TJ project fail to be realized? What are the primary criticisms of past TJ cases? To take a prominent example that has become a classic case in TJ textbooks,[16] the South African Truth and Reconciliation Commission has received a series of critical evaluations. Several of the criticisms have addressed shortcomings of the mandate and the commission's inability to involve the perspectives of all citizens. With respect to the framework of the TRC process, Mahmood Mamdani's (2009) criticism of the responsibility of the beneficiaries (i.e., those who did not directly commit injustices but benefited from them) is crucial. Mamdani focused on the definition of "perpetration" by the TRC, arguing that only actual criminal deeds were addressed while the systematic perpetration of the apartheid regime was ignored (pp. 472–473). For Mamdani, the TRC should have incorporated mandates such as addressing more systematic injustices as well as the role of the beneficiaries who stood on the side of the perpetrators in supporting the ruling party that had established the policy of apartheid.

Similarly, Ruben Carranza (2008:313) noted that the TRC could not address the corruption that occurred during the apartheid era because "corruption fell outside its mandate." Undoubtedly, most types of corruption or institutionally unfair economic gain involved white public-service personnel, thus again illustrating the impunity of the beneficiaries. Therefore, a request for a TJ project to address more economic injustice in times of conflict led to an appeal for involving certain social groups such as state officials.

Furthermore, the statistical data on testimonies collected by the commission generated various criticisms. Foremost among them was a concern that the statements were not collected equally among population groups. There was little doubt that the TRC collected many statements from Africans, particularly those who supported the African National Congress. Some have observed that several South African NGOs, including churches, offered a good foundation for local cooperation and criticized the TRC for not mobilizing local stakeholders and developing close relationships and lasting cooperation with these local NGOs (van der Merwe 2003:110–112; van der Merwe and Chapman 2008). Beneficiaries, former state officials, certain ethnic groups, and NGOs should have been involved in the TJ attempt. Further, the criticism of lack of involvement is not restricted to stakeholders, or to the TRC. Tim Kelsall's (2013:3) scathing criticism of the special tribunals in Sierra Leone cites the failure of the process "to adjust to the local culture in which it worked."

Positions that pursue the empowerment of victims are also criticized for their failure to implement essential provisions. The myriad forms of victimhood in TJ projects in general also remain a fundamental dilemma. Van der Merwe and Laurel Fletcher (2014:3) point out that these myriad forms led to "competing demands of victims":

> Some may want perpetrators punished, others prioritize full disclosure of state policies, and still others struggling to reestablish lives and livelihoods want material reparations. Particularly where resources constrain what demands may be satisfied, how are these competing demands to be reconciled? . . . Transitional justice needs victims but is incapable, even discursively, of recognizing them in their infinite variety, let alone satisfying their competing and conflicting needs.

The solution to this problem depends on a political process rather than a principle, inevitably resulting in complaints from those whose expectations are derailed by the TJ operation.[17] Thus, when evaluating past TJ activities, regardless of the discussant's position, almost all cases have been negatively assessed because they have not fulfilled formal expectations or lacked implementation of the essential elements, such as improving the rule of law in a local context and the realization of substantial victim empowerment.

In one such example, a negative report on the Serbian TJ program stated, "Today, eight years on, we witness the failure of this transition" (Dimitrijevic 2008:11). In another such case, Jelena Subotić (2009:38) stated, "The experience of transitional justice in Serbia has been one of great disappointment for international justice promoters."

Guatemalan judicial reform has also been dismissed as a failure: "A decade—and $165 million—later, the results of the reform programme are not impressive. The World Bank, one of its main donors, has rated the achievement of the goal of creating a more effective, accessible and credible judicial system performance as moderately unsatisfactory" (Zunino 2011:106).

Civil society shares this view:

> Fundación Myrna Mack has claimed that the reform of the judiciary delivered scant progress; Asociación de Investigación y Estudios Sociales has concluded that the strengthening of the judicial system has not been significant; and Grupo de Apoyo Mútuo has pugnaciously stated that the Guatemalan justice system is weak and unable to adjudicate according to law. (Zunino 2011:106)

Similarly, the Nigerian program has been described as "fundamentally flawed from the outset [due to] a deliberate ploy on the part of the government" (Yusuf 2007:269). In Sri Lanka, several attempts by postwar governmental commissions to disseminate the findings of their inquiries have failed because of internal political conflict. As a result, the nation has become indifferent to inquiries (Anonymous 2011:39).

One scholar lamented that no previous TJ program had achieved its goals:

> We have focused entirely too much on the notions of closure and reconciliation. Member states of the UN and European Union have expended considerable amounts of money and human resources on chasing a will-o'-the-wisp, adopting buzzwords that have no consistent definition or conceptual clarity and promoting mechanisms to achieve these obscure outcomes with little evidence that they will make a difference. (Weinstein 2011:3)

Another author echoed these critical choruses, wondering "whether there is anything we can do to lessen the disappointments and frustrations that often result from our attempts to pursue transitional justice" (McAdams 2011). As a policy, TJ cannot escape the success-failure debate; however, in the scholarly field, evaluations have almost always been on the side of failure. Should we, then, naturally perceive that future TJ needs to be replaced by another policy option? A hasty person may think that I have tried to dismiss the past TJ cases based on an arbitrary accumulation of critical notes. We can, however, inquire into the basis of these criticisms. Put differently, having a tendency to be criticized as failure is a specific condition of TJ, or of a social/political context in which TJ is implemented.

If one assesses the results of TJ activities in light of the official objectives, a TJ project will always be insufficient and incomplete because of a lingering shortage of resources, politically unstable circumstances, and the variety of victims' needs as mentioned above. However, is there another avenue for further consideration of the aspects that have been evaluated as failures? An auxiliary line of argument in this chapter is to replace the term *failure* with a discussion of deviations and derivatives from the expected steps of TJ activities.

Deviations and Derivatives from Expected Steps

Use of the concept *unintended consequence* in this volume is closely aligned with the earlier arguments that proposed seeking latent eufunctions of TJ. This interpretation invites describing TJ as having the possibility of being a "kinetic social institution" (Clark 2010:7), which may have indirect social influence as "unanticipated effects" (Orentlicher 2013:541), particularly for locals who are then allowed to behave as "positive deviants" (Duggan 2010:322). All these scholars distance themselves from the general stereotype or official self-justifying phrase that paints a TJ as promoting people's healing. Rather, they propose that people have found their own path for self-recovery in the course of involvement with a TJ process, a recovery outcome that was not anticipated or prepared by an official TJ body.

I have referred already to locals' *self-recovery*, yet wandering into a murky argument on how to define the word *recovery* might not be productive, given a general understanding of psychoanalysis. This field, particularly the Lacanian discourses, teaches us that we can neither predict when a traumatic symptom will appear on the surface of human consciousness nor identify what actually constitutes the traumatic experience as an objective fact.[18] Therefore, even if a patient insists that he or she has been healed, a reversal could still occur. In accordance with this view of trauma, the status of self-recovery should not be defined as fixed. Nevertheless, it can serve as a landmark for describing locals' various attempts to reconstruct their sense of life.

The self-recovery of locals thus represents one of the aspects of unintended consequences of TJ implementation, but we need a more substantial and observable reality that can be translated into a *symptom* of self-recovery. I suggest in this volume that autonomous meaning-making by locals can hold such a position, by which we can infer locals' self-recovery from their condition. *Meaning-making* incorporates various attempts by which locals remember and digest past experiences. It can take the form of resistance or challenge to an official TJ scenario, further deviating from the official stage to a unique amalgam with factors external to a TJ in a local context. These two terms, *self-recovery* and *meaning-making*, are not connected by an equals sign, and the gap between them, in theory, cannot be bridged intentionally by anyone, including the person who seeks recovery. I assume in this volume that the meaning-making is not supplied by an official TJ service, as it publicly seeks to do, but could happen in the unexpected or unplanned reactions of locals to the TJ, including deviations or derivatives from the official scenario. As described above, a contemporary TJ, or an institutional TJ at a normalized stage, would be shaped based on existing public expectations, yet these expectations would usually not be realized through the TJ's activities.

How the deviations and derivatives work will be discussed in relation to the four implementation steps of an institutional TJ, and each step (or derailment from the step) will be depicted in reference to sociological frameworks. These are deviant perception of the public message, divergent mobilization from official mobilization, an official stage with several scenarios, and commonality without a common marker. Below, I outline the theoretical frameworks that will be applied in Chapters 3 through 6.

Deviant Perception of the Public Message

Locals do not always receive public messages from an official TJ organization in a positive manner. These messages, reflecting the project's public character, have been colored by moralistic or surface ideals. Locals might react intentionally or unintentionally to those messages by challenging, ignoring, or tactically attempting to utilize them for their own benefit.

This pattern of recognition in the deviant perception of public messages by recipients, or the gap between official messages and their collective acceptance, has long been a research topic in the field of sociological inquiry. I will refer to works by Max Weber, Paul Willis, and Michel de Certeau to illustrate a variety of deviant perceptions of public or formal messages. Deviation can appear in a covert form (Weber), a challenging form (Willis), or a tactical form (de Certeau), and each form brings about unexpected or undesired outcomes from the viewpoint of the sender of public messages. By following the approaches laid out in these works, one can perceive local deviation as something other than a sign of project failure. Rather, the issue is how the recipients collectively distance themselves from the public or formal messages.[19]

Max Weber's *The Protestant Ethic and the Spirit of Capitalism* (originally published in 1905) properly fits into this pattern of analysis. Protestant reformer John Calvin argued that a follower could not affect God's final choice of salvation through worship or know who was destined for salvation.[20] However, at a deeper level of consciousness, followers secretly—subconsciously, to some extent—translated the pedagogy into a game with the goal of seeking out and confirming a prediction of the Last Judgment. Secular success—or the appearance of luck—was thus used by serious followers as a sign of their salvation. This secret individual game, Weber contemplated, would in time bring about a social change in the economic sphere in northern Europe once it was collectively implemented. Thus, the birth of a primitive form of capitalism is understood to appear through the latent eufunction of Calvinist dogma.

Paul Willis's *Learning to Labour* (1977) effectively illustrates this pattern of deviant acceptance of an official message in public education. A school in a democratic society is based on an ideal of equal educational opportunity for every child and communicates a public message that studying harder helps you rise higher in society. However, according to Willis, that official message, or social rule of fairness, is not directly accepted by students, particularly those from the working class.[21] Their resistance and rejection of the school norms, which equate formal knowledge and skill with worldly success, deny them the opportunity to climb up the ladder of social stratification, thus bringing about the reproduction of social class. School, in theory, provides the opportunity for these boys to demonstrate their competence in counterasocial activities such as chauvinistic masculinity and "street wisdom," which is opposite to the school's formal objective. This pattern is radical and is not generally witnessed in the TJ project, although it has appeared to some extent in a form of politics of victimhood.

Michel de Certeau's *The Practice of Everyday Life* (first published in 1980) contrasts the term *tactic* with *strategy*. The former represents the nature of the everyday practices of consumers (ordinary people), whereas the latter explains "the typical attitude of modern science, politics, and military strategy," which constitute "the calculation (or manipulation) of power" that isolates itself from the context and tries to control objects from "its own place" (de Certeau 1984:35–36).[22] The text basically talks about ordinary people's soft resistance to and casual deviance from the disciplinary social system in general, yet it can also be read from the perspective of how locals develop tactics to behave in a dualistic manner, that is, appearing on the surface to be subject to the norm while the substantial meaning of their behavior lies under the surface.[23] Responses to formal, public messages are not necessarily logical and overt, yet missing such subtle and casual signs from recipients may put an observer in a closed circuit with a self-referencing enlightenment scheme.

Chapter 3 will discuss these patterns of deviance, with the goal of revealing people's unpredictable ways of accepting official messages, which are derived from the formal expectations of an institutional TJ.

Divergent Mobilization from Official Mobilization

A TJ, often in the middle of contentious circumstances, engages in mobilizing as many locals as possible to participate in its official public events, regardless of whether they are victims, perpetrators, or bystanders. Recently, this approach has been indispensable among institutional TJ programs, and the topic of localizing TJ has become a major research topic.

Mobilization is translated into *local ownership* and, in a practical context, is described as *outreach activity*. Even if a high-caliber judicial inquiry and examination have been conducted, a TJ program without sufficient local recognition is seen as unlikely to have any positive impact on the affected society. Moreover, an elite pact, which alienates vast numbers of ordinary locals, and top-down declarations regarding past events have provided a source of continuing animosity, thus setting the stage for a likely future conflict. The ICTY in The Hague and the International Criminal Tribunal for Rwanda in Arusha have repeatedly referred to the concern that a TJ may have no positive effect on the very society to heal, despite the spending of huge amounts of resources and securing expert participation, because of its failure to connect with local circumstances and needs (Ciorciari 2009; Orentlicher 2013; Simić and Daly 2011; Subotić 2009). The ECCC, one of the most recent international justice initiatives, has specifically been described as a mechanism that has accommodated local ownership, in comparison to previous international tribunals in The Hague and Arusha, which have allowed victims to participate in the court process as "civil parties."[24]

Outreach programs have gained greater prominence in the context of TJ projects, based on both an eagerness to engage deeper insights into a post-conflict society and cost-benefit calculations on behalf of donor countries supporting TJ projects. In societies where legislative and judicial institutions routinely sanction severe human-rights violations by the authorities, and in a context where people no longer trust these institutions, courts need to mitigate "entrenched local suspicion and cynicism" and let them access, observe, and evaluate the "internal activities of the court" (January 2009:210, 225). A court, or any other official body, that is not perceived as legitimate will not be able to have its decisions perceived as truthful or legitimate. Outreach programs are increasingly relying on a technique of public mediation in these circumstances.

TJ entities thus begin their activities in negative circumstances, with people being suspicious of their messages. Obviously, they need to change these circumstances. Just announcing authoritatively one day, at some official place, "In a spirit of national reconciliation, we have decided to hold a forum (or court) to transcend past conflict; please come to the venue and join us if you agree with this idea," is insufficient. If any TJ organization were to conduct public relations in this manner, it would have no significant influence on the locals.

Therefore, mobilization of locals becomes a second mission for any TJ body, in view of the inevitable presence of negative local reactions to the initial announcement. Where a public announcement does not work, more direct communication, in the form of outreach, is required. A TJ project needs to ask for help from and coordinate with local agents such as churches, local media, and other NGOs to disseminate related information and to encourage locals to participate in such events as preparatory forums, seminars, and statement-taking meetings, all of which lead up to the project's main public events such as trial hearings and public-testimony forums.

These requirements and the difficulties of an institutional TJ project may well have the result that the organization begins to resonate more with the realities of local attitudes in identifying with social movements rather than with the policy implementation agenda of state or internationally authorized organizations.

Social-movement theories offer several theoretical frameworks such as *resource mobilization theory*,[25] which seeks social resources that sustainably maintain and develop a movement; *political opportunity structure theory*,[26] which considers political factors that facilitate the birth, deployment, and deterioration of a movement; and *framing analysis*, which has concentrated on how a movement expresses its aim, the background context of the movement, and future scenarios, all of which affect both whether and how fully people accept the movement. This volume mainly adopts a fourth approach, that of *propagation of movement repertoires*.

A social movement is not just a genuine expression of complainants but a calculated collective action, sometimes drawing on deliberate learning from prior movements. Information and episodes of movement in other areas are delivered and circulated among actors inside a movement. Thus, one can perhaps identify an action being successfully implemented at a different place from the original context, where the project had finished in failure. Propagation is surely open to a change in performance depending on the new situation, reminding us of the term *syncretism* in religious studies.

Incorporating the idea of propagation of movement repertoires has merit for deepening an understanding of local reactions to an institutional TJ program. The mobilization of a TJ body does not necessarily cause a positive reaction among locals, who may view the process with indifference. Yet there is another type of local action that appropriates, imitates, or develops an official program for its own interests and objectives. If we were to concentrate only on the internal activities of the TJ process, we would overlook these occurrences. In contrast, if we take the view that a TJ resonates with the public position of a social movement, which lacks established authority in the society, a TJ's ideal or motive implemented in a different place would be a subject for further inquiry.

Local actors do not always respond directly to the official calling. A TJ has no plan to generate local derivatives from its own official programs. However, when a similar motive, a developed program, or a more contextualized activity is deployed at an indirectly related space in the society concerned, these appearances can be captured by the term *propagation of repertoires*.

For TJ staffers who have confidence in the organization's authority and legitimacy, these appearances may be perceived as deviant. They might cause discomfort partly because they can be considered evidence of the dysfunction of the official program. But from a wider perspective grounded in the basic TJ principle—to make the affected society better—they should be recognized as a by-product of the TJ process, and a proper assessment of positive and negative impacts will require their contextual examination. Chapter 4 thus incorporates the framework of social-movement theory to widen our recognition of the influences of the TJ process and to deepen our understanding of these local reactions, including any symptoms of unintended consequences.

An Official Stage with Several Scenarios

A significant public event such as a trial hearing of an international or internationalized court, or a public testimony hearing of a truth commission, usually follows the official announcement of the new project and collective mobilization of locals. The mobilized people would be expected to experience the agenda at the official venue, which should be executed along with a directed scenario. In such a scenario, participants at a public trial or hearing understand the principle of the rule of law, respect the authority and expertise of the legal profession, are patient in listening to the lengthy professional discussions, and accept the final decision. Another desirable result is acknowledgment of the realization of justice and healing through overcoming trauma.

One may expect that in a routine scenario of a truth commission, people are transformed into subjects who cooperate willfully with the statement-taking procedure, display compassion and support for the speaker on the stage of the public hearing, and agree with the commissioners' concluding comments (though they are often criticized as part of a master narrative, to use Chidester's term), which tend to refer to the people's victimhood as an inevitable step in the country's democratization or political change.

However, reviewing the detailed records of past TJ public events shows that the above scenario seems to have changed its orbit. A variety of happenings—what anthropologists have called messiness—have intruded onto the stage, including audiences' challenges to the judges, fabricated statements, emotional outbursts, witnesses dropping into silence, or the uncontrollable excitement of the audience, followed by discontinuation of the proceedings. These happenings demonstrate the actual conditions of the program and its title of "transitional." They remind us that the public event is not undergirded by stable authority and legitimacy in the concerned society, is often held before sufficient human and other social resources have been secured, and has suspicious people in the audience at the venue who are not really aware of, or are not content with, the official scenario.

The term *scenario* is appropriate because the social context of a public TJ event is much like a political drama. According to David Apter, an *official drama* is most required in a society in transition:

> Political theatre becomes most significant in politically rupturing moral moments. That is, when political theatre aims at far more than ritual exercise, when it seeks to capture and encapsulate in performance such solemn occasions as the founding of new societies and states, or moments of revolutionary transformation, or redemptive moments, it becomes most important, especially in establishing when it is that old orders transgress and purifying alternatives come into being. (Apter 2006:250)

Specific roles are allotted to the participants, or performers, in this political drama, causing them to become subject to the official scenario. Yet the motif of deviation and derivatives has consistently appeared; even though official messages overtly or covertly request participants to behave in accordance with the rules and norms of the venue, or the *official theater*, the allotted roles are not necessarily performed as the scenario plans. As Erving Goffman (1959) observed, role performance often deviates from the norm. Or the prescribed roles are misunderstood by either the performer or the audience. Thus, a public drama may continue toward an unplanned, unexpected, or undesirable place by a strange path.

From the beginning, the condition of transitional society, where social norms are unstable and ambiguous, implies that not all performers will function in the roles allotted to them. The paradox that a normalized policy is implemented in a situation where the norm that should endorse the policy is not shared among actors surely sets the stage for diverse results.

Those who are in charge of managing the official scenario are not really in a secure position. They do not embody enough authority and legitimacy, yet they need to control these deviant actions. Some court officials (such as judges) have misunderstood their position as having established authority and have executed forcible power. As a result, the venue has been spoiled by the perception that it is an exclusive stage for elites. Such authorities cannot deal with local expectations, and they cannot take a completely open stance, welcoming any request. In the course of stressful negotiation with the complainants and balancing between the official scenario and the substantial needs of victims, participants become aware of the emergence of a principle different from either legal logic or a humanitarian sense of empowerment.

The framework of a dramaturgical approach might be beneficial in such a situation where the people gathered seem prepared to maintain the stage and the process of drama; however, in this instance, some participants do not completely understand the scenario or consciously attempt to disturb it. Some people appear at the venue with the clear intention of challenging the official scenario; their purpose is not to destroy the stage but to reshape it in their intended direction.

Goffman (1959) provided the example of passengers in a train car who are unknown to each other. These passengers may share in a drama by pretending to see nothing when a passenger in front of them performs a shameful deed. The term *role-playing* thus does not explain only how each performer performs for his or her benefit. Even while some participants' acts can be viewed as (negative) deviance from an official scenario, others can be interpreted, from the dramaturgical perspective, as derivatives of role-playing according to, or subject to, the local context. Those unwelcome performers from the TJ's official viewpoint might behave as they do, not for their own profit but rather to try to contribute to a TJ drama, albeit with misunderstanding or misconceptions about the stage and scenario. The theoretical framework, by presupposing layers of motivations or understanding among actors at a public event, is conducive to addressing the participants' inconsistent and sometimes paradoxical surface behaviors.

Commonality Without a Common Marker

An institutional TJ would seek to guide the various societal constituents toward sharing the official interpretation of the past collective experiences by constructing its authority and legitimacy parallel to the implementation of a program. However, as we have seen above, this process is messy and confronts indifference and challenges from locals. The process is beyond the total control of TJ organizations. But in a practical sense, if the public slogan or official objective is assessed as having been achieved, the policy and staff can be given a hearty sendoff. Is this expectation feasible?

As already mentioned, the epithet *transitional* appears in (institutional) TJ because an ordinary justice system cannot function in the society. Yet to prevent the recurrence of armed conflict or of return to the prior nondemocratic, authoritarian regime, the following elements are regarded as crucial for such a conflict-affected society:

- violence and political connections are no longer viewed as the primary means to solve social problems;
- animosity and distrust, which could provide the source of another outbreak of violence, are mitigated; and
- interaction and mutual recognition among former enemies is ongoing, or the role of a trusted mediator, such as the government or the UN, is accepted.

In TJ terminology, these elements are translated into the adoption of the following expressions: democratization and rule of law, victim empowerment, and collective identity.

Yet these assumed requirements for preventing the recurrence of violence are, in reality, interconnected, standing in a relationship in which they require each other as preconditions for their enactment. These requirements are subsumed under the term *national reconciliation* or *social (re)integration*, which signifies the realization of a shared national identity. For this goal to be realized, a society must be perceived not as a divided one where an excluded group, which might be the target of armed attack, still remains, but as a unified society in which collective bonds (norms, values, and identity) are shared among people. The series of external expectations of and internal self-justifications for an institutional TJ project culminate in this point. Authorized texts such as court judgments or truth commissions' final reports can become symbolic objects through which people would be expected to discover a unified, collective identity. But, as the previous discussions have repeatedly stressed, a process filled with deviations, challenges, and derivatives will rarely leap to the desired goal.

For instance, many observers have described the South African TRC as a positive example of a TJ program. But Brandon Hamber, who has been engaging in reconciliation work in South Africa and Northern Ireland, has reservations about crediting the South African TRC with bringing about national reconciliation. To assess it, he proposes a "five-strand reconciliation model," consisting of (1) developing a shared vision of an independent and fair society, (2) acknowledging and dealing with the past, (3) building positive relationships, (4) acknowledging significant cultural and attitudinal change, and (5) promoting substantial social, economic, and political change (involving equity and equality) (Hamber 2009:159–161; Hamber and Kelly 2005:38–40). Hamber's assessment of the TRC, based on these criteria, was that "South Africa could be said to be strong on strands 1 and 2, mediocre to poor on strands 3 and 4, and particularly weak on strand 5" (Hamber 2009:161).

The TRC's final report did not contain either a definition or an interpretation of the abstract goal (national reconciliation), whereas another ambiguous term, *truth*, was explained. The report presented four dimensions of truth—namely, factual or forensic truth, personal and narrative truth, dialogical truth, and healing and restorative truth. The final report's understanding of truth is without doubt open to various interpretations by readers, and it does not claim to be the single authorized version of the historical script. The editorial tone was reinforced by President Mandela's speech at the report's publication ceremony in October 1998. But it is believed that the report's message did not actually reach many South Africans[27] and remained merely symbolic.

External donors usually expect that national reconciliation or social integration will be realized through official TJ processes, and the institutional TJ body itself has used this criterion for the self-justification of its programs. Yet after several years of implementation, observers usually come to realize that actually accomplishing that objective can hardly be proved empirically. As a result, when reviewing assessments of the degree to which national reconciliation has been achieved, we may need to watch for an intentional focus on a specific topic or maneuver of discourses by specific actors.

On the contrary, the past tendency has been to conclude that the results of published attitude surveys on the outcomes or effectiveness of TJ projects have consistently been negative, particularly with regard to mutual recognition between formerly antagonistic parties. It may not be surprising that bringing warring groups to the point of national reconciliation or social integration after a lengthy conflict would take a longer time than the period of the official TJ process; however, for those who had believed in any possibility of transformation in a radical manner, the survey results could create further distrust.

This evaluation is primarily based on criteria that require, in theory, all the social constituents to share a common marker of "us." Many theoretical bases of sociological inquiries presuppose the existence of shared norms to achieve the collective dimension of human interactions.[28] The term *social norm* covers many forms of actual appearance in a public space, such as collective identity, traditions or customs, common sense, and discourse on faith or values, including justice. Collective identity has been explained as a social construct that can be achieved through people sharing a unified writing script style (Benedict Anderson), authorized symbolic materials entitled to tradition (Eric Hobsbawm), or an attitudinal code of collective forgetting of past conflict (Ernest Gellner). These arguments converge in that they all envision people collectively sharing a specific form of behavior. Reaching a point where people cannot present any suspicion, inquiry, doubt, question, or challenge prepares the society for the achievement of the collective dimension of human interactions as a form of national identity, leading to successive social effects being deployed under the guise of nationalism.

A basic logic of these orthodox explanations of nationalism seems suitable for assessing the people's progress toward social integration through an institutional TJ program, because TJ is formally recognized as a way to open opportunities for locals to do the following:

- to experience a specific stage collectively by being part of the drama on it;
- to witness others behaving in accordance with their official calling and to confirm that a norm is publicly shared; and
- to listen to or read the authentic text, which is open to anyone who wants to access it.

However, these directed steps for encouraging locals to share a common marker of "us" have unexpectedly invited derivations. To address this reality, I adopt an alternative theoretical framework on the issue of social integration or national reconciliation, particularly concentrating on the sphere of sustainable interactions among conflicting parties.

Another approach loosely connected to the framework of social cohesion has been explored through the arguments on *substate nationalism* (Will Kymlicka), *contentious coexistence* (Leigh Payne), and *mimetic desire* (René Girard). These views all explore a paradoxical relationship in a lasting condition as well as the possibility of social cohesion, especially among conflicting people who do not necessarily share a unified status.

These interpretations are not included in the official perspective of an institutionalized TJ because of their emphasis on the continuing presence of conflict, but they represent a specific aspect of social dynamics that can be expected to characterize the interaction and experience of locals during a TJ process. How these deviations or derivatives from the official TJ process are or are not associated with the concept of unintended consequences will be further explored in Chapter 6.

Notes

1. This general remark has been empirically supported by the surveys conducted by organizations such as the World Bank and Transparency International. The former's *Worldwide Governance Indicators* provides indicators on the governance of each country by measuring six dimensions: voice and accountability; political stability and absence of violence; government effectiveness; regulatory quality; rule of law; control of corruption. When searching weak countries in regard to the status of their rule of law in 2016, the ranked countries match the social conditions of politically conflicted or authoritarian regimes (http://info.worldbank.org/governance/wgi/#home; accessed on December 15, 2017). The latter's *Corruptions Perceptions Index 2016* (Transparency International 2017) shows the correlation between corruption issues and political conflict or authoritarian political status. Signs of corruption do not stem only from political conflict and authoritarian political status; however in this index, countries with such conditions as political conflict and authoritarian status are not ranked for political transparency because of corruption issues. These data allow us to infer the rule-of-law status of those societies.

2. The following interview with an Argentine military official illustrates well the gap between regulation and operation: "We live in a civilized country [Argentina] without law . . . This country is a caricature of democracy, and it always has been. All of these institutions are false, because they exist artificially . . . If Argentines woke up one morning and they were living with the laws of the United States, they would feel like they were in a dictatorship. Punishment for violating the system? . . . There is no such thing as equality under the law" (Payne 2000:59).

3. *Gacaca* is a type of community court in Rwanda, organized to deal with genocide suspects. It can be loosely translated as "justice on the grass." Gacaca rendered sentences on lower-level cases, whereas more serious crimes were put before the national court and the International Criminal Tribunal for Rwanda.

4. Duggan writes of "those victims who manage to coexist in close proximity with perpetrators and reconstruct their life projects despite disappointing truth commissions and undelivered reparations. Admittedly, this will be difficult in the aid world given the multiple accountabilities at play and the different set of reasons why admitting failure is less than appetizing to donors" (Duggan 2010:322).

5. An example of "unanticipated effects" is as follows: "One of the most valuable effects of the ICTY's work in the former Yugoslavia was not foreseen: it has helped spur the development of domestic war crimes chambers" (Orentlicher 2013:15).

6. In Max Weber's interpretation, Christians reinvested the benefits derived from their labor in their personal enterprises. Without intending to affect society at large, they viewed the secular success of their business as a sign of their redemption. Yet the accumulation of such motivation and behavior on a social level generated unintended consequences in the form of early capitalism (Weber 1930). This classic and representative work on unintended consequences at a collective level demonstrates that the sum of many individual behaviors may generate uncontrollable outcomes at the collective level that actors cannot calculate or even foresee. (Furthermore, these uncontrollable outcomes, which people unintentionally produce, may later control their lives in various ways.) This explanation has no connotation of an opposite relationship in value between the followers' endeavors, based on their unique spiritual interpretation, and the birth of an early system of capitalism, because the followers were still obedient at a behavioral level to the norm regarding their *beruf* (calling). Rather, the social change was understood as the uncontrollable and unforeseeable collective effect of individual reactions to Protestant dogma.

7. In a sociological context, paradoxical social phenomena that do not conform to ordinary cause-effect logic have been keenly pursued in analyses of collective activities. How can something negative have any positive function in the public space with a collective dimension? Emile Durkheim proposed one answer by considering the function of *halfway belonging* and *inversion of meaning* between different social dimensions. Latent eufunction is, at a glance, not given further logic in itself, yet the following explanation provides some patterns that permit us to take this concept further in analyzing social issues.

Durkheim's classic works on the social context of suicide and the collective function of particular categories of crime are conducive to clarifying the logic of paradoxical functions. In terms of suicide, people usually take bipolar positions, which are not actually incompatible with each other. They claim that either a close human relationship or individual freedom will help a person not to feel complete desperation. The former avoids leaving someone in total loneliness, and the latter allows someone to seek new human contacts, which may open up new communication and an idea for restarting one's life. However, Durkheim's analysis of the collective data on suicide demonstrated that neither close human relationships nor expanded freedom was conducive to lowering the suicide rate, whereas the areas where these factors were recognized as neither high nor low showed a lower rate. The finding suggests that a situation of being neither too closely connected nor too liberated might function best to prevent people from making such an ultimate decision. In other words, a specific incomplete, insufficient, or ambiguous situation, which could be regarded by modernists and traditionalists alike as "not enough," might have paradoxically worked to direct people's action.

Durkheim's argument on the function of the (social) category of crime also takes a parallel route in arguing for a paradoxical effect of negative representation, or a "signifier," in a public space. A social procedure in which a criminal is punished in public and alienated from a public space prepares for collective solidarity among noncriminals. This logic indicates that a socially negative factor could paradoxically bring about another collective effect, which can often be accepted as a positive function. This can be an exemplar of a latent function of crime, or of a category of crime.

8. This "normalization" may match the contemporary change in armed conflict that Mary Kaldor (2006:4) describes: "The new wars involve a blurring of distinctions between war . . . organized crimes . . . and large-scale violations of human rights."

9. This surely shares a common idea with the concept of restorative justice in terms of the reintegration of former perpetrators for a more stable and connected community.

10. This information was obtained from the ICTJ website, https://www.ictj.org.

11. Partly because of how the NRC was created, many Muslims in the southern region expected it to affect state policy in an immediate and positive manner. Yet twenty-four of the twenty-eight main meetings that the NRC held between April 2005 and April 2006 took place in Bangkok, mostly as a means of editing the final report, and the so-called Bangkok elite dominated most discussions. Malay Muslims, the stakeholders on one side of this conflict, "were often less comfortable speaking in Thai and found the presence of so many senior figures—including leading security officials—rather intimidating" (McCargo 2010:78). The commission could not agree on its fundamental direction with regard to the goal of reconciliation contained in its title, as it was trapped in a dilemma between justice issues and Malay Muslims' desire for greater autonomy. In addition to these institutional flaws, popular media, such as the *Thai Rath* newspaper, expressed their deep mistrust of the commission as likely to defer to the position of Malay Muslims. This view that the NRC was "leasing [radical] Muslims" was connected with suspicions about the ideal of one indivisible kingdom (McCargo 2010:85, 87).

12. A hybrid tribunal such as a Cambodian court is formally established as a domestic court with international input in terms of legal regulation and staff. It is not formally an international court but is commonly described as "internationalized," as it is substantially an international institution supported by foreign staff.

13. A visual image is available at http://www.eccc.gov.kh/en/media-center/photos/tag/outreach?page=1, accessed on January 22, 2017.

14. John Paul Lederach shares the methodology for interpreting the word *reconciliation*. "Engaging the sides of a conflict with each other as humans-in-relationship," "finding ways to address the past without getting locked into a vicious cycle of mutual exclusiveness," and "envisioning the shared future" are the important assumptions he proposes (Lederach 1997:26–27).

15. One of the most crucial steps in the sequence is (2). What is the alleged mechanism of change in mutual understanding and acquisition of new identification of the self or the other? How does this model explain that such a change can be induced in parties that are deeply estranged? Ronald Fisher insists that continuing dialogue gives participants increasing information, which induces cognitive dissonance in regard to their simplified beliefs or stereotypes of the other. It is difficult for participants to ignore this cognitive dissonance, and they come to adjust their attitude to one compatible with the new information (Fisher 2001:31–32). A change in one's identity is also assumed to ensue, as participants reach a "higher level of inclusiveness [so that] they may see themselves as belonging to the same group" (Riek et al. 2008:261). Such a desirable outcome is brought about when participants recognize "more of the total field of forces acting on their adversary in both the past and the present" and where participants are expected to come to see that "each party has been making difficult choices in this complex environment" (Fisher 2001:33).

16. Judith Renner (2013:2) describes the South African TRC in the following manner: "Since the South African experience, scholars and political practitioners have been fascinated by the idea that truth-telling in a truth commission might be a way to national reconciliation. Today, long after the end of its existence, the South African TRC remains, as Claire Moon puts it, the 'indisputable *locus classicus*' (Moon 2008:1; emphasis in original) for the global quest for reconciliation. The underlying assumptions and the working processes of the TRC have constantly, and often uncritically, been reproduced in the scientific discourse, and the assumption that public truth-telling in a truth commission leads to reconciliation has been established as a relatively stable knowledge." See also Fletcher (2015), Hayner (2001), and Minow (1999).

17. Van der Merwe and Fletcher (2014:3) continue: "And so we are left with victims and their advocates pressing transitional justice to be more and do more. Transitional justice should be more responsive to victims, should do more to meet their desires for how societies respond to mass violence and their experiences of it, and should do a better job at implementing the promises made by transitional justice mechanisms. These are mechanisms that rely on victims to function and to be considered legitimate. Therefore, there is an ongoing negotiation or struggle between transitional justice mechanism and victims."

18. "Consequently, the ultimate goal of psychoanalysis is not the confessionary pacification/gentrification of the trauma, but the acceptance of the very fact that our lives involve a traumatic kernel beyond redemption, that there is a dimension of our being which forever resists redemption—deliverance" (Žižek 2000:98).

19. There can be another viewpoint on this topic, namely, the possibility of no influence. In terms of this, an argument from the field of media studies is suggestive. In that field, scholars have long considered how the mass media influences an audience. At the earliest stage of understanding the mass media, ideas such as the "magic

bullet model" or "hypodermic needle model," both of which anticipated direct acceptance of the intended message by the audience, were proposed. This simplistic assumption was soon discarded, giving way to a more moderate conception of agenda setting, priming, and framing. Although the similarities, differences, and relationships among these concepts are still under discussion (Entman 2007; Rill and Davis 2008; Scheufele and Tewksbury 2007; Weaver 2007), they basically all presuppose correlations between media coverage and public perception, yet the logic is more indirect. Agenda setting asserts a "transfer of salience from the media to the public" (Kiousis 2011:360). The idea behind so-called first-level agenda-setting hypotheses is that the news media's salience has an impact on the audience's change of attitudes and opinions: "When mass media emphasize a topic, the audience/public receiving the message will consider this topic to be important" (Walgravel and Van Aelst 2006:88). In light of the assertion that the mass media have minimal impact on public attitudes and opinions (Klapper 1960, cited in Kiousis 2011:361), the idea appeared in the 1970s that second-level agenda setting "examines the relative salience of attributes of issues," whereas the first level is "focused on the relative salience . . . of issues" (Weaver 2007:142).

Scholars do not necessarily expect the media to mold the opinions of audiences or readers, but they assume that the media exert their influence to make people prioritize among several issues and take more interest in some specific issues to which the media attributes salience. Nevertheless, we need to be careful of the tone of the argument, being vigilant to the point that people do not accept the prioritization given by the media even while the media influence people's attitudes toward prioritization.

20. For Calvin, "God does not exist for men, but men for the sake of God. . . . Everything else, including the meaning of our individual destiny, is hidden in dark mystery which it would be both impossible to pierce and presumptuous to question. We know only that a part of humanity is saved, the rest damned. To assume that human merit or guilt play a part in determining this destiny would be to think of God's absolutely free decrees, which have been settled from eternity, as subject to change by human influence, an impossible contradiction" (Weber 1930:59–60). On the other hand, a secular vocation was taught in the form of the doctrine that one ought to accept one's calling (*beruf*) or sacred duty. Thus, a follower was religiously compelled to concentrate on living a diligent life, with no desire to use the surplus profits from his or her work for personal pleasure but only for further investment in his or her economic mission.

21. Although those boys are not actually inferior to other students, they prefer using the school as a social space to demonstrate their competence in countercultural activities rather than conforming to the "work hard, move forward" mentality. The counterculture entails preference for factors such as chauvinistic masculinity, practical knowledge or "street wisdom," and hard manual labor, which are without doubt familiar to the boys' surrounding world.

22. An ordinary person, a user of a given rule, or a consumer in the capitalist market, who is also subsumed under the term "the weak," continues to "operate," utilize, or reappropriate the space "organized by techniques of sociocultural production" among the "forces alien to" the person (de Certeau 1984:xv, xx).

23. Scholars of cultural studies who have intensively addressed receivers' creative way of reading the messages contained in films, advertisements, and fashion modes have shared a similar motive. The accumulation of arguments in cultural studies can also be read as inquiring into a deviant perception of public messages in a wider sense.

24. A civil party is the official status given to officially recognized individual victims in Cambodia, allowing them to be involved in the court process in more substantive procedural ways. That status gives them the same rights as other parties to the case file and to be present in hearings, where they can question suspects

and witnesses (through a civil party lawyer) and seek compensation for their losses during the Khmer Rouge regime.

25. Various complaints by various people are always present within a society (McCarthy and Zald 1977). However, some movements become real and others fade out. The result is identified with the concrete factors and conditions that a movement possesses, such as money, place, (potential) human networks, and availability of staff for broadening, accelerating, and sustaining the movement.

The analytical point of view is how and what resources are acquired by the particular movement. This theory understands a collective movement as a rational and strategic project.

For example, Freeman analyzed the feminist movement in the United States in the late 1960s from the perspective of resource mobilization and focused on the necessary strategy and tactics and mobilizable resources used to attain the movement's goals. The resources in the analysis included feminist publications, letters sent to governmental bodies to apply pressure to policy planners, and institutional resources such as labor unions (Freeman 1979). Other scholars dubbed the movement body's strategy and tactics "mobilizing technology" (Oliver and Marwell 1992:256).

26. This approach is based on the political process model provided by Charles Tilly (1978) and Doug McAdam (1982), who considered environmental variables such as political accessibility and the possibility of cooperation with political elites. Sidney Tarrow defined political opportunity structure theory as describing "consistent . . . dimensions of the political struggle that encourage people to engage in contentious politics' (1994:19–20). For others, the concept of political opportunity includes certain broad factors, such as (1) the relative openness or closure of the institutionalized political system; (2) the stability or instability of that broad set of elite alignments that typically undergird a polity; (3) the presence or absence of elite allies; and (4) the state's capacity and propensity for repression (McAdam 1996:27). Kriesi et al. (1995) proposed the concept of social cleavage between center and periphery, urban and rural, and labor workers and bourgeoisie in applying the term *political opportunity*, which is composed of interconnected factors such as the structure of political institutions, dominant strategy, and allied structure.

27. See the argument on Reconciliation Barometer Survey of IJR in Chapter 4 for this topic. By comparison, the report of Argentina's truth commission, *Nunca Más* (Never Again), has been a bestseller in the country; however, it is unclear whether those who bought the book really read its whole contents or how the text has been read by those who obtained it.

28. Sociologist Talcott Parsons discussed the term *double contingency* in his social system theory (Parsons and Shils 1951; Parsons 1968). He explained that a fundamental contingency exists between actions and reactions in all relationships because the initial action expects a reaction. However, the reaction cannot be foreseen. It is contingent on the action but also theoretically open to several possible options. Therefore, the reaction occurs under contingent conditions. In his social system theory, Parsons (1968:437) stated that individuals rely on social norms when they make logical attempts to remedy this unstable condition. Social norms prevent people from becoming trapped in endless vacillation before they take action.

3

Goodwill and Ideals in the Face of Resistance

Institutional TJ programs are established with certain expectations, such as resolving the social problems caused by adverse relations, mutual distrust, political unfairness, and corruption, and helping a society proceed toward a correct future based on the ultimate ideals of justice and national reconciliation. An institutional TJ project is, and must be, an official organization that is formally, at least on its surface, based on the *goodwill and ideals* of a new government. In this sense, a proper TJ program tries to behave as a trustworthy mass medium that announces authentic information and leads social constituents in the right direction.

The character of TJ as an *authentic and ethically correct mass medium* seems to be legitimized by the assumption that a TJ program can promote citizens' trust in the state by exhibiting improvements in state morality (de Greiff 2010:23–25; Winter 2013:232). The logic of this legitimization is close to that of the old-fashioned "hypodermic needle model" or "magic bullet model" in media studies, which assumed that audiences generally react to information precisely as intended by the producer of the information. The idea that a nation becomes subject to a government as a caring guardian does not correspond to any of the power models advanced by Max Weber: charismatic authority, traditional authority, or rational legal authority. Whereas Michel Foucault critically explained the pastoral mode of power in a modern society (in contrast with the sovereign mode of military power held by feudal kings), which involves caring for and acquiring a reputation among the flock, the expectation of TJ programs is that they will gain the spontaneous support of locals. In the same vein, some argue that TJ can be a pedagogic medium,[1] providing an opportunity for civic education through which people in a post-conflict society learn public rules in general, such as those embodied by justice and democracy.

However, this cause–effect logic has not necessarily been realized in past TJ cases. Thus, this chapter considers why and how such forms of formal goodwill, presented in the form of a new government and new social ideals, are challenged and dismissed by audiences. The following section starts by identifying several senders of the official message.

The Untrustworthy Preacher

Among TJ options, a local government is often the sender of a positive message at the first stage of establishing a truth commission (TC). In the case of an international or internationalized tribunal, however, the international community tends to be the first messenger. The international community (typically the UN) calls on the local society to change its social conditions in a correct manner through the establishment and operation of an international judiciary. Those who still believe in the hypodermic needle model or magic bullet model may foresee a smooth reception of that international justice norm by the local society. Yet past TJ cases demonstrate that conflicts can arise in this doctor-patient relationship even at this stage, before the establishment of any official entity.

For instance, locals in transitional Egypt criticized this international goodwill-and-ideals approach toward the establishment of a TJ project. Reem Abou-El-Fadl (2012:320–321) indicated that locals complained about the TJ option suggested by the international community, particularly the United States and European countries that had supported Hosni Mubarak's regime but swiftly accommodated the new status quo without scrutinizing their own responsibility. One example cited international governments' involvement in the "extraordinary rendition" implemented in collaboration between intelligence officers of the Mubarak government and other governments: "One of the many victims was an Egyptian citizen Ahmad Agiza, who was kidnapped by Swedish security and American intelligence personnel in Sweden while seeking asylum and deported to Egypt as a terror suspect after the 9/11 attacks, where he spent over ten years in jail without charge" (Abou-El-Fadl 2012:321).

TJ projects, up to this point, have not included in their agenda the issue of responsibility for past abuses by such international governments. It is reasonable to predict that locals in the concerned society will doubt the claims of goodwill, or any positive messages, emanating from such an international agency. Local doubts about the selective justice of any TJ attempts thus become a baseline influencing local responses to international peace interventions.

As in the Egyptian case, where locals faulted what they considered the unprincipled approach taken by the international community to the regime change, the UN and other supportive countries were not able to gain trust and legitimacy from many Cambodians when they proposed the establishment of an international(ized) court (Extraordinary Chambers in the Courts of Cambodia, or ECCC) to try former Khmer Rouge (KR) cadres. When the international tribunals to try former KR cadres were adopted, the court's legitimacy, which would be guaranteed by the international standard of justice through the UN's backing, was questioned by ordinary locals.[2]

For example, one participant in a local NGO forum said, "I don't understand why they [the KR leaders] have to go on trial [when] one of the seats at the UN was given to [the] KR. It is very confusing."[3] Another participant wondered, "What did the UN do to stop the killing? Why didn't they stop it? [Why did the countries with UN seats] even recognize a UN seat occupied by the KR?"[4] These questions showed that the ECCC could not gain legitimacy through the backing of the UN alone.[5] The participants painted the UN as a duplicitous entity that supported the KR until 1990 and was responsible for the long-lasting Cambodian conflict, but was now prosecuting the KR leaders. (The UN had also committed to providing a defense team for the KR leaders and judges for the court, but forum participants often did not consider these aspects when opining on the tribunals.) If people dispute the legitimacy of the UN, court officials will lose the authority to educate them.[6]

As one looks back at the process of political negotiation between the UN and the Cambodian government on the establishment of the ECCC, it becomes clear that widespread questioning of the lead organization's hegemony in implementing a TJ policy among stakeholders was the first societal reaction to the formal goodwill-and-ideals approach.

Let us further explore this issue in the case of the Cambodian court. The idea of establishing the KR tribunal became a realistic possibility in 1999, when the UN finally responded favorably to the Cambodian request for the UN's assistance in setting up such a court.[7] However, the Cambodian government's plans for the tribunal diverged greatly from those of the UN task force, and difficulties emerged in balancing the applicability of domestic and international laws with the mandate of the ECCC.[8]

Notably, the Cambodian government had previously asked the UN to establish an international tribunal. This request occurred in 1990, when the State of Cambodia suggested that the UN create such a tribunal to try the Pol Pot perpetrators in the Nuremberg style; however, the conflicting parties in Cambodia and other countries were in the process of negotiating a possible settlement of the civil war, which finally led to the Paris Peace Agreement of 1991. Few countries at that time accepted the idea of an international tribunal as a suitable option for pursuing social stability.

However, by the time of the surrender of the top KR leaders, Ieng Sary in 1996 and Khieu Samphan and Nuon Chea in 1998, priorities in domestic politics had shifted. An internationally assisted court was not the imperative any longer, and the need to adhere to the political deal, expressed under the slogan of national reconciliation, came to the foreground. In informal negotiations between the government and top leaders of the KR, such as Nuon Chea and Khieu Samphan, it was agreed that the government would not try those former cadres in an international court and would instead use a domestic mechanism whereby the process would end in a pardon. On December 25, 1998, following these private negotiations, Nuon Chea and Khieu Samphan surrendered unconditionally, and Hun Sen responded to them with his "warmest welcome" and thanked them for their "precious will to end war and seek peace, national reconciliation and national union" (Fawthrop and Jarvis 2004:134).

As the domestic political scene had thus changed, the Cambodian government was wary of sanctioning the establishment of a fully internationally controlled tribunal. In July 1999, the Royal Government of Cambodia (RGC) rejected the UN's proposal for a hybrid tribunal with a majority of international legal experts. The Cambodian prime minister insisted that Cambodians hold the majority of these positions. From the outset, the RGC and the UN experts had different motives for the possible tribunal. The Cambodian side sought to minimize the UN's influence over legal decisions, whereas the UN officials expected a more internationally inclined operation in terms of judicial standards and the large numbers of people accused (see Ciorciari 2009:67).

After the introduction of the concept of a hybrid tribunal, the topic of "balance of influence" (Ciorciari 2009:72) emerged as the focal point of contestation for negotiations on the precise mechanism: Which side would have a majority of judges, whose law would govern, and who would stand trial? Whereas the UN secretary-general announced that he would agree to such a mixed court only if it had a majority of international judges and an independent international prosecutor, the Cambodian government did not change its stance. Finally, on August 10, 2001, the RGC enacted the ECCC law, which included many clauses that the UN had rejected, without seeking an agreement with the UN negotiators. According to the International Bar Association (IBA), "UN negotiators believed that what the Cambodians really wanted was to maintain complete control, making few, if any, concessions to the UN, while gaining the hallmark of the UN to add legitimacy to the court" (International Bar Association 2011:17). Eventually, the RGC's position was confirmed by the UN General Assembly. The secretary-general's warnings "were ignored by the Member States. The General Assembly, despite 'taking note of the report of the Secretary-General,' approved the draft with no changes on 13 May 2003" (IBA 2011:19).

The ECCC was eventually established in 2006 as a composite of both international and domestic laws, with local and foreign staff members. At the beginning, it was deemed to reflect the principle of local ownership at the institutional level, like the tribunals for Sierra Leone and East Timor. However, as of 2018, after twelve years of operation, appraisals of the ECCC's hybrid structure as a realization of local ownership are now far more uneven. The hybrid system had initially been conceived with the intent that institutional local ownership would be secured, and that the related institutions and actors in Cambodian society would be empowered. Instead, retrospectively, the system created an arena wherein Cambodian and international experts continued to experience tensions and conflicts along national and international lines. In sum, the tensions over the ECCC's composition, visible during negotiations to establish the court, continued to center on the RGC's preference for a greater role for the local judiciary, whereas UN officials preferred as much influence as possible over the prosecution. This basic tension remains a defining feature of the hybrid model.

Even when the idea of TJ is finally accepted, the society involved—the RGC in this case—might exhibit a great deal of resistance to a proposed program because it does not want the international community (the UN in this case) to execute the program as it desires under the banner of justice. Even though the establishment of TJ has been officially decided, what mechanism of TJ should be adopted and in what manner becomes a point of conflict and lingering political negotiation. Furthermore, these conflicts and negotiations affect the original idea of TJ, which is reshaped in the political context of the specific society so as eventually to take on a different image from the one announced in the beginning (characterized by fairness and neutrality).

Normative Compliance as Window Dressing: Serbia

Local responses to such international bias may take on a complex appearance. A society that accepts a TJ program can behave in a very strategic way in response to international political pressure. A transitional government understands certain biases of international politics and accepts, actively or passively, a proposal by the international community to implement a TJ project. They know that the game is biased, yet they dare to enter the arena with a specific purpose.

Recognition of the Biased Ideal

Jelena Subotić criticizes arguments that attribute the acceptance of global norms by local political elites to their positive intention to comply with them, because many states "show signs of normative compliance . . . for window dressing in order to ease international pressure while in fact continuing, and even stepping up, normative violations at home" (Subotić 2009:29). Local political elites can be divided into three types of respondents: norm resisters, instrumental norm adopters, and true believers. The last category tends to be occupied by local civil society groups or other political coalitions.

According to Subotić's classification, norm resisters are political elites who ideologically or politically oppose the norms of the international liberal order because it fundamentally undermines the legitimacy of their polity. However, these actors might still adopt the international norm to "pursue cosmetic changes to their domestic practices and tactical concessions in order to obtain international benefits and payoffs" (Subotić 2009:34). Radical critiques of the Cambodian government's reaction to the UN proposal place it in this category. Instrumental norm adopters use international norms to attain a better position politically than their rivals by describing themselves as "internationalist and reformist forces" in order to gain favorable responses from the international actors upon whom they depend (Subotić 2009:35). A more moderate critique would place the Cambodian government's position in this category, suggesting that the RGC could depict the TJ event as a positive national symbol to its citizens. Finally, true believers are usually found in the political opposition, expecting international support for political change. Therefore, the sustainability of their movement is affected more by international attention than by the extent of true believers' motivation.

In this framework in international politics, the variation in the acceptance of global norms by local political elites is theoretically grasped as a competition among adherents of these three positions. Based on this classification, Subotić has traced the case of the Serbian government and its strategic acceptance of ICTY, considering how the formal goodwill and ideals of the international community were accepted by government representatives.

Manipulating Justice Discourse in Domestic Politics

The Serbian government's engagement in the ICTY process has not been straightforward. Consider the case of Slobodan Milošević, formerly president of Serbia (1989–1997) and the Federal Republic of Yugoslavia (1997–2000), who was charged by the ICTY with war crimes. At first, Milošević's arrest and extradition were justified by Serbian prime minister Zoran Đinđić, who used highly pragmatic expressions such as "entrance ticket to the democratic world" and took the position that "refusal to extradite Milošević would lead to the suspension of financial aid, which would bring the country to the brink of economic collapse, complicate the repayment of foreign debt, and prevent Serbia's membership in international financial institutions" (Subotić 2009:47).

The comment about entering the democratic world was likely tactical rhetoric, deployed to help Serbia become a European Union (EU) member state. Čedomir Javanović, the former deputy prime minister, was more outspoken: "We wanted American money, we wanted EU money" (Subotić 2009:46). It was enough to make Serbian citizens come to see the situation "as a business transaction and not an issue of justice" (Subotić 2009:46). The Serbian government thus followed a policy of dualism: on the one hand, cooperating with the ICTY for pragmatic purposes, and on the other hand, distancing itself from justice norms in its local communications. Justice was not a transcendent ideal but just a convenient political choice to advance a secular agenda.

The government was forced to clarify its position in this dualistic approach when, in 2003, the ICTY indicted four generals who had been active in the army and police for crimes against humanity during Serbia's war in Kosovo in 1999. The Serbian police minister promised that "he would do everything in his power to prevent the generals from going to The Hague, 'except as tourists,'" and the government issued a public statement accusing ICTY chief prosecutor Carla Del Ponte of having "humiliated the Serbian government and the entire state"; it left the accused untouched for a year (Subotić 2009:48).

However, the government was again compelled to calculate the cost of its nationalistic maneuvers against foreign intervention in 2005 when the US ambassador in Belgrade announced that "substantial portions of U.S. aid were to be cut, and technical advisers were to be withdrawn" and "the EU foreign policy chief cancelled a planned trip to Belgrade in protest over continuing Serbian noncooperation with the ICTY" (Subotić 2009:48–49). Facing this open challenge, the government introduced a new policy concept of "voluntary surrenders." This meant that a deal would be guaranteed for those surrendering on their return from The Hague; they would face charges while on bail and their families would receive financial assistance (Subotić 2009:49).

The Serbian government finally agreed to send the accused to The Hague, but it constructed a tactical story striking an exquisite balance between nationalistic discourse and sanctions by the international community. Even after the indictment from the ICTY was provided, the Serbian side kept silent, with no movement toward compliance. However, it swiftly changed its stance two days before the EU's completion of a feasibility study for Serbia's EU accession, having one of the four accused generals, Nebojša Pavković, turn himself in. His voluntary surrender was arranged as "a huge media event," and the Koštunica government issued a statement praising the decision as "moral, responsible and patriotic" and promising to provide ongoing assistance to his family (Subotić 2009:49–50). The accused wartime criminal had thus been treated as a hero inside Serbia while at the same time, in the international arena, the state behaved as though it were moving closer toward democracy and the rule of law. The situation actually became quite farcical, even though the international community had to formally accept Serbia's compliance:

> Another member of the group of four generals, Vladimir Lazarević, had an even more VIP send-off. After deciding to surrender, Lazarević was met by the patriarch of the Serbian Orthodox Church and Prime Minister Koštunica, who both praised Lazarević's heroic decision. Koštunica went so far as to say that "the general acted in line with a long-standing tradition of the Serbian army, namely, that our officers fight for the interests of the people and country until the bitter end." As in the case of Pavković, Lazarević's surrender was cast as an act of supreme patriotism, as a "difficult decision in the interest of the homeland." Lazarević was flown to The Hague in a government jet, accompanied by the justice minister. (Subotić 2009:50)

An ideal of justice to be realized in a post-conflict authoritarian society was thus implemented as requested by the international community—but what were the actual implications of this case? The Serbian government complied with international norms, but its dualistic manner of acceptance was evident and the veneer of morality and righteousness completely vanished in the local context. This strategic behavior became yet more apparent in another suspect's case. Even though the arrest of former Serbian deputy interior minister, Sreten Lukić, was conducted in a way that suggested a voluntary surrender, he was in fact forcibly arrested in a hospital while being treated for heart disease. The government explained that "the surrenders worked as acts of soldiers' devotion to their country at a time of need" (Subotić 2009:50). Subotić also cites an interview with a state official regarding the importance of cooperation with the ICTY "for Serbia's struggling textile industry" (p. 50). In short, the Serbian government's compliance with international justice norms was pragmatically justified to its people as linked to important deals such as acquiring EU membership, along with "$100 million in direct U.S. aid and U.S. support for International Monetary Fund and World Bank loans to Serbia" (Subotić 2009:45–46). Finally, the compliance was explained away as something exchangeable for the protection of a specific trade field.

Subotić concludes that the Serbian government used the ICTY tribunals as an opportunity to create a patriotic atmosphere inside its society while not substantially addressing past abuses. No police or judicial reform was made. Serbian courts remained unskilled in dealing with war-crime prosecutions, and Serbian lawmakers refused to incorporate the concept of command responsibility into national law (Subotić 2009:51). When local NGOs found evidence of mass graves in Serbia in 2005, containing the bodies of Kosovo Albanian civilians killed in 1999,

> the Serbian Ministry of the Interior, the Ministry of Justice, and the security services all covered up the findings and began a campaign of silencing and intimidating witnesses by forcing them to sign statements on "spiritual peace," admitting in writing that they did not "feel psychological pressure to disclose what had happened . . . in May 1999." (Subotić 2009:52)

Transitional justice in Serbia consists, according to Subotić's analysis, of "effectively removing the substantive issue of addressing past wrongs from the public debate," preserving "the grand narrative of Serbia's victimization and the need for its vindication," and finally contributing to gaining "great international awards" (Subotić 2009:52).

These are episodes of state-level maneuvering even when accepting TJ initiatives proposed by the international community, and the government of the concerned society took the lead in constructing a dualistic public discourse on the TJ program. The local political landscape was not changed, and in fact a negative status quo was intensified, as Paul Willis (1977) described in the context of public schooling. What promoted this dysfunction? A formal message or an official device? If the past cases involving the goodwill and ideals of international justice norms have always witnessed such deviant reactions, we must consider whether the logic inherently contributes to such outcomes.

In the same vein, an anthropological observation compared local politicians' use of TJ in Sierra Leone with court officials' unfulfilled promises. According to Gerhard Anders, despite Chief Prosecutor Crane's rousing statements that "we mean business" and "no one is above the law," the Special Court for Sierra Leone and the TRC "were, in fact, not extraordinary from the perspective of political and military leaders who were doing business as usual, trying to outmaneuver their rivals in spite of grand announcements of a new beginning" (Anders 2014b:525, 527). Anders used the expression "business as usual" to represent a strategy "to convert their military strength into political and economic capital after the end of the war" (p. 540). The use of the expression is apt, as this case also demonstrates the strategic utilization of TJ, or TJ discourse, by local political elites facing pressure to accept an internationalized TJ initiative.

These two cases cannot be termed fake TJ because a foreign organization was a leading stakeholder in each case, maintaining surface-level legitimacy. However, the value that supports the legitimacy of TJ has never been shared with these local stakeholders. Justice, or justice in the service of reconciliation, has appeared to local political players to be an unavoidable path to take reluctantly in the course of ongoing conflict. The moralistic discourse of the formal goodwill and ideals of TJ is thus accepted as a new circumstance against which they have to struggle.

Local Ownership Dismissal: Cambodia

The Serbian case demonstrates that a TJ institutionalized by external initiatives can expect to face high-level political manipulation in the domestic realm. In this case, political resistance and maneuvering were observed in a country's attempts to maintain a political and institutional status quo without engaging in any sort of systematic reform.

On the other hand, the formal goodwill and ideals of TJ are also challenged by ordinary local people with no specific political intention. The case of Cambodia provides suggestive examples of local people's perception of an international court. The stage for this section is an open forum that was organized by a local NGO parallel to the ECCC. Local participants' expressions at these forums had no intention of vindicating a specific political regime or governmental policy, yet they exhibited a different channel of resistance to the imposition of international norms from the pattern of strategic resistance demonstrated by the Serbian government.

Local Perception of International TJ at an NGO Forum

The Center for Social Development (CSD) in Phnom Penh began a series of twenty-one public forums called "Justice and National Reconciliation" in 2006, with funding support from the German Development Service (DED). The series continued for four years. At the outset of this time period, the ECCC was preparing to open public hearings in Case 001. Other Cambodian NGOs, such as the Documentation Center of Cambodia (DC-Cam) and the Transcultural Psychosocial Organization (TPO Cambodia), had implemented similar forums, which primarily included the following activities: publishing basic information about the ECCC, calling for civilian participation in court proceedings, collecting testimonies on past experiences, and facilitating dialogue on various topics such as reconciliation, justice, and healing. However, the court itself had not yet started similar public-relations activities. The ECCC began mimicking these activities in 2009, shortly after these local NGOs had fully established their outreach format.

The CSD forums had between 150 and 200 participants, with balanced representation by age and gender. Although these participants were by no means representative of the Cambodian population as a whole, their responses nevertheless provide enlightening examples of the local people's perceptions of the ECCC. In addition to the CSD staff, court officials and representatives from other NGOs were present at each event. For instance, at the forum in Pailin, the former Khmer Rouge stronghold, on October 24, 2008, local people attended a question-and-answer session featuring an ECCC judge, a co-prosecutor, a public-affairs officer, a defense-section officer, and a witness-protection-unit officer.

The first half of each CSD forum opened with a short introductory film, which briefed viewers on the court's general background. The forum was mainly an opportunity for ECCC court officials to outline the objectives and regulations of the court. The legal terminology used to explain the ECCC objectives and mandate must have seemed like a foreign language to ordinary local people who were unfamiliar with such parlance. This may have hindered them from asking questions, although court officials provided detailed and dedicated speeches and answers. However, a close reading of the proceedings of all the forums reveals roughly two standpoints in the questions posed by participants to the ECCC officials: "I want to obtain some basic information about the ECCC because I do not know much about it," and "I know that the ECCC will try some of the KR leaders, but I don't know why it is dealing with past atrocities in this way." (I exclude comments that were critical or supportive of the ECCC.)

The questions in the second of these two categories were not as easy for court officials to answer as those in the first category, because they were beyond the court's mandate and regulations. Such questions could be divided into the following subclasses: (1) the responsibility or involvement of foreign countries; (2) persons to be prosecuted; (3) the time span of the atrocities; (4) doubts regarding the prosecution of older leaders; and (5) the legitimacy of a hybrid court. See Table 3.1 for specific examples of the questions asked.

ECCC officials could answer questions in the first category by simply referring to or quoting ECCC regulations, but how were they to answer questions and comments in the second category? These questions were arguably being addressed to the wrong persons, but they are significant for inferring local people's perceptions regarding the conditional legitimacy of the ECCC. We should therefore focus on how these questions were framed.

Local Acceptance or Dismissal of the Justice Ideal

During morning sessions, ECCC officials were given seats on a stage at the front of the venue. Their role was to enlighten—rather than to share information with—the local participants. They performed readily when asked questions that fell into the first category ("I want to obtain some basic information about the ECCC . . ."), but they always showed hesitation when addressing questions in the second category ("I don't know why it is dealing

70   Unintended Consequences in Transitional Justice

Table 3.1 Questions Posed to ECCC Officials by Local Participants at the CSD Forums

Subject	Contents
1. The responsibility or involvement of foreign countries	"Did some countries or some foreigners [get] behind [the] KR to give it weapons and ideological training? . . . Why are we only putting [the] KR on trial?"[9] "As I read the law, I felt dissatisfied and regretful because the foreigners will not be brought to trial . . . after Liberation Day, people said China had supported the KR regime because [there] were a lot of weapons from China."[10]
2. Persons to be prosecuted	"The subordinates killed people, too. So they must go on trial. . . . Actually, the practitioners sometimes did not follow the leaders. They were asked to kill one, [but] they killed ten."[11] "Why [does] the KR tribunal sentence [only] a few leaders?"[12] "I believe that people who used to command guerrillas and soldiers in the KR regime are now working in the government and business. Will they be brought to trial?"[13]
3. The time span of the atrocities	"Why is the court only [addressing events that occurred] between 1975 and 1979 and not the bombardments of pagodas, bridges and schools . . . by B-52s?"[14] [B-52s are Boeing B-52 Stratofortress bombers that operated from 1970.] "Which international body determined the three-year jurisdiction? Thousands of people were killed before 1975. . . . I am despairing of what the court is doing."[15]
4. Doubts regarding the prosecution of (older) leaders	"[The] KR leaders . . . are very old. . . . What benefits will this trial bring? . . . What are the benefits for the Cambodian people?"[16] "Why do we have to try [the] KR people?"[17]
5. The legitimacy of a hybrid court	"We use both Cambodian and international law. Is it necessary to have two types of law?"[18]

with past atrocities . . ."), because such questions fell outside their jurisdiction. Therefore, they tended to produce replies such as the following: "I am a law practitioner and I don't want to go over what is not stated in the law."[19] Responding to a question regarding the determination of guilt, another officer could say only, "The law [does] not allow [them] to be sentenced. Why doesn't it allow them to be sentenced? An agreement was reached for them not to be sentenced. That's all, thank you."[20]

Some officers adopted a legalistic principle, namely, that the rule of law is superior to all else: "Everyone has to bear in mind [that] it is very important to follow the law and regulations to find justice . . . trying to find justice without following laws and regulations is useless for people everywhere."[21] Others displayed passive acceptance: "A four-legged chair can't become a five-legged chair naturally. Now that it [the tribunal] has been established, we have to make the best results [that we can make] in accordance with it . . . everything is in the process."[22] One even deflected the question by saying, "Why is the court good for Cambodia? I think it's a question that the people of Cambodia and Pailin need to answer for themselves."[23]

The local people did not question the need for or the application of the law itself, but they had reservations regarding its preconditions and restrictions and how justice would be meted out. Prosecutors and investigating judges were appointed to their positions in accordance with certain mandates of the ECCC statute. They possessed the professional knowledge and skills needed to deal with the atrocities allegedly committed by the KR, but their official positions also required them to have only a limited standpoint on the matters being examined. In most cases, they were left with no option but to resort to the standard phrase, "the law defines such and such thus." One participant at the Siem Reap forum replied to such answers in the following way:

> I don't have any questions to ask, but I wonder. Many questions [have been] asked, but the answer is still that the law doesn't allow [foreign actors or other stakeholders] to be sentenced and the agreement [between the UN and the Cambodian government] doesn't allow [them] to be sentenced. In this regard, can the tribunal [bring] justice to the victims? . . . Whether only answering that the law and agreement don't allow [them] to be sentenced will give justice and please the Khmer people or not, [I'm not sure].[24]

Another participant inquired, "Was the law to try the KR leaders established with the consultation of the people? Do the government and foreign countries use this method?"[25] These questions challenged the officials' desire for forum participants to understand and accept the principles and mechanisms of the ECCC. Some foreign officials sometimes behaved as if the Cambodians should simply accept the officials' directions and values because they were proceeding with their mission on a righteous basis. The participants did not always react in line with this reasoning; despite the officials' best efforts to justify ECCC procedures, some questioned how the ECCC judicial system had been instituted and by whom.

The important point here is not the specifics of any one expression, but the frame in which the participants expressed their discontent. Forum participants tended to judge the legitimacy of the ECCC by the preconditions used to establish it, even while ECCC officers emphasized the ongoing legal procedures. Dissenting or doubtful reactions may have been provoked by foreign officials' growing adherence to technical accuracy in their legal explanations, because these details all felt like a house of cards, concocted with no consultation process with the substantial number of victims. "Buttoned up unevenly" is one way to describe such interactions in local-international encounters. In this way, official messages to the locals failed to communicate their senders' reassuring intent.

Acceptance, Consultation, and Local Ownership

The problem of a limited—or nonexistent—consultation process with ordinary locals at the design stage of TJ has also been reported in the case of East Timor. The Serious Crimes Process, mandated to prosecute those individuals "most responsible" for serious crimes (with no high-ranking members of the Indonesian military being brought to trial), began with no substantial outreach preparation because of "chronic resource deficiencies, understaffing, and poor management" (Kent 2012:79). The absence of public outreach likely molds public perceptions of the TJ program. Even if the program is open to the public, people cannot come and perceive it positively without substantial public relations. This is what happened in East Timor, where no court dates for the first trial were publicly listed or otherwise publicized by the court and there were rarely more than a few East Timorese present in the public gallery (Kent 2012:79). It is hard for locals to offer any positive comments on a program, given such a situation.

Legal justice is not a panacea and usually entails various political, monetary, and human restrictions. However, starting without substantial consultation or an information-sharing process inevitably causes these restrictions to seem larger in the eyes of local people. As a result, the "prosecution of a selected number of low-level East Timorese militia members has left the experiences of large numbers of victims unrecognized and . . . has been overwhelmingly perceived by the community as an unfair targeting of the 'little people,' instead of those who planned and instigated the violence" (Kent 2012:79).

Inadequate resources and resource management, lack of substantial public relations or a consultation process, and a sense of alienation create a vicious cycle. Moreover, a TJ process cannot avoid selecting a few perpetrators or victims for its agenda. The unfortunate pairing of these elements—not enough public relations and the selection of only a few individuals to suit its agenda—gives locals the sense of a biased project.

On the other hand, East Timor's TRC (Comissão de Acolhimento, Verdade e Reconciliação de Timor Leste, or CAVR) was established after some consultation with "targeted communities, political parties, jurists and human-rights organizations and victims' groups" (Robins 2012:88), but they were still limited in scale and scope. Therefore, "None of the needs [of the families of the missing and the dead] articulated resonates with the stated goals of transitional justice processes rooted in truth and reconciliation and the trope of 'healing' that drove CAVR" (Robins 2012:96–97).

A Consultation Process: South Africa

A TJ project is always a new agenda and an unknown organization for most people in the concerned society, as they have neither an image of nor a consensus on what TJ is. Therefore, sharing information on future policies with the people as much as possible should be an urgent agenda item for policymakers. In this regard, the South African case might work as an operational manual for people in charge of TJ design.[26]

The South African TRC started its PR activities by demarcating geographical subareas within the region allocated to each regional commission office. The branch offices of political parties, civil society organizations, churches, and local municipalities were targeted as bridging actors between the TRC and local residents. Pamphlets, leaflets, and posters were printed for dissemination, and preparatory hearings in communities were announced. The local preparatory hearings were held one month before the TRC hearings. A three-hour session was allotted for a summary explanation of the TRC activities, a question-and-answer session, and comments submitted on feedback forms. The sessions not only provided information but also encouraged people to become testifiers. TRC staffers were given a fifty-six-page operations manual and attended a training course.

At the preparatory hearing, thirty minutes were used for the general explanation of the TRC, of which the first ten explained why the commission was established, what it would deal with, and what issues or periods it would focus on. The topics "What does human rights mean?" "Gross violation of human rights," "Political context [of perpetration]," and "Application deadline" were then each allotted five minutes, including time for questions and answers.

The manual also offered model ways of answering in certain simulated situations. Following are some of its instructions:

- When demonstrating the process of a human-rights violation hearing, staff have to take on the role of participants. Do not allow participants to play a role because it may draw out their memories and role-playing will become impossible.
- Amnesty is a difficult matter to explain. Therefore, even when a participant comments negatively on the amnesty clause, do not become involved in a debate on whether amnesty is right or wrong.
- When a participant tries to dominate the floor and speak for a long time, courteously inform the person that he or she will be given the opportunity to raise the issue at another time in another place.
- If a participant begins to speak about his or her personal experiences at the meeting, let him or her speak officially to the commission.

As an example, the Cape Town regional office demarcated eleven subareas that would be in charge of public relations. For each area, preparation steps, opening steps, and follow-up steps related to the public hearing were set up within a ten-week period. Statement taking from the locals was planned for each step. Each statement was expected to require from thirty minutes to three hours. When there was a shortfall in the number of statement-takers, local volunteers such as church staff were asked to help after attending a brief preparatory session. The PR unit supported the statement-takers' fieldwork with printed materials. In light of the relatively low literacy rate, it also made use of local radio programs. For instance, one month before a public hearing in a certain area, local radio stations were asked to provide slots for a one-week talk-show program. Radio stations were considered a symbolic medium for many nonwhite people because the stations had worked underground to create communication and solidarity among activists in the apartheid era and during the emergency, when television and newspapers were strictly censored. The testimonies gathered by statement-takers were brought to the research unit, which analyzed the recorded memories and selected a few of them for the upcoming public hearings.

Knowledge Production

However, a counterargument can be proposed regarding the positive role of a consultation process: consultation or information sharing with citizens in advance may not necessarily secure local support and understanding of TJ activities. Locals' refutation of the formal goodwill-and-ideals approach of TJ can arise even after such preparation.

An institutional TJ process needs to be as formally neutral as possible, because tension remains among various political positions, particularly in a society where democracy is still under pressure. But no public organization in a transitional society can be free from some appearance of political inclination, selective preference, and prioritizing of activities, simply because of restrictions of time, budget, and human resources. Furthermore, a government often pursues its own political agenda under a façade of neutrality. Even when the government has no surreptitious intention, an official production of specific, legitimized information on the past always entails selecting, editing, and admitting raw information into public discourse.

This critical probe can continue at a deeper level, in questioning how such information about locals' memories and experiences can be represented in the public sphere. Before being selected as significant episodes and addressed in an official report, locals' testimonies are recorded by official staff. What experiences are recorded as human-rights violations? What is the officially accepted period of victimhood? How are locals allowed to speak of their experiences, and in what settings? How long does each statement-taking session last, and how many times can it be repeated? These issues are institutionally sorted out in the form of legal regulations and the mandate of an organization. However, that fact means that the law and mandate that create and endorse a TJ body are already reflected in a specific political decision. These decisions may reflect prioritization after assessing limitations on various resources, but they are often also a product of negotiation among competing stakeholders in balancing conflicting views. More likely, they may reflect certain political preferences and motivations to manipulate public representations. An official decision is thus set out in a forced manner, and in theory, there will remain dissidents opposed to the decision. A public discourse can be viewed retrospectively as a series of configurations of these dissident voices, negotiation among competitors, molding ambiguous consensus or hegemony of a certain meaning in public, and sometimes forceful decisions by powerful authorities, particularly in the case of political issues discussed in a transitional society.

Discourse Analysis and the Matter of Power

Michel Foucault (1982:27) encapsulates the basic orientation of discourse analysis in this simple question: "According to what rules has a particular statement been made?" In greater detail, his inquiry into the mechanism for producing public knowledge, which entails a normative sense of legitimacy, identifies the essential filters through which the knowledge becomes public. First, with the term "surfaces of their emergence" (p. 41), he observes that a certain discourse is allotted a specific channel such as an academic field or genre where the basic character of information as well as official status is given. Discourse, which appears as publicly authentic information, cannot be produced by just anyone who wishes to do so. Usually, a specific profession possesses "the authority of delimitation." For example:

> in the nineteenth century, medicine (as an institution possessing its own rules, as a group of individuals constituting the medical profession, as a body of knowledge and practice, as an authority recognized by public opinion, the law, and government) became the major authority in society that delimited, designated, named, and established madness as an object. (Foucault 1982:41–42)

Therefore, to incorporate Foucault's method in the dissection of discourses in the TJ process, the following questions become a practical guide:

> Who is speaking? Who, among the totality of speaking individuals, is accorded the right to use this sort of language (langage)? Who is qualified to do so? Who derives from it his own special quality, his prestige,

and from whom, in return, does he receive if not the assurance, at least the presumption that what he says is true? What is the status of the individuals who alone have the right, sanctioned by law or tradition, juridically defined or spontaneously accepted, to proffer such a discourse? (Foucault 1982:50)

The persons identified as qualified, privileged, and legitimized have their own "institutional sites," such as a hospital, for doctors (Foucault 1982:51).

Thus, legitimate information, or truth in general at a certain time, appears as a form of public discourse, communicated through the specific social devices of that era. From the beginning, what should be spoken and shared socially has been demarcated by specific people. Information that lies outside that framework cannot receive public attention. Legitimate information is produced by certain professionals who possess their own authentic place. There, the people who are involved in the relation with such authentic agents need to accept specific roles, along with rules regarding the restriction of communication. The institution of information production regulates its own pattern of arrangement in questioning and recording. In modern societies, hospitals, courts, churches, and universities have all functioned to produce discourses.

When we apply Foucault's analytical structure to TJ experiences, we see that the international courts and truth commissions are comparable to these other legitimating institutions. Peter Manning explains the characteristics of the TJ process by using the term *memory politics*, highlighting the fact that the basic motivation to deal with the past is itself formed by that institutional initiative:

> Transitional justice mechanisms are a form of memory politics because they intervene in the past in two ways. Firstly, in the way they act on memory and (re)construct an account of "what happened." . . . Secondly, transitional justice mechanisms are principally rationalised and validated by situating memory and the past as a problematic field that must be ameliorated. In doing so, memory is positioned as an "object" of political practice. (Manning 2014:38)

From the viewpoint of knowledge production, any TJ body's public announcement of goodwill and ideals needs to be examined for a certain bias in the authentic social agents in charge of setting the mechanism. Yet an institutional TJ program is not firmly established in a transitional society, as is a domestic court in a stable modern society, so analysis of the process of knowledge production might be particularly important here to grasp the constellation of discourses. Such discourses tend to engage in more competitive exchanges in those societies that are still defining themselves than in stable societies. Especially in transitional settings, an announcement of a new social value is more likely to trigger public disputes than peaceful acceptance by subjected audiences. And finally, the public slogan, which was once thought to reflect goodwill and ideals, is interpreted as a political pretext for the imposition of a unique or bizarre arrangement on a given society after a period of heated debates, tactical maneuvers, and gloomy compromising.

Limitations of the Consultation Mechanism

In theory, any TJ project's ideals are thus challenged by dissidents because of its inevitable process of official agenda setting and production of public knowledge. For instance, the institutional objective of the South African TRC was to bring dissidents around to endorsing the goal of national reconciliation. Even in the relatively elaborate preparation stage of outreach, the family of charismatic activist leader Steve Biko filed a court case, accusing the TRC of violating the South African constitution. The basic criticism of the TRC mandate was that it excluded systematic violations of human rights by the apartheid regime such as the pass law, which prohibited nonwhite South Africans from moving around without a bulk of ID certification (a *pass*) and permitted police officers to detain people and ship anyone found without a pass to compulsory labor farms. Mahmood Mamdani (2009) observed an institutional deficiency in the TRC's failure to consider the responsibility of beneficiaries—that is, ordinary white civilians with no power-enforcement occupation.

Claire Moon (2008:77–78) pointed out that the elimination of black-on-black violence—which occurred primarily between the Inkhatha Freedom Party (IFP) and the African National Congress (ANC) in the early 1990s—from the TRC proceedings was an outcome of the commission's internal demand to "fit within the broader morality tale the TRC sought to tell about South Africa's past." Although affirming the positive connotation of the ideal of reconciliation, both the National Party (NP) and the IFP retreated from the TRC process, saying that pursuing reconciliation in this setting was impossible. NP leader F. W. de Klerk announced the party's withdrawal from the TRC process in May 1997 because of alleged discrimination by the TRC. The IFP criticized the TRC for its tone of a "witch hunt against opponents of the ANC" (Moon 2008:13). Even though Nelson Mandela, then South Africa's president and leader of the ANC, strongly promoted the TRC's activities as a high-priority policy in the course of political transition, other younger top ANC politicians such as Thabo Mbeki opposed the TRC principle that all political positions should be dealt with equally. Many ANC officials stated publicly their view that the TRC should be "a forum for perpetrators from the former regime to give their accounts of the past in return for amnesty" (Moon 2008:12).

These tensions among literally all the political parties led to a disturbance in October 1998; just before Chairperson Desmond Tutu publicly presented the TRC's official report to President Mandela, both the NP and ANC brought suits against the TRC because of the injurious descriptions of their past activities in the reports. The attempt by the ANC failed, but de Klerk's objection was upheld and the concerned pages were painted over with black squares. In addition, the representatives from all the major political parties were absent at the presentation ceremony for the official report. Mandela could not help but make the following speech at the ceremony:

> Many of us will have reservations about aspects of what is contained in these five volumes. All are free to make comment on it and indeed we invite you to do so. And for those who feel unjustly damaged, there are remedies. It will seem artificial to some to place those fighting a just war alongside those whom they opposed. It will be difficult for the victims of gross violations of human rights to accept the philosophical account of the trade-off between punitive justice and a peaceful transition. . . . I therefore take this opportunity to say that I accept the report as it is, with all its imperfections, as an aid that the TRC has given to us to help reconcile and build our nation. The Commission was not required to muster a definitive and comprehensive history of the past three decades. Nor was it expected to conjure up instant reconciliation. And it does not claim to have delivered these either. Its success in any case depended on how far all of us co-operated with it.[27]

The Legitimate Target of Transitional Justice

Disagreement and conflict surrounding the formal goodwill and ideals of institutional TJ have been found even among the victims who are assumed to be the people most served by TJ's empowerment policy. When a TJ entity is expected to be an authentic form of mass media, audiences are assumed to be uniform subjects. Those behind the TJ operations hope that these subjects will be tamed by any state announcement, thus behaving as "ideal victims."

Nils Christie (1986:18) defines the concept of an "ideal victim" as one who is given the complete and legitimate status of a victim when affected by a crime. What matters is the social image or pressure that comes with the concept of victim, which can often take the form of either hero or traitor. An ideal victim is characterized by the following attributes: weakness, carrying out a respectable project, not worthy of blame, and exposed to further victimization by an unknown offender (van Wijk 2013:160).

In writings related to this conception, Luke Moffett warns against the general use of the term *victim* in a TJ context because it brings with it a labeling of who should be a victim or who deserves recognition: "The victim label can bestow sympathy, praise, or benefits on an individual as it recognises that they have suffered" (Moffett 2014:3). Moffett expresses further concern that the ideal image of victims also induces "others to use victims politically, without considering their agency and autonomy to help themselves or contribute to wider political or legal processes" (p. 3).

In addition, representations of victimhood have always entailed a residual category as well as tension and conflict between those entitled and not entitled to victim status. The tension among recipients of reparation takes the form of "contestation by victims' groups over who has the right to the status of victim" (Brewer 2010:164). This contestation may be generated around a hierarchy of suffering in terms of levels of harm, physical and medical status, and political contribution to the regime change or to the past struggle.

Referring to the context of Northern Ireland, Marie Smyth uncovered a taboo on the hidden side of the public image of ideal victims: getting recognized as a victim is a convenient way of escaping responsibility.

> Victims are never guilty, responsible, or strong. If victims harm others it is supposedly understandable in the light of their suffering, and above all, those who claim victimhood are not to be blamed. . . . [As a result] currently there is a tendency on the part of diverse groups and individuals to claim victimhood. This willingness is not matched by a corresponding willingness to own responsibility in relation to the hurts and harms that have been done in their name, or that we have inflicted directly by our own actions. (Smyth 1998:36)

The Politics of Victimhood

This form of politics appears as "victimhood as a social construct" (Druliolle 2015). In Cambodia, Mahdev Mohan and Sangeetha Yogendran heard the stories of several survivors, all of whom insisted that there should be a hierarchy of suffering and that theirs should be treated more seriously than that of others:

> Sum Rithy is a former prisoner, and Chin Navy a widow. Each arrogates centrality for his/her individual pain and claim to victimhood. Each feels he/she suffered more than the other did. This is not a phenomenon peculiar to these two victims, but a trait common to many other victims we interviewed as well. (Mohan and Yogendran, 2017)

Contrary to this tendency, according to Mohan and Yogendran, the victims on the side of the Khmer Rouge, who in the present context are generally categorized as former perpetrators, tended to suggest that all the Cambodian victims should be treated equally.

It can be presumed that the victims who have experienced more severe damage than others tend to seek greater compensation or public recognition for their special status. Those who are not publicly viewed as victims, however, or the Khmer Rouge in this case, usually hope simply that all victims be treated equally. Thus, indirectly linked to compensation issues, the identification of victimhood moves on into a debate about hierarchical measurement:

> He [Sum Rithy] believes that a distinction should be drawn between innocent prisoners like him—"true victims"—and those who were interred for a short period of time, others who were spared imprisonment, and still others who suffered psychological or material harm rather than physical harm as a result of what happened to their property or their loved ones. To Sum, the title of civil party [in the ECCC judicial process] is an emblem of victimhood that he feels deserves a special status. . . . He said: *"I was told that a civil party is a special victim. Now that I am a civil party, I want the court to respect me as a special person.* . . . The court should make a card for me that says I am a civil party, a former prisoner, so that no one will look down on me. Since the court treats the defendants as very important people, shouldn't we be treated as people who are even more important?" (Mohan and Yogendran, 2017; emphasis added)

Another victim, Chin Navy, proposed a different standard, suggesting that those who suffered psychological harm (as Navy did by losing her husband to execution and having to flee her village) have as great a claim to victimhood as anyone. Things become worse and more complicated when local NGOs, which should be helpful bridges between ordinary locals and an official entity, apply a similar sense of hierarchy among victims in their competition with other rival NGOs while upholding "their own people."

The politics of victimhood thus becomes more problematic when a reparations policy is implemented. Moffett addresses the case in Peru, where the Comisión para Verdad y Reconciliación, or Truth and Reconciliation Commission (CVR), recommended reparations and the Comprehensive Reparation Programme (PIR) was in charge of their realization. When the CVR defined victims, it did so broadly, counting anyone who suffered human-rights violations, including those associated with subversive nonstate groups. However, the CVR adopted a slightly more complicated definition of who qualified as a recipient of reparations, excluding members of subversive groups (primarily Sendero Luminoso, or Shining Path) who had suffered damages in armed clashes when fighting against the democratic government. These victims were officially "not considered victims and thus not beneficiaries of the programs enumerated in [Article 4 of the 2005 reparations law]" (Theidon 2013:390). On the other hand, Moffett indicates, "Such presumption on the legitimacy of state violence allows state forces to be included as 'victims' in reparation programmes on the basis that they were protecting the community, despite documented widespread and systematic human rights abuses" (Moffett 2014:13).

With such a policy in place, the PIR has to screen every reparations applicant to check whether the person formerly belonged to any illegal armed groups such as the Shining Path, and this process takes years of examination. Moreover, this procedure inevitably runs the risk of errors in judgment, whereby someone is identified wrongly as a former member of a subversive group. In addition, "Such a broad distinction also prevents vulnerable individuals within such communities [from accessing] an effective remedy, who did not have the freedom or capacity for the violence they committed, such as children who were members of illegal groups at the time" (Moffett 2014:14).

In the context of the politics of victimhood with normative discourses aiming at national reconciliation, for the Peruvians in the former Sendero Luminoso stronghold, "The less they portray themselves as protagonists then, the more persuasive their demands on the state are today" (Theidon 2013:389). This circumstance compels those who supported Shining Path to "construct their life histories at a sizable distance from any sympathy whatsoever with Sendero" (p. 389). Competition for "a higher rank on the hierarchy of victimhood" through pretending to be a serious victim has also been observed in such a context (Theidon 2013:390).

Because of the lingering problem of scarce resources, a TJ program cannot meet all the demands of victims, but the concept of empowerment of victims always raises questions around the possibility of measuring suffering and degree of victimhood. The status of victim is an entitlement given to a qualified actor in a TJ process who, according to the prevailing narrative, should be cared for more than those who do not qualify as (or are a lesser degree of) victims. A public image of ideal victims in an affected society thus overtly or covertly influences how qualified victims are demarcated. In this sense, it seems at first glance that conflict among those who already officially qualify as victims is something that external supporters do not wish to witness; however, the essence of this problem might be understood along the same lines as an official's determination of a TJ mandate. It articulates distinctions between people with complicated and not easily differentiated experiences.

This institutional articulation often brings about a more negative impact: the politics of victimhood does not necessarily confine itself to the compensation framework, presupposing the end of conflict. Lia Kent (2012:175) warns of the TJ's potential reverse function to worsen the politics of victimhood "between different kinds of victims, and between victims and other marginalized groups, as they compete for recognition of their unique claims" because of the potential explosiveness of these disputes.

Even after the end of East Timor's CAVR in December 2005, an armed clash around the hierarchy of suffering occurred. According to Kent, it coalesced around the notion of "who contributed the most to the resistance struggle" (pp. 130–131). In 2006, this conflict between young men called Lorosa'e (Easterners) and Loromunu (Westerners) escalated, leading to the killing of more than thirty gang members on both sides, the looting of thousands of houses, and the displacement of around 140,000 people. Initially, Loromunu soldiers complained that they were not as well treated in the military as the Lorosa'e were, because, as they stated in their petition to Prime Minister Alkatiri, they had been labeled as "untrustworthy." The name Loromunu (Westerners) meant that they were closer to the Indonesian border, so "they were perceived not to have fought as hard in the resistance as Lorosa'e" (Kent 2012:130–131).

Media Influence on Transitional Justice

These negative perceptions among locals can be amplified by local media coverage. Scholars have noted the important role of local media in achieving TJ outcomes, influence that is heightened because of the limited extent of formal TJ outreach. Many locals cannot access information directly from a TJ entity. Local media coverage is thought to fill the communication gap between TJ initiatives and audiences.

Patrick Vinck and Phuong Pham (2010:431) reported that in the ICC's project in the Central African Republic (CAR), its "outreach strategy relies in part on the media as an intermediary to disseminate information regarding the Court to the general public." They stressed "information poverty" in the country and the significance of "understanding how individuals gather information" (p. 431).

In agreement with these findings, Lisa J. Laplante and Kelly Phenicie (2010:207) emphasize the influence of media coverage on TJ outcomes as a primary factor in determining people's perception of TJ. Based on this presupposition, they pose the question whether the media in a post-conflict society should support TJ to promote human rights and democracy by helping to shape public opinion or whether the media should take a neutral stance, even if the latter approach entails revealing the errors and shortcomings of the TJ program (p. 208). Laplante and Phenicie maintain that a situation in which the media could serve as tools of both repression and resistance, much as in wartime, does not permit pursuing "the classic aims of journalistic objectivity," which promote "a fruitful discussion that leads to the establishment of a collective memory and national reconciliation" (p. 208).

Looking back at the South African context, the South African Broadcasting Corporation (SABC) can be assessed as having played a relatively neutral, positive role in keeping the public informed regarding the TRC process. The case of SABC provides insight into how a TJ project needs an external media device to complement its work.

When the TRC was active, SABC radio conducted live broadcasts from 11:00 a.m. until 4:00 p.m. on each day of the public hearings. These broadcasts, without any editing or commentary, may have given listeners the sensation of being present at the venues. SABC aired the programs in each major language (Zulu, Xhosa, Afrikaans, and English). SABC television aired daily news spots as well as the *TRC Special Report*, which ran on Sunday evenings from April 1996 to June 1998. The producer explained the television program's objective as providing contextual understanding of each case, reflecting the local background in the footage, and critically examining the TRC's activities. The TRC guaranteed SABC full editorial independence (Truth and Reconciliation Commission 1998a:356). Moreover, the print media continued to cover the daily output from the TRC, appointing "specialist correspondents to cover the Commission, virtually on a full-time basis" (p. 356). The continuous and intense media coverage of TRC activities offered South African citizens an arena for ongoing discussion and contestation. In this way, the media provided effective agenda setting.

However, a transitional society may often have a narrower space for local media to report political events. Reporting a TJ process is not necessarily praised as a positive support to the process. The following case study on Cambodian local media will illustrate the unique difficulties and unintended agenda-setting activities generated by local media coverage. The local media thus can become embroiled in a complicated situation in which they cannot always support TJ.

Local Media Ambivalence in a Transitional Society

When reading the ten or so local newspapers available in the Khmer language at newspaper stands in Phnom Penh, one quickly recognizes the clear differences between pro-government media and publications of the political opposition. *Rasmei Kampuchea (RK), Kampuchea Thmey (KT),* and *Koh Santepheap (KO)* generally support the government; *Machas Srok Khmer (MS), Moneaksekar Khmer (MO), Khmer Scientific (KS),* and *Khmer Nation (KN)* typically take an opposition stance (Wagstaff 2010:29).

Not only is there a disparity between the two groups in appearance, with the pro-government newspapers printed on rich, colored paper, but also in the contents, particularly regarding the Khmer Rouge Tribunal (KRT, also known as the ECCC), where they differ sharply from each other. The pro-government media give court issues much less coverage than their rivals. When they do cover the KRT, they allot only a very small space to the article on the front page, giving more attention to the day's murders or government programs. In contrast, the newspapers that generally side with the opposition cover KRT-related issues in depth. Not only are the court proceedings of the previous day reported, but so is the background and career of the accused (e.g., *KS,* June 26–27, 2011; *MS,* June 28, 2011), the mechanism of being recognized as a civil party (*KS,* June 26–27, 2011), the reason for a complicated court decision such as the one about the treatment of Ieng Tirith, who suffered from psychological problems (*MS,* September 22 and October 18, 2011), and some supplemental information to help the audience understand the prosecutors' explanation (*KS,* November 22, 2011).

However, the most significant feature of the opposition newspapers' coverage of the tribunals is that they have never ignored the problems inside the court. The ECCC has faced many problems, including internal conflict between domestic and foreign experts and between prosecutors and investigating judges, suspicions of corruption, and accusations of political intervention by the ruling party. The following discussion contains only a limited set of such critical articles, but it illustrates the tone of these media sources' coverage of the ECCC, which allows us to infer how local readers may perceive the nature of the courts.

Critical Newspaper Coverage of the KRT

Conflicts inside the ECCC. Conflict has been one of the leading characteristics of this hybrid tribunal's proceedings and historical background. In particular, 2011 witnessed a vehement battle between foreign prosecutor Andrew Cayley (from the United Kingdom, who resigned on September 16, 2013) and co-investigating judges Siegfried Blunk (Germany, resigned on October 10, 2011), and You Bunleng (Cambodia) over the investigation of Case 003/004. Throughout most of the year, virtually the only news outlets to cover this issue continuously were those of the political opposition. *MS* introduced this conflict as a battle between the prosecutor and the investigating judges; the latter insisted that they had investigated sufficiently, whereas the former demanded further investigations (*MS,* May 5, 2011). *MS* wrote in detail on the conflict, focusing more directly on the key stakeholders Cayley and Bunleng. Disagreement over Case 003 also surfaced between the co-prosecutors, Cayley and Chea Leang (co-prosecutor, Cambodia), at the very basic level of whether they should engage in the prosecution or not. *MO* (May 27, 2011) also addressed this conflict, adding the claim that Chea Leang was protecting some high-ranking government officials who would be summoned before the ECCC on issues related to Case 003. Chea Leang was even reported as saying that the events related to Cases 003 and 004 did not happen during the relevant period (*MS,* October 27, 2011). Images of Cayley, Blunk, and Bunleng appeared on the front pages repeatedly with an explanation of their professional battle, which undoubtedly shaped readers' impression of the internal dynamics of the ECCC.

The story of conflict between the prosecutors and investigating judges had not finished unfolding before a new one emerged regarding the Office of Co-Investigating Judges (OCIJ) itself. Five foreign staff of the OCIJ resigned in protest over a directive from their bosses—two co-investigating judges—and the judges reported that they were happy with the subordinates' resignations (*MO,* June 14, 2011). This conflict inside the OCIJ developed following the resignation in November 2010 of the former foreign investigating judge, Marcel Lemonde (France), allegedly because four top political leaders in Cambodia (Hun Sen, Norodom Sihanouk, Chea Sim, and Norodom Ranariddh)[28] had ignored a summons by his team (*MS,* June 23, 2011). *KN* (on June 17, 2011) reviewed the earlier resignation of former foreign prosecutor Robert Petit (Canada) on September 1, 2009, indicating that Petit had resigned for the same reason as Lemonde.

The power balance of this conflict changed when Blunk resigned his position on October 31, 2011. He continued to make comments about political interference, saying that the information minister and a government spokesperson had threatened him and told him to pack his clothes and go home if he wished to continue with the investigation of Cases 003 and 004 (*MS,* October 20 and 22–23, 2011; *SP,* December 2, 2011). Blunk clashed with Cayley during the first half of 2011 but finally resigned from the ECCC after a conflict with the Cambodian ruling party, according to the coverage. Yet the ruling party denied its commitment to the OCIJ's investigation of Cases 003 and 004, so Blunk's resignation put this lingering conflict in a new light.

Patricia O'Brien, undersecretary-general for legal affairs (the legal counsel of the United Nations), reportedly demanded that Sok An, deputy prime minister of the Royal Government of Cambodia, not interfere with the ECCC process (*MS,* October 22–23, 2011; *MO,* October 25, 2011; *MO,* October 28–30, 2011). This story has never appeared in *RK, KT,* or *KO.*

Furthermore, political interference by the ruling party was among the grounds brought in the lawsuit by the defense lawyers for Nuon Chea. They filed a complaint in Phnom Penh Municipal Court against eleven senior Cambodian officials, alleging their political intervention in a form contrary to the ECCC regulations (*MO,* October 25 and 28–30, 2011; *MS,* October 25, 2011). The defense lawyers for Ieng Sary commented on this lawsuit, saying that the ECCC should render justice to the survivors and the family of the deceased; however, the court was filled with internal conflicts and was far from achieving justice (*MO,* October 28–30, 2011). Herein lay a strange paradox: those accused of atrocities in the Khmer Rouge era, who were usually seen as the target of the citizens' condemnation, were supporting the cause of justice for citizens as a new conflict between senior government officials and defense lawyers became public.

Moreover, newspaper coverage included direct, critical comments on the ECCC as well: "They got out of one scrape only to fall into another" (*MS*, September 8, 2011); "The court is filled with problems" (*MS*, August 10, 2011); "Imbroglio inside the court prevents its smooth running" (*MO*, October 25, 2011). The information reported was all factual; the media created no fictitious charges. Yet these reports by media sources sympathetic to the political opposition may have fueled the impression that the ECCC was itself a source of successive conflicts in the process of reaching final decisions about right and wrong.

Negative evaluations of the court. The critical tone in the coverage of the issues surrounding the KRT went so far as to question its legitimacy. Typical expressions included these: "The ECCC cannot bring justice to the families of the deceased," and "There is no justice in the court process." Besides the references to various conflicts inside the court as mentioned above, many other factors and episodes that deprived the court of legitimacy were cited. Following are some examples.

"The court is corrupt so justice cannot be realized." Suspicions of corruption by Cambodian officials have been repeatedly aired. Some senior officials of the ruling party were exposed for having taken bribes in return for providing a position on the court (*MO*, October 25 and 28–30, 2011). The bribe is itself a matter of disgrace, but in this case it also undermines the supposed political independence of the ECCC. The court, under the strong influence of a ruling party, may be suspected of not investigating issues thoroughly before rendering its decisions. The ruling party's influence over the Cambodian court staff was evident when Cambodian prosecutor You Bunleng was selected by the ruling party, and the party also chose a reserve judge for the pretrial chamber, Pen Pichsaly, who had no prior experience as a judge[29] (*MS*, October 20, 2011).

"The court only takes care of the physical condition of the accused." The due process of law must be reflected in dealing with the accused as well, all of whom were quite old—some over age ninety. The trial itself is not a punishment, and until the judges give a final decision, in principle, the accused are not criminals. So they needed to be kept in healthy surroundings and, in case of a medical emergency, to be swiftly sent to Calmette, the large and expensive hospital in Phnom Penh. Given the severe economic disparity among Cambodians, it is understandable that people viewed this as special treatment, especially because victims could never expect to receive the same consideration. A critic said, "The ECCC is always worrying about the health status of the four accused" (*MO*, October 5, 2011). Receiving medical care at a proper hospital at all is beyond most ordinary people's resources in Cambodia. *KN* (September 7, 2011) cited DC-Cam director Youk Chhang's comment that not only are the accused old, but so

are the victims, so the court should consider the physical condition of victims, too. The court's special decision on the psychological disorder of Ieng Tirith, because of which it ruled that she would not attend the trial, drew similar complaints. (She passed away in August 2015.) The ample consideration given to the health of the accused was contrasted with the lack of improvement in the victims' living conditions (*MS,* November 21, 2011).

"The court is introducing foreign viewpoints." This concern also appears only in the print media of the political opposition. Foreigners, including journalists, politicians, and human-rights observers, tend to take a critical stance when describing the KRT process, so their comments are familiar to the readers of Cambodian English newspapers such as the *Phnom Penh Post* or *Cambodia Daily*. However, that is not the case in the coverage provided by *RK, KO,* and *KT.*

Brad Adams, executive director of Human Rights Watch's Asia Division, is a prominent character in the opposition newspapers *MS, MO,* and *KN*. His comments criticizing Prime Minister Hun Sen for political interference (*MS,* May 6–7, 2011) and indicating that Cambodian nationals could not trust the court because the investigating judges were not fulfilling their obligations (*MO,* October 5, 2011) became commonplace phrases in Cambodian discourse during 2011. Amnesty International's sharp accusations of political interference were also quoted (*MS,* June 10–11, 2011), as was the same charge by an officer of the French embassy (*MS,* September 9–10, 2011). As of 2011, US legal scholars lamented that the ECCC had handed down only one sentence (against Duch in Case 001) after spending $200 million over five years (*MS,* October 28–29, 2011). The editorial decision to report criticisms of the ECCC by foreigners, including UN legal counsel Patricia O'Brien, was a remarkable feature of newspapers supporting the political opposition.

The KRT is a spectacle in pro-government print media. In contrast to the critical opposition by news outlets such as *MS, MO,* and *KN,* those seen as pro-government did not actively cover the issues surrounding the KRT. Certainly, they could not fail to follow the events that held people's attention, such as when the judicial decision in Duch's case was handed down or at the beginning of Case 002. However, as a whole, they reported in depth on only a few events, so that few articles are available to depict the pattern of their coverage. Yet this fact in itself indicates their framing of the KRT, namely, that the trials were not really a significant issue and did not merit routine coverage. On the other hand, failure to cover the trials at all would give the impression that the government did not support the activity. They needed to reflect the government's position, finding a balance between supporting and distancing themselves too far from the ECCC.

Yet we can trace a discernible pattern in these pro-government newspapers. *KT* reported on May 6, 2011, that foreign executives (officials from the

Swiss and Israeli embassies) visited the ECCC, and the court officials exchanged ideas with them. At the beginning of Case 002, *RK* (June 28, 2011) reported that more than 600 observers from across the world were in attendance. One well-known survivor from S-21 (a torture center in the KR era), Vann Nath, was cited as saying that he was very happy for the moment. Theary Seng, quoted later as a strong critic of the KRT in the opposition newspapers, was reported to have been visibly moved and to have trembled with emotion. The ECCC's PR officer, Neth Pheaktra, expressed the opinion that Case 002 was the most important trial in Cambodian history. He wanted the world to know the proceedings of Case 002, the article said. One senior official of the Cambodian government commented in the article that this was a very important day for international society as well as for Cambodia. On the first day, when the four persons accused in Case 002 spoke, *KT* counted 900 observers and *KS* estimated 1,000, whereas *MS* and *MO* estimated an attendance of 700 (*KT,* November 23, 2011; *KO,* November 22, 2011).

RK also discussed (on May 1–2, 2011) the difficulties and conflicts surrounding the prosecution of Cases 003 and 004, but its tone was quite different from that of *MS* or *MO* in that it just addressed the prediction by government officials that Case 003 would cause a civil war. In terms of descriptions of the court proceedings of Case 002, the paper only reported who said or did what, without comment (e.g., "Nuon Chea insisted that he would comment through his lawyer . . . his lawyer asked if Nuon Chea could put on a cap during the deliberations because the air conditioner was very cold," *KS,* June 28, 2011).

The pro-government media coverage showed a definite pattern of depicting the ECCC as a symbolic national event through which Cambodians could share in the achievements of their society and confirm that foreign countries admired it. The newspapers included the opinions of some who referred to many Cambodian people positively supporting this historic ceremony. Analytical or critical articles, therefore, do not appear because *the event was a ceremony* and the very existence of the court represented an achievement. The positive tone praising only a particular moment without covering the complicated details suggests the implicit framing.

Can the media report the truth of TJ in a transitional society? The opposition media coverage stressed the complicated power balance and conflicts inside and outside the court, which helped to explain why the court process was so lengthy. Its reporting accurately reflected the court's actual status, although the framing and editing decisions likely gave a critical impression of the court to readers. On the other hand, pro-government news media limited their coverage in terms of both the space allotted and the discourse conveyed. *Spectacularization* might be an apt word to explain their framing—or, actually, lack of framing. At a certain moment that holds people's attention, these media outlets tended to use the present perfect tense, implying that something valuable has already happened and is complete (so any criticisms are unnecessary).

In sum, reporting that heavily reflected the realities, challenges, and difficulties facing the court caused its processes to appear illegitimate, whereas limited reporting gave the impression that the government did not want citizens to follow the process and preferred to frame the court as a symbolic ceremony. The latter approach implied that the court's actual decisions were politically illegitimate.

Conclusion

At the beginning of the launch of a TJ project, declared from a position full of moralistic disguise, comes a proclamation of the establishment and execution of rules called TJ to allow for a departure from the past. The moral tone is stipulated by a choice of nonviolent means of verbal communication pursuant to the ideal of justice or reconciliation.

However, suspicious eyes have often been cast on the moral legitimacy of the senders of such messages. Some directly dismiss the messages as a political maneuver, and others partly agree with the messages' orientation but demand other means to realize that ideal.

As demonstrated by the cases of Egypt and Cambodia, when the international community sends such a moralistic message, it tends to reshape the message to deflect attention from its past duplicitous engagement in state conflict or abuse, painting itself as blameless. Or, as the Serbian case vividly illustrates, while completely dismissing TJ's moralistic purpose, local political actors can adopt and commandeer a TJ regime to pursue their own utilitarian benefits, even deploying the preventive tactics of TJ's moralistic influence in a domestic context.

Although the Cambodian court featured institutional local ownership, in contrast to the ICTY case, it was established without substantial consultation with local stakeholders, leaving ordinary locals dissatisfied. The more the court's law experts stressed due process and the importance of maintaining the rule of law, the more ordinary locals demonstrated their suspicions of the reliability of the judicial mechanism.

The South African TRC contrasts with these cases in terms of its planned outreach to locals to build internal support before embarking on its work. Nevertheless, it also faced various criticisms after its inception. Families of deceased activists sued the TRC in constitutional court because the TRC had blocked their rights to prosecute the perpetrators, and all the major political parties boycotted the ceremony commemorating the publication of the TRC's report in 1998.

Ordinary local victims, in contrast to tactical political elites or activists, have also expressed their dissident opinions of TJ, despite its appearance of empowering victims. They complain that the TJ program does not deal with them in a proper manner. Some feel that TJ does not serve their needs; others engage in competition with fellow victims for social recognition as being "more serious" victims. When such complaints escalate, they can even lead to the eruption of a new armed conflict, as exemplified by East Timor.

Thus, TJ's moralistic message has not necessarily been accepted by its receivers in the way its senders expected. One can infer that the negative reactions occurred because TJ's PR backers lacked the ability to deliver the desired message to locals. Local media have thus come to be seen as a desirable counterpart to the TJ body. This view may partly reflect an expectation or assumption that locals would be interested in and cooperate with TJ programs as long as they are given sufficient ongoing information to be active stakeholders in the process. Yet the case study from Cambodia demonstrates the unique and complex difficulties of agenda setting by the local media as they publish political information during a time of post-conflict instability. A straightforward outcome in the causal scheme, namely, that more information will lead to more acceptance and understanding, cannot be expected in a transitional society.

The episodes described above illustrate that TJ's moralistic messages have been questioned in multiple ways, depending on the local context. Negative reactions may even appear, as in the cases of South Africa, Serbia, and Cambodia, on the side of local government, which should normally be a leading supporter of TJ in the local context. Or, sometimes political elites can utter dual messages to local citizens, pretending to support the process but rejecting substantial change. This can happen implicitly, as in Cambodia, or explicitly, as in Serbia. In other places, ordinary local stakeholders publicly deny the official moralistic message.

These reactions may be evaluated negatively or perceived as a fault of the sender's public relations efforts. But what would we think of a situation in which people are not permitted to express these dissident ideas that deviate from the intended message of TJ? Such a situation would resemble the authoritarian and conflict-ridden past from which TJ tries to help a country distance itself. In this sense, TJ projects face a dilemma. Whereas they expect receivers to agree with and internalize their message, if people were to blindly accept that message, their behavior would suggest a continuation of old ways rather than a break from the past. So far, however, this dilemma has not appeared often in transitional societies. Rather, TJ—and its message—tends to have become a target at which locals have felt comfortable aiming their dissident opinions. Why has this happened? There have undoubtedly been various contributing factors, yet TJ's lack of authority needs to be identified as one primary cause. Furthermore, the negative conditions of transitional societies, such as the malfunction of legal norms, may also have had an effect. These factors have inevitably produced a situation in which TJ tolerates deviations from its public message by the intended receivers. However, the function of such deviations calls for further consideration, given the fact that such behavior has been banned under the nation's previous social conditions, the very ones with which TJ attempts to deal.

Notes

1. "Rather than assuming the role of objective observer or passive reporter, many journalists saw the TRC hearings as an opportunity to engage in a form of civic education" (Goodman 2006:183).
2. For instance, one participant at a Center for Social Development (CSD) forum in Mondolkiri on May 4, 2007, wondered whether "the international prosecutor and judge [will] use their expertise and heartfelt emotion to do this work, since they do not have relatives or friends who were killed during this regime."
3. CSD forum, Kampot, June 14, 2006.
4. CSD forum, Mondolkiri, May 4, 2007.
5. Such views were repeatedly propounded in other forums, even after the court's verdict on Case 001 had been returned. See the Documentation Center of Cambodia's publication *Searching for the Truth* (*SFT*, First Quarter, 2010).
6. The people of Sierra Leone had a similar reaction to the international judiciary in the Special Court for Sierra Leone, as documented by court records for January (2009).
7. The direct reason for establishing the ECCC was a letter from the Royal Government of Cambodia (RGC) to the UN in 1997. Since 1990, Hun Sen and his colleagues had repeatedly appealed to the UN for a tribunal to try Khmer Rouge cadres (Heder 2011:4–15).
8. For details of the negotiation process between the UN and the Cambodian government, see Heder and Tittemore (2004), Heder (2011), Chhang (2007:157–172), and Dacil (2010:4–6).
9. CSD forum, Kep and Kampot, August 31, 2007.
10. CSD forum, Kratie, September 28, 2006.
11. CSD forum, Kampot, June 14, 2006.
12. CSD forum, Siem Reap, March 2, 2007.
13. CSD forum, Kratie, September 28, 2006.
14. CSD forum, Svay Rieng, June 8, 2008.
15. CSD forum, Phnom Penh, November 20, 2008.
16. CSD forum, Kep and Kampot, August 31, 2007.
17. CSD forum, Kratie, September 28, 2006.
18. CSD forum, Svay Rieng, June 8, 2008.
19. Chea Leang, co-prosecutor, CSD Forum, Kratie, September 28, 2006.
20. Reach Sambath, public relations officer, CSD Forum, Siem Reap, March 2, 2007.
21. Robert Petit, co-prosecutor, CSD Forum, Kratie, September 28, 2006. He resigned from his position on September 1, 2009.
22. Peter Foster, public affairs officer, CSD Forum, Kratie, September 28, 2006. He left the ECCC in December 2008.

23. Andrew Mace, British ambassador to the Kingdom of Cambodia, CSD Forum, Pailin, October 24, 2008.

24. CSD Forum, Siem Reap, March 2, 2007.

25. NGO guest staffer, CSD Forum, Siem Reap, March 2, 2007.

26. The following description is based on the interviews with TRC staff (August 1998, TRC Johannesburg office, Braamfontein) and the commission's internal documents.

27. Mandela's speech was accessed at http://www.mandela.gov.za/mandela_speeches/1998/981029_trcreport.htm, accessed January 12, 2018.

28. *MS* (October 20, 2011) mentions six persons cited in the summons by Lemonde's team on October 10, 2009.

29. On the ECCC web page, he is introduced as a judge sitting since 2001: https://www.eccc.gov.kh/en/persons/judge-pen-pichsaly-reserve, accessed January 12, 2018.

4

Going Beyond Official Mobilization

The previous chapter depicted past TJ cases as failing to function successfully as authentic forms of mass media or effective educators. Although TJ entities have always associated themselves with the concepts of goodwill and ideals, at least formally, some people have publicly challenged TJ entities' legitimacy, as the family of Steve Biko did. Additionally, other political organizations that should serve as affiliates of a TJ body, such as the ANC in South Africa, have even brought lawsuits against TJ entities. A more radical case occurred in Serbia, where top politicians aggressively designed a strategic campaign in collaboration with TJ programs, but with an intention far removed from any TJ principle or value. These past cases demonstrate that locals, regardless of which social stratum they belong to, are not necessarily subject to the ideals and values of TJ.

Institutional TJ entities have thus begun their activities in negative circumstances, among people who are suspicious of their messages. They need to change this mood. Sincere staffers inside a TJ body might seek spontaneously to solve this problem. Moreover, donor countries and organizations can pressure a TJ organization to demonstrate positive performance. These benefactors do not want to expend huge amounts of money on a project that has no substantial influence within the society in question. Moreover, observers, including foreign donors, would view a TJ program with no serious public relations or outreach effort as simply a cosmetic initiative by the domestic government, which would be only pretending that it had organized a TJ program for democratization and human-rights reformation.

Therefore, outreach has become a crucial part of any TJ project. In other words, direct and sustained outreach to locals is required above and beyond official announcements. An important role of institutional outreach is to achieve as great a mobilization of locals as possible at official events such as public hearings of a tribunal or a truth commission's forum. Mobilization has also become increasingly important in recent TJ situations because it is a convenient and objective way to demonstrate a project's influence within the local society to foreign donors. However, local citizens have not always been responsive to invitations to formal events, sometimes creating their own alternative gathering spaces. This chapter reports on such instances in South Africa, Sierra Leone, and Cambodia.

Outreach Is Required

While acknowledging negative reactions by local people to the initial announcement, an institutional TJ body adopts mobilization of locals as its mission. Staff of truth commissions, internationalized (hybrid) courts, and the International Criminal Court travel nationwide to explain their purpose, mandate, and requests to locals.

Sativa January has described the work of the press office of the Special Court for Sierra Leone in this regard. This press office spent considerable time encouraging civilians to view the trials as truthful by establishing that they were accessible. Yet physical and geographical conditions did not allow locals in remote areas to attend court sessions in Freetown, the coastal capital city. Therefore, the Special Court itself moved out of Freetown and traveled around the country. The press office created a video documentary to introduce the court and screened it in all thirteen of the country's provinces, followed by a question-and-answer session. Radio programs summarizing the proceedings were aired (January 2009:210–211). In recent times, Cambodian NGOs and, later, the ECCC have also adopted this style of outreach to disseminate information on the court to locals. In this behavior, we can recognize a line of TJ public-relations methodology dating back to the South African TRC.

Conversely, the International Criminal Tribunal for Rwanda has been referred to as an example of a TJ entity that no future program should follow. According to a survey conducted by Timothy Longman, Phuong Pham, and Harvey Weinstein of respondents in Rwanda, 87.2 percent were not even aware that the tribunal existed.[1] As for survivors' experience of the ICTR process, Emily Haslam (2011:229) wrote that the ICTR's outreach program "has been charged with focusing too much on information exchange at the expense of engagement."

The phrase that expresses Rwandan victims' criticisms of the ICTR most succinctly is "a wasteful parody of justice" (Musila 2010:45). Based on this negative view, the Rwandan survivors' groups boycotted the tribunals. According to Haslam (2011:229), "The introduction of victim participation and compensation at the ICC can be seen as recognition of the substance of at least some of their complaints."

Overly Controlled Mobilization

In the context of another TJ option in Rwanda (the gacaca court), the matter of mobilization has been discussed differently from the case of the ICTR. In gacaca, mobilization was rather conducted in a *too perfect* way. Phil Clark explained the reports from the early years of gacaca:

> An important feature of several gacaca hearings observed by the ASF [Avocats Sans Frontières, or Lawyers Without Borders] is the extent to which some communities have instituted ad hoc procedures to punish local people who fail to attend gacaca hearings. In one cell in Kigali Ville, gacaca judges maintained a list of habitual absentees. In a cell in Kigali Ngali, the general assembly discussed whether it should impose fines on those who arrived late to hearings or failed to attend altogether. The PRI [Penal Reform International] reports that some communities have discussed sanctioning the owners of bars and other businesses that open while gacaca hearings are underway. (Clark 2010:139–140)

These sanctions were justified on the grounds that gacaca was "government work" that required citizen participation. To the local residents, such government work meant that the action was obligatory: "The government says we must go to gacaca, so we will go" (Clark 2010:141). These answers not only express the source of locals' motivation but also suggest, according to Clark, the presence of severe social pressure. Locals may fear being marked as divisive if they do not participate; detainees who encourage participation in gacaca may simply be trying to gain favor from government officials and earn an early release (Clark 2010:141).

The situation is similar in East Timor, where nonparticipation inevitably carries a negative social connotation and participation becomes obligatory even though no official control exists:

> Regina, who lost her husband in 1999, suggested that she only participated in the CRP [Community Reconciliation Process] because "people might think I don't want peace if I don't." ... Regina's comments also allude to the extent to which there could be an element of pressure involved in gaining people's participation in the CRP process, either from community leaders or from CAVR staff. (Kent 2012:157)

This style of high-pressure mobilization does not cause a problem in itself, because the gathering also provides opportunities for significant interaction or forms of self-help among participants. Yet a mobilization that is too active—other scholars use the term *conscription* (Thomson and Nagy 2011:28)—tends to be linked to other compulsory mechanisms. The Rwandan gacaca, created to address the suspects with the crimes related to the genocide, has been widely criticized for its degree of state control. For example, the government allocated Hutu people the sole position of testifying as perpetrators and gave "official direction" for their testimonies in advance:

> Joseph, a Hutu peasant and former prisoner, said from his home in western Rwanda in August 2006, "Gacaca is just for show. We are told how to tell our truth about what we did during the genocide at gacaca. Me, I killed, and I even went through ingando [an educational program or solidarity camp organized by the government]. I have done everything this new government told me to do to get reconciled. So you might think peace is part of my life. I did what I was told to get free but really there is no peace in my heart. (Thomson and Nagy 2011:22)

However, a mobilization that is too perfect may have political objectives other than the goodwill and ideals of TJ: "For many Hutu men and women, the gacaca process is simply a means 'for this government to get rid of us [in public life]. They are trying to eliminate us from society. It is like they are killing Hutu through excessive punishment'" (Thomson and Nagy 2011:27).

The new Rwandan government, led by Tutsi politicians, has been consistent in bringing an ethnic hierarchy to the process of gacaca. Thomson and Nagy reported the case of the Twa, Rwanda's third and smallest ethnic group (composing less than 1 percent of the population), which was excluded from the gacaca process. According to the authors, local officials did not give them a chance to testify. Théogène in western Rwanda said:

> I went to ask [the local official] if I could tell my truth because I knew that the accused killed my wife in 1994. He laughed and said, "You don't need to waste our time talking because you are not part of the genocide. Your people did not kill or get killed." I was so angry with him. I lost also my mother and sister and I even hid some Tutsi in my home! (Thomson and Nagy 2011:28)

While indicating that state control was not necessarily perfect in areas distant from the capital city, Kigali, and that people's sense of obligation had changed through the course of gacaca, Clark (2010:151) also observed that the government has imposed official interventions and controls, and that the dialogue at gacaca "is not as open and undirected" as some commentators have suggested.

The compulsory nature of mobilization, regardless of whether it takes an authoritative or spontaneous form, needs to be considered not only as a negative condition for local participants' engagement in the TJ process but also as a continuation of a societal context in which mass atrocities occurred. What I mean by that rather serious expression of concern is that joining in collective activities out of fear of being labeled by others as traitors to the community or disloyal to a certain value has served as one strong social-psychological mechanism that has driven people to participate in mass atrocities. Such a dynamic was doubtless present in the Rwandan genocide and the mass atrocities in Cambodia. Ultimately, the activities themselves or the justifications for those activities do not matter for those involved; a certain type of membership is crucial for such mobilization. In these contexts, not only those in power but even ordinary residents label people who are not mobilized as a danger to the community. In this way, truly totalitarian situations develop. Regardless of whether a TJ program is directly connected with a forced mobilization mechanism, the tendency to retreat to old forms of mass mobilization often lingers.

Reasons to Testify

In such situations of social control, people's positive comments on their participation may need to be taken with some reservations, because they may have uttered the comment to please their audience. Clark heard many positive comments from locals, but given what we now know about the process, how can we accept them as authentic?

> "Gacaca is the best way for survivors to find out the truth about the past and for us to learn about living in peace," said Christiane, a widow in Kigali Ville with three young children whose husband was killed during the genocide. "I'm not sure if we can live together again after what has happened. But at gacaca we will learn how to talk together again, and maybe then we will be able to live together peacefully." Muvunyi, a thirty-seven-year-old survivor in Nyabihu district of Gisenyi, said, "If the people can talk face to face at gacaca and learn how to be together again, then they will live peacefully in the future. . . . We lack peace in our hearts but gacaca allows us to bring out the anger." (Clark 2010:225–226)

These are answers that TJ officials may be pleased to hear, because they serve as evidence of the positive influence of TJ mobilization. Indeed, the literal meaning of their words may contain some truth. However, one cannot shake the sense that they are guarded answers, seemingly drawn straight out of a textbook. This reminds us of C. Wright Mills's (1940) concept of *vocabularies of motive*, whereby the discourse does not truthfully connect the act with the reason it was performed. Rather, the comment abandons the usual cause–effect logic of explanation or reverses it, because the actor, particularly a person suspected of executing a negative act, is seeking to be accepted as legitimate by other people through the use of vocabularies of motive to justify himself or herself. Mills explained:

> It [diplomatic choice of motive] merely indicates that an appropriate vocabulary of motives will be utilized—that they are conditions for certain lines of conduct. When an agent vocalizes or imputes motives, he is not trying to describe his experienced social action. He is not merely stating "reasons." He is influencing others—and himself. Often he is finding new "reasons" which will mediate action. (Mills 1940:907)[2]

This idea of vocabularies of motive seems to be present when one reads Clark's reflection on the process in Rwanda:

> In my interviews, it is not always clear how genuinely suspects express this level of confidence in gacaca. It is possible that some detainees, for example, express confidence in gacaca because they wish to please the officials who oversee the ingando or other state officials, or because they wish to convince themselves that they will receive a warm welcome from the community. (Clark 2010:318–319)

In a paper titled "Why Testify? Witnesses' Motivations for Giving Evidence in a War Crimes Tribunal in Sierra Leone," Shanee Stepakoff et al. (2014) observed that being mobilized or testifying in a TJ program is not as natural for locals as many TJ supporters expect. On the contrary, this is a special or unusual experience for participants. Stepakoff et al. (2014:450) classified the motivations for testifying in the following ways: as a response to a direct experience of suffering, as a sense of contributing to indirect values such as the rule of law, as a way to prevent harm to potential future victims, and as a way to honor the dead.

Stepakoff et al. (2014:430) further elaborated their viewpoint by citing the following five factors that encourage people to testify: fulfilling a moral duty, seeking retributive justice, reducing psychological pain, confronting the accused, and obtaining material benefits. In this way, their research agenda has gone further than assuming the simple expectation that locals are pleased to testify in TJ settings. However, one can still view these motivations as illustrating a pattern of locals who feel compelled to explain the reason for their engagement. The first three of these five reasons constitute a socially positive or scientific mode of explanation and thus qualify as *proper vocabulary*. Such explanations from the Sierra Leonean context include the following:

> "To respond to and denounce the wrongs committed against me during the war"; "The rebels captured me and I have come to testify about what they did to me"; "I testified because of my son who was ampu-

tated . . . so when I had the opportunity to come [to] testify before the Court I did it with all my heart"; "Because my sister's daughter was raped to death"; and "I saw them torture people, and kill people, and burn houses . . . so when the Special Court came . . . I said let me go and testify." (Stepakoff et al. 2014:442–443)

Stepakoff et al. asserted that these statements serve the purpose of fulfilling moral duty and contributing to justice, but one can interpret these statements in that way without knowing the details of their participation or of the proceedings. Moreover, it is possible that locals casually attended the program with no special motivation, answering in that manner retrospectively when contacted by foreign researchers who requested legitimate explanations. The more abstract and universal answers especially raise this suspicion because these may not be rooted in the vocabulary of the residents' daily lives: For example: "I testified for the Court to wipe away impunity and the perpetrators to be punished for the wrongs they did to us," and "I wanted the culprits to be dealt with properly" (Stepakoff et al. 2014:443). Considering these answers with the notion of vocabularies of motive in mind, one arrives at two basic understandings. First, the answers socially and culturally fit the domestic context. In this case, one must consider the possibility of locals being pressured into giving such statements. The second understanding is that locals accessed the TJ body without detailed knowledge of it or any strong motivation for doing so. They may have visited the place to gain concrete information and ended up participating unexpectedly in the process (by testifying). In both understandings, the assumption that mobilization by a TJ entity to cultivate locals' own motivation works, and that therefore the locals give positive comments about the TJ process, is dismissed. In the former interpretation, they are offering the proper mode of comment in their local context. In the latter interpretation, they make the proper mode of comment when researchers are listening.

Proper Vocabulary, Institutional Justification

Paying critical attention to locals' vocabulary regarding participation is demanding, because locals' support and satisfaction is a key aspect for a TJ organization's self-justification. This chapter began with a summary of Chapter 3, critical responses by locals to a TJ promotional campaign. These reactions require TJ entities to change local perceptions. We observed that outreach and mobilization have, therefore, become essential tools for TJ success. By conducting outreach and mobilization, a TJ entity aims to increase the number of local supporters of its activities. An increase in the number of people who express satisfaction with the TJ project's work will be a positive sign for the donors.

Currently, outreach and participation mechanisms are considered essential elements of justice activities (Vinck and Pham, 2010:423).[3] Comments by the United Nations High Commissioner for Human Rights, who was formerly a judge at the ICC, affirm this understanding: "Over the course of the last thirteen years, as a judge on the [ICTR] and now the ICC, I learned to listen to different voices, both within and outside the courtroom, and I have slowly developed a growing awareness that rendering justice after mass conflicts is an undertaking that extends well beyond the courtroom" (Pillay 2007:314).

This trend fits the contemporary global, liberalist justice regime, which presupposes a combination of local engagement and objective measurement as basic requirements for Western intervention in a transitional or fragile state. In terms of intervention, international society is required to support a local society when the local government is about to pursue democratizing policies based on goodwill and ideals. The factor of local ownership is incorporated into this undertaking because it is thought to stabilize local political conditions in the long term. TJ projects require huge budgets, so in order to satisfy those funding the project, proof of positive outcomes is inherently the first agenda item in program design. Initially, the obligation appears in the form of a time restriction: "UNTAET's [the UN Transitional Administration in East Timor] budget was financed by assessed (or nonvoluntary) contributions from UN members, [so that] meant there was pressure to complete the mission as soon as possible and, by early 2001, the date for independence was set for 20 May 2002" (Kent 2012:49).[4]

Then, outcomes need to be presented using concrete figures that support the staff's claims of success. Thus, if you are a staff member inside any TJ entity, the need for outreach, PR, and mobilization is now obligatory not only for the substantial satisfaction and healing of locals but also to verify your achievements to foreign donors. TJ policies are planned using a specific cause–effect perspective that can be considered "policy as usual," even though the prediction of effectiveness is only assumed.

Pablo de Greiff makes the following observation in this regard:

> The external challenge of transitional justice . . . is the pressure, manifested most immediately in a "results-oriented" attitude on the part of both governmental and nongovernmental funders, to quantify its impact. There is nothing that puts transitional justice in a distinctively poorer position than other justice-related interventions to speak about its impact. . . . Questions about impact are as legitimate as they are unpostponable. (de Greiff 2013:551)

Further, in the context of neoliberalism, the presentation of outcomes to donors using reasonable figures may be more and more necessary. In other words, institutional TJ entities have been facing increasing pressure from foreign donors to demonstrate their positive influence on local societies through statistical data. The data might then be converted or translated into decisions on the amount of fiscal support awarded. Scholars and experts have criticized this "numbers game," but TJ staff cannot afford to neglect this responsibility in their hectic schedule.

A Cambodian case is illustrative. Since the beginning of the tribunals in 2006, survivors as well as foreign observers have joined in a chorus of complaints about delayed justice in the courts. Indeed, as of January 2018, only two final judgments had been rendered, and two of the original five accused have passed away. The years of resistance by the RGC had limited the number of accused to no more than five. Although four additional defendants were added in 2014, their status had still been under investigation as of January 2018. With so few defendants, the cost per defendant was estimated to be $112.7 million (Bates 2010:45), far higher than that of any other international judicial body.[5] In a society where the monthly income of a schoolteacher or a police officer is around $150—and even a well-paid professional soccer player expects $300—it is easy to see why the sheer expense of these proceedings, purportedly carried out on behalf of the people, alienated many Cambodians from the process.

Investigating events that occurred during the Khmer Rouge era, more than thirty years ago, poses a serious challenge. Understandably, when legal experts pursue more rigorous logic to avoid any ambiguity, more time for legal examination is needed both before and during court hearings. Consequently, the elaborating examinations at longer proceedings become too detailed for ordinary audiences to follow without particular legal knowledge. Here a dilemma emerges. Long court examinations occur because of the sincerity and professional ethics of legal experts, but for a person outside that legal circle, the examinations are too obscure. Facing such a dilemma, a convenient option for a TJ body (in order to prove its ongoing "success") is to produce data on locals who have been officially mobilized. Outreach and mobilization themselves are neutral notions, so either positive or negative consequences might result from them. If locals might be disappointed by the court's deficiencies, having no such outreach or mobilization might be regarded as preferable to mobilizing one's future critics. But for now, such concerns seem to have been set aside. The naive and unproven assumption that mobilized people experience internal positive change has been a cliché used to justify TJ entities. It surely links the ideas of the court as a pedagogic medium and of local participants as ideal victims, as argued in Chapter 3.

On the other hand, in the short history of the ECCC, and even though it was set up with a victim-support mechanism, for the most part since 2006 only a small budget has been allotted for this task and no substantial work has occurred. Christoph Sperfeldt (2012:156) explained that "only in 2009, after receiving earmarked funding from the German Foreign Office, was the Unit able to operate at a higher level." Although the ECCC's Victims Unit (later renamed the Victim Support Section) was mandated to conduct victim aid activities, they were substantially and informally passed on to local NGOs for implementation. This role included providing general information about the ECCC and helping victims to complete the court's victim participation form, which developed into comprehensive victim support projects involving notifying survivors about the status of their applications, facilitating victims' legal representation, and regularly informing civil parties about and supporting them in attending trials and meeting with their lawyers. But in 2009, the ECCC changed its internal focus and became active in informing the public. It seems that the ECCC formally recognized the value and role of outreach and made it a priority, once it realized that judicial outcomes would not be expected to be produced in the near future. A substantial number of mobilized people, which can be produced and demonstrated by outreach programs, may help their self-justification against the critical chorus objecting to court delay.

"Something Has Been Constantly Increasing"

Data showing that "something has been constantly increasing during a certain period" fit the norms of this neoliberal era, regardless of the specific content. This trend can be found in various places in the contemporary world.

The host of an internet site not only enjoys seeing the number of people his or her idea has reached but also receives economic benefits from this number, because advertising companies that link to the site pay affiliate fees. By way of comparison, equity investment might be in essence a method of supporting a company's vision and projects through stock purchase, but this occurs after the calculation of complex indicators, such as the constant increase of several technical indicators as well as profits in each quarter. Positive data trends are simply the best evidence of the company's effort and reliability. Even scholars must constantly produce in this way, accumulating a large number of published studies if they want any public research funding, even though the quality and content of their research may not contribute meaningfully to society. Tactically citing each other among fellows or in peer circles to achieve a higher impact factor may seem scientific (!) within the context of the scheme itself but is ultimately unscientific in the sense that this attitude induces unproductive outcomes at a collective level. Regardless, third parties in many social sectors view increasing numbers as the fairest and most objective way to assess someone's social legitimacy.

Within this schema, we do not necessarily scrutinize the meaning of goal setting. We treat this in a relatively liberal manner. In the present context, an explanation that outreach and mobilization bring positive consequences to all participants is an assumption that raises a question: Exactly how do outreach and mobilization improve locals' understanding and motivation to engage in the process? However, in actual practice, an assumption or an expectation does not substantially affect a policy decision. The expectation of a self-fulfilling prophecy (Robert Merton) is used here as a kind of self-legitimization. Rather, effective operation of processes in the service of goals is required. If a reasonable figure is submitted in a persuasive presentation, we view that as a sign of success. Impressive-sounding statistical data can be made brilliantly clear and transparent even to those with no legal knowledge. Specific numbers can be provided for: how many locals visited the court; how many lectures the TJ staff held at local schools; how long each participant spent in the capital on a court tour; how many pamphlets and T-shirts the TJ body distributed, and in how many villages; and how big the budget was. Yet how locals perceive the court will still be unclear. I remember an ECCC court hearing where locals from a remote area were occupying most of the seats in the public gallery. The court PR unit had prepared buses for their trip. After the long hours of cross-examination in the courtroom, which might make anyone unfamiliar with legal language sleepy, one of the participants muttered, "I don't know who is accused. I have just come to see Phnom Penh."

Finding signs of the numbers game in other TJ cases is not difficult. Third parties assessed the ICC trial of Jean-Pierre Bemba in the Central African Republic based on the number of victims who participated, whereas the legal process itself seems to have been slow, just as in the Cambodian case: "The sheer number of applications for victim participation in ICC proceedings somewhat puts a stamp of legitimacy on proceedings . . . even if Bemba is so far the only person prosecuted by the ICC for crimes committed in the CAR" (Ndahinda 2013:495). Gacaca's outcomes in Rwanda were also justified by the numbers of people mobilized:

> Tharcisse Karugarama, the Minister of Justice, underscored gacaca's achievements. . . . "Look at what gacaca has accomplished," he said. "We now have only 53,000 detainees in prison [compared to 110,000 as of 1995], including genocide and other cases. Where are the rest? They've been reintegrated into the community." (Clark 2010:241)

Comparing TJ Mobilization to a Social Movement

Scholars have depicted TJ entities' mobilization in terms of dilemmas and reservations. Whereas an institutional TJ body wants to gather as many participants as possible, mobilization should not assume a compulsory nature if the TJ body expects participants to experience positive psychological and emotional change. Locals' positive comments are a criterion for measuring the success of TJ mobilization; however, some comments may be uttered using a certain code of expression. Scholars then categorize them as a socially and culturally filtered vocabulary of motive. Strict obedience to legal professionalism might be inevitable, particularly in the context of a post-conflict transitional country. But this may lead to no visible outcomes in a certain time span with which all observers, including nonlegal experts, can be satisfied. Therefore, the number of locals mobilized becomes convenient and proper evidence of a TJ organization's demonstration of a positive influence on the affected society.

In theory, with these reservations in mind, the mobilization of TJ bodies should appear in the form of *mechanisms to ensure that the greatest number of individuals engage in the process based on their own initiative.* Usually an organization, a social group, or collective activity with that orientation is called a social movement. Taking that need into account, this chapter proposes that TJ bodies can helpfully be compared with social movements, rather than being treated as policies or state organizations employed in non-post-conflict societies.

Spontaneous Participation as a Central Agenda

Although various scholars have attempted to define the term *social movement,* Sidney Tarrow has offered the generally accepted definition. He stated that social movements consist of "collective challenges, based on common purposes and social solidarities, in sustained interaction with elites, opponents, and authorities" (Tarrow 1994:4). If this definition is adopted, an institutional TJ program would not seem to be a social movement because authorities do not normally establish social movements. But the concept has been expanded from that classic picture. Some scholars have offered more flexible views of social movements that do not require the acquisition of social resources as primary goals. In his study of ecological and peace movements, for example, Alberto Melucci (1996:165) focused on "a transformation of the relations between society and its survival." Movements, he said, should not be categorized primarily by the distribution of social resources, or as political or institutional reflections of protesters' appeals for rights. What matters more is the meaning or framing of public discourses:

> The problem raised by contemporary movements rather concerns a redefinition of what democracy is, can be, and ought to be in a world where information becomes the central resource and where individuals and groups are offered the possibility of themselves constructing their

identities instead of remaining simply recipients [of the identities] assigned them from the outside. (Melucci 1996:203)

This approach to a better understanding of contemporary social movements has been extended further. Kōichi Hasegawa and Takashi Machimura (2004:19) defined a social movement as "a transformation-oriented collective action, which derives from people's discontent with the present conditions or certain prospective situations." Although they stressed three key terms in their definition (orientation toward transformation, collective action, and discontent), they deleted the terms *contention, protest,* and *collective identity.*

The vector that extends the concept of social movements appears to parallel the changing status of authorities that remain unstable with respect to their mandate, legitimacy, durability, and power to control social members in a rapidly changing world. This presence of unstable authority in the so-called postmodern world is also central to an understanding of a post-conflict society. A TJ project has frequently been adopted because it can offer a different approach from de facto public services, such as the provision of domestic courts in societies where governmental authority is unstable and does not enjoy a legitimacy supported by locals.

It is possible to compare social movements and TJ from another angle. A social movement contains three invariable elements: (1) attempts to change a society through channels other than established institutional ones (e.g., a domestic judiciary or parliament), (2) attempts to establish values and meanings that have not yet occupied the position of a social norm, and (3) attempts to mobilize the greatest number of people. If the action lacks the first element, then it will be subsumed under the normal political work performed by political parties. If the second element is not considered, cultural conservatism could qualify as a social movement. If an action lacks the third element, it will be impossible to distinguish a social movement from the work of elite bureaucrats.

In summary, if we view a social movement as a "transformation-oriented collective action" (Hasegawa and Machimura) that includes a "redefinition of democracy" (Melucci) through channels that differ from de facto judiciary and parliamentary channels and attempts to mobilize and involve the greatest number of people, then this definition is compatible with the ideal of TJ mobilization in practice.

Questioning the "TJ as a Social Movement" Model

To enable locals to engage in public communication through their own will and to give them a sense of relief, spontaneous, noncompulsory participation is crucial. In this regard, a social-movement model is a better fit than a policy model. But this model faces several limitations related to the issue of a movement's ability to mobilize the greatest number of individuals.

One of the basic concerns is gender. Several scholars have indicated that the experience of sexual violence does not suit the style of TJ that encourages victims to speak about their experiences and share them with others (Ross 2003:17–19; Truth and Reconciliation Commission 1998b:285). The South African TRC recognized this problem in the preparation stage, so it developed a mechanism for anonymous testimony at a public forum, which was delivered over a blind wall with only female commissioners present. It also adopted a method whereby a "wise woman" in a residential community would gather statements from victims and then testify in public as their representative. Despite such considerations in program design, many women still felt reluctant to testify in public and retreated from the process.

The same problem was reported in East Timor. According to Kent, even though the CAVR included gender violence on its agenda, many women declined to participate in the public victim hearings or give statements because they did not want to testify to men, or they just prioritized housework over attending to CAVR activities. Some women may have thought that their story was not worth telling, or a family member may have prevented them from testifying, as was reported in the course of the South African TRC. One woman who retreated from the process did so because "she felt that others had suffered more than she had" (Kent 2012:101). This pattern of withdrawal by women from the TJ process, regardless of their social background, has been broadly witnessed.

Eligibility for mobilization in the TJ movement is not unconditionally open. Indirect resonance with the politics of victimhood, first presented in Chapter 3, appears here. Table 4.1 shows the number of people in each racial

Table 4.1 Number of Victim Statements Collected from Each Population Group by the South African Truth and Reconciliation Commission

Population Group	Number of Statements	Statements from Each Group (%)	Total Population in Each Group (%)
African	19,144	89.9	76.1
Colored	354	1.7	8.5
Asian	45	0.2	2.6
White	231	1.1	12.8
Total	21,297	100	100

Source: Truth and Reconciliation Commission 1998a:168.
Note: There were 1,523 statements from people whose population group is unknown, making the total number different from the sum of each population group.

group who gave victim statements to the South African TRC. The TRC can be presented as an example of a TJ entity that allowed participation on a relatively voluntary basis. Despite this openness, those classified as Colored and Asian (mostly referred to as Indians) remained silent bystanders, tending not to utilize the opportunity to announce their victimhood in the public arena. That tendency is clear in comparison to the aggressive dissenters (white people), who are generally labeled as former perpetrators or a beneficiary group.

Despite an institutional TJ body's effort to integrate disparate political positions in an attempt at nation building, the former adversarial relationship lingers during the period of transition. That fact may reflect the unbalanced configuration among participants. However, describing this tendency as reflecting a direct continuation of the former political conflict would oversimplify the matter, because, as we will see in the next chapter, political opponents and adversarial actors opposed to TJ often enter the TJ arena and seek to achieve their goals there. The conflict continues, but in a different fashion.

In considering this issue, Jelena Obradović-Wochnik (2013:340) brings up the case of Serbia and indicates that the Serbian public is frequently constructed as a subject that needs to be (re)educated. She describes the enlightenment campaign run by the Belgrade Center for Human Rights in 2010:

> In general, it is made clear that one of the things that has to change is "the Serbs'" perception of their own community as victims. However, such projects assume that "the public" is misinformed and uncritically subscribes to the "Serbs as victims" view. This view constructs the public as a subject that has to admit publicly its ignorance and engage with TJ initiatives on those terms. This contributes to the "silent dilemma," as individuals may be reluctant to engage on this basis, preferring to keep silent in order not to be labeled "ignorant." (Obradović-Wochnik 2013:340)

Why were South African whites, Cambodian former Khmer Rouge soldiers, and Serbian citizens not mobilized in TJ programs? The reason was that the prevailing human-rights tone, under the guise of neutrality and universality, excluded a specific political position from the beginning. Obradović-Wochnik (2013:341) writes that many Serbs held complex feelings alongside their regret about the loss of ethnic lives and "the horror they felt at knowing that Serbs committed war crimes." But the public conditions for them to speak had already set up the agenda to require locals to admit "that 'Serbs' committed war crimes." In such a context, locals naturally felt that "their stories lack[ed] an audience."

This observation that some groups felt they lacked an audience directly resonates with the argument about the public production of knowledge in

Chapter 3. In a venue of public knowledge production, the group of people that is able to speak with a certain code of expression is predetermined to wear the guise of correctness. Someone who finds himself or herself alienated from that condition can only remain silent, because making any utterance would earn the label of ignorant perpetrator. Whereas the reference to this concept in the previous chapter was aimed at illuminating selective victimhood in the TJ process, here we are dealing with an ambiguous group identity as beneficiary, or with a more general view of one group as on the side of the perpetrators. In the Serbian case, for example, Serbians' diversity is disregarded and "the Serbs-Serbia-Serbian society or 'the public' exists primarily as an imagined audience, constructed through expert narrative" (Obradović-Wochnik 2013:343). Consequently, those who recognize their effective exclusion from TJ discourses based on goodwill and human rights quietly withdraw from the TJ movement.

Relationships with Other Movements

Institutional TJ bodies that appear to function as pseudo-social movements, even when attempting to increase spontaneous support in the concerned society, have often been derailed. On the other hand, TJ bodies' cooperation with local NGOs has tended to be crucial to the outcomes of TJ activities. Priscilla Hayner (2001:223–24) notes how cooperation with NGOs will "determine the success of any truth commission." This expression reminds us of the role of local media in TJ activities, examined in Chapter 3. Here we will review the case of Kenya's TJ body, which has been negatively assessed partly because of the unfruitful relationship between the Truth, Justice and Reconciliation Commission (TJRC) of Kenya and civil-society organizations (CSOs).

Lydiah Kemunto Bosire and Gabrielle Lynch addressed two institutional TJ attempts in Kenya, in 2003 and from 2008 to 2013. Both cases are depicted as having been closely connected with NGO engagement. The CSOs in the former case spearheaded a wider reform agenda, although in the latter case they demonstrated very limited support for the TJRC. The CSOs' scarce support of the TJRC, Bosire and Lynch (2014:258) assert, brought about the TJRC's "credibility crisis, public scepticism, media disinterest and donor distance from the project," leading to their evaluation that "the TJRC process is widely considered to have been politically unsuccessful." What they mean by "politically unsuccessful" is that the TJRC has routinely conducted several TJ activities like other commissions, such as public hearings, witness statements, lawsuits, and writing reports, but these programs are assessed as "increasingly [having become] a technical exercise" (Bosire and Lynch 2014:276). Bosire and Lynch highlight several reasons for the loss of CSO support, such as the selection process of commissioners with no substantial reflection on CSO recommendations, the appointment of a chairman with a politically weak record on human-rights abuses and violations, and the repeated postponement of publication of the final report. This decreased support from local CSOs left "only *GIZ* [the German *Gesellschaft für Internationale Zusammenarbeit* or Corporation for International Cooperation] and the UN Development Programme offering substantial technical and financial support for much of its lifespan" (Bosire and Lynch 2014:275). Ironically, the Kenyan government initially established this commission with the consultation and advice of Priscilla Hayner, who must have arranged the technical matters. Yet the commission would later be criticized as being merely technical. Thus "most ordinary Kenyans knew very little about the Commission beyond the headlines about its [scandalous] chairman" (Bosire and Lynch 2014:275), who was indicted at the ICC and escaped sentencing only on a technicality. The Kenyan case suggests that a TJ body bearing the nature of a pseudo-social movement seems necessary to develop networking and working relationships with other, more recognizable social-movement bodies.

Propagation of Movement Repertoire

I have proposed an analytical approach that compares TJ bodies to social movements partly to reveal their unstable position as well as their basic need to gather as many proponents as possible. The concept of propagation or diffusion of movement repertoire is useful in understanding the TJ body's unique but informal influence on the concerned society. Charles Tilly (1986) used this term to describe a contentious demonstration taking place in the form of "a limited set of routines that are learned, shared, and acted out through a relatively deliberate process of choice." Contentious demonstration was thus identified as rational expression, although on the surface there might have been irrational explosions. A collective expression, properly accepted by many others in a society, would then be mimicked by another group for another movement because this might enhance the capability to mobilize people. Knowledge and skill on how to frame an appeal and how to behave in public will become a common currency among those who interact with or are inspired to action by a previously existing group that possesses this currency. Using this framework, a TJ body becomes directly comparable to other social-movement entities.

In the next step, we can assess its influence by examining how the propagation of movement repertoire to other entities occurs. In this section, some examples of such "spontaneous" engagement of locals that diverged from the official mandate and program are introduced, beginning with cases from South Africa and Sierra Leone, which are characterized by their voluntary changes to compensate for official TJ bodies' deficiencies. In South Africa, the TRC provided a potential space for participants to engage in the process because of its all-encompassing terms of "truth and reconciliation." However, its all-encompassing character did not fit the various needs of victims. As such, many participants diverged from the official stream of TRC, creating a new space where shared memories and mutual assistance among survivors could ensue, which neither the TRC nor the government could anticipate or control.

The Khulumani Support Group

Khulumani, which means "speak out" in Zulu, began its work in 1995 at the time of the establishment of the TRC and grew to be the largest victims' association in South Africa with more than 100,000 members (Kesselring 2017:27). Its participants were victimized in myriad ways: torture, detention without trial, sexual assault, abuse, harassment, mutilation of body parts, banning and banishment by order, deliberate withholding of medical attention, denial of food and water, the destruction of homes, and loss of family members. In the beginning, the Khulumani Support Group's core activities mirrored the TRC's agenda, including spreading the commission's information, offering proposals for victim reparations, and making public appeals on amnesty judgments. Yet it did not limit its activities to lobbying for the TRC. Soon the organization staged a play that focused on the tensions and contradictions in the TRC process, taking the performance to many townships. In critically focusing on the TRC process, Khulumani developed its own strong bonds with local communities and its own role. In Hayner's view:

> The founders of Khulumani realize that the group never would have formed without the truth commission, though it has now taken on a life of its own. Those who work closely with victims have seen the positive effect of Khulumani and similar organizations and a much lower likelihood of retraumatization symptoms for those who are members of such groups. Many maintain that Khulumani's support provided a much greater sense of healing than the commission itself. Reverend S. K. Mbande, in Daveyton, told me that these support groups were "one of the fruits of the commission. People coming together and healing themselves—that never would have happened before. Fear was the order of the day. Since the truth commission, things have come out, and it's made people come together." (Hayner 2001:148)

Khulumani thus formed initially as a positive derivative from the official institution, but over time it became closer and more tactically responsive to specific victims. The TRC had never planned to create such a supplementary branch or independently functioning unit, but Khulumani did not appear out of thin air; the motivation for the movement and its repertoire of activities came in part from its predecessor. As an official organization, the TRC had to be open to all political groups, including those in conflict with each other. This meant that the commission could not be expected to provide a space for closed, and therefore safe, communication. However, once the TRC was identified as an incomplete space, the need for a complementary space became clear. Khulumani, sensitive to this need, developed its unique style in response. Rita Kesselring (2017:164) assesses Khulumani's role among members as molding their subjectivity: "By teaching members how to articulate their pain in public settings, the leadership plays a constitutive role in coding members' victimhood." If the TRC had been considered almighty and sufficiently complete, such an organization as Khulumani would not have developed out of the TRC process.

During the period while Khulumani was developing, the TRC's most crucial unfinished business lay in justice issues pertaining to symbolic and financial reparations. Therefore, Khulumani and another group, Jubilee 2000, brought a lawsuit in US federal court in New York in 2002 on behalf of victims of apartheid (*Khulumani et al. v. Barclays National Bank et al.*, Case No. 02-CV5952, S.D.N.Y. 2002). The accused were twenty-three foreign multinational enterprises, including British Petroleum, Shell Oil, Barclays, Credit Suisse, Deutsche Bank, Ford Motors, and IBM; they were alleged to have aided and abetted the perpetration of gross human-rights violations in South Africa by collaborating with the apartheid regime and providing military and other strategic equipment to its security agencies. President Thabo Mbeki expressed his strong opposition to the lawsuit in 2003, stating that it interfered with the "sovereign right to determine, according to internal political and constitutional order, how best to address Apartheid's legacy." In 2004, the banks and oil companies were freed from the case because "District Judge John Sprizzo said that no direct link could be proved between the firms' actions during Apartheid and human rights violations of the era."[6] Justice Minister Penuell Maduna affirmed this position, indicting to the US district court that the case should not be dealt with because it had the potential to discourage foreign investment in South Africa. However, the Zuma government reversed its previous position in September 2009 and expressed support for the lawsuit. When General Motors, which had declared bankruptcy and been reorganized in 2009, opted to settle the case with a payment of $1.5 million in 2012, Khulumani called on other defendant companies to follow suit. However, the remaining actors, Ford and IBM, were found by the US district court in August 2014 to be not responsible for apartheid-era abuses. In July 2015, the Second US Circuit Court of Appeals in New York dismissed the case because Ford's South African subsidiary—not the US company itself—had cooperated with the apartheid government and because it had not been proved that IBM had the clear purpose of supporting human-rights abuses.[7]

The TRC has often been criticized for not bringing legal justice to victims, as typically illustrated by the decision by the family of Steve Biko to sue the TRC (see Chapter 3). A debate over whether reconciliation or justice needs to be prioritized was one of the controversies in TJ studies in the post-TRC period. This argument seems to have converged to a middle-ground position that the proper combination of reconciliation policy and judicial initiative should be pursued. Cases in Sierra Leone, East Timor, and Peru have all officially followed that option. Yet efforts to pursue both reconciliation and justice are compatible, for instance, in the paradoxical manner exemplified by the South African TRC and Khulumani. Such paradoxical compatibility cannot be institutionally planned, and it can be assessed only retrospectively. It is not clear whether an official court established by a government or a justice movement with no governmental support, like Khulumani, more strongly and substantially supplies a real sense of justice.

The South African History Archive

Having begun its work in the 1980s in close connection with the United Democratic Front, the Congress of South African Trade Unions, and the ANC, the South African History Archive (SAHA) now operates as an independent human-rights archive that specializes in documenting and publishing a broad range of information on the liberation movement, political transition, and freedom of information in contemporary South Africa. Among its various projects, the following three are prominent in regard to the documentation of TRC activities.

The first project, the Preservation and Access to Records and Stories relating to the TRC, is an archive established in 2006–2009 in cooperation with the Historical Papers of the University of the Witwatersrand Library. This archive is unique in light of its interpretation of TRC activities, which SAHA believes should expand to "the ever-shifting stories about the TRC carried by a myriad people," so that "internal records used by the TRC as well as external documentation of the TRC process by a wide range of individuals and organizations, within and outside of South Africa" are required.[8]

Based on the idea of the TRC as a social phenomenon, the archive includes:

- interviews with sixty-three individuals who worked for the commission in various capacities and in different locales;
- the TRC's *Select Bibliography to the South African Truth and Reconciliation Commission Debate*, identifying key published articles,

books and book chapters, theses, and online and audiovisual resources about the TRC, from conception to aftermath; and
- digitized copies of key archival materials organized into five broad categories—background, human-rights violations, amnesty, reparations, and aftermath—with accompanying narrative, in an attempt to contextualize, compare, and contrast these archival fragments to enrich "social memory."

The second project is a digital web resource, launched in 2013 centering on the South Africa Broadcasting Corporation television series *Truth and Reconciliation Commission Special Report*, which comprised eighty-seven episodes and was aired weekly from 1996 to 1998. A multimedia platform containing all episodes of the series was created in conjunction with SABC Digital News and SABC Business Development. Moreover, the episodes are linked to relevant sections of the TRC's final report and other documents, "to form a seamless searchable resource intended to make the work of the TRC more accessible and to support on-going transitional justice and reconciliation work in South Africa."[9] The project also digitized a collection of cartoons related to the TRC, drawn by Zapiro between 1995 and 2004.

The third and latest SAHA project was initiated in 2015 following the official release of TRC Section 29 records. The TRC conducted closed hearings, called Section 29 hearings, at which those subpoenaed divulged the full extent of their knowledge of gross human-rights violations. Based on a freedom of information law passed in the year 2000, SAHA has repeatedly challenged the Department of Justice for access to the full transcripts of these hearings. SAHA's requests in 2003, 2006, and 2009 were denied mainly because of concerns that releasing such information would have a negative impact on cases being investigated and prosecuted by the National Prosecuting Authority (NPA). However, the NPA has prosecuted no cases related to Section 29 hearings since 2009; thus, in 2014, the department provided SAHA with 174 records from the hearings. In addition to publishing the full hearing records,[10] SAHA has been continuing to contact individuals who interacted with Section 29 investigations.

The Institute for Justice and Reconciliation

The Institute for Justice and Reconciliation (IJR) is a Cape Town–based NGO established in 2001 under the patronage of Desmond Tutu; its first director was the former head of the TRC's research unit, Charles Villa-Vicencio. As of 2018, three former TRC commissioners serve on its board of directors: Pumla Gobodo-Madikizela, Dumisa Ntsebeza, and Glenda Wildschut. Among the projects implemented by the IJR related to community healing, youth leadership, and arts and culture, its Reconciliation

Barometer Survey warrants particular note. To understand the status of progress toward reconciliation, the IJR has conducted "an annual national public opinion poll that measures citizen attitudes towards reconciliation, transformation and national unity" by means of six main indicators: human security, political culture, cross-cutting political relations, race relations, historical confrontation, and dialogue.[11] Particularly in terms of race relations, the IJR's Reconciliation Barometer 2014 Report provided contradictory but significant survey data for the ten years since the TRC's final report was published. This report compelled a reconsideration of the meaning of reconciliation and of people's complex perceptions of reconciliation in the context of their everyday lives.

The IJR's survey on "Interracial Talk and Socialisation Across Race Lines" illustrated a gradual increase in socializing and talking with other racial groups, even though the curve of the graph is modest (Wale 2014:21). One related result, on interracial mistrust by race, portrayed a positive trend in that more respondents, both white and black, have described other groups as more trustworthy (Wale 2014:17). Notably, people of Asian (Indian) and Colored identities have maintained their vigilance toward other groups (a sense of trust in others has low status), which was once reflected by their relative indifference to or distancing from the TRC proceedings in the 1990s. This finding calls for more consideration of the collective tendency toward national reconciliation. Also notably, Colored people dramatically showed their collective disappointment in interracial relationships, with nearly 70 percent desiring interracial talk in 2003 but only 20 percent doing so in 2013, while the other three groups remained around 20 percent to 30 percent over that period. In addition, the percentage favoring the "desirability and possibility of creating one united South Africa," an idea directly related to the sense of national identity or the nation-building project, has been steadily declining, thus demonstrating a gradual trend toward *living together separately* (Wale 2014:16). The report cautioned against a quick assessment of these data, pointing out that they "could mean either that South Africans are indeed becoming less keen about the idea of a unified nation, or it may also suggest disillusionment with the interpretation of the concept of unity and nationhood as used in our political discourse" (Wale 2014:20).

In any case, these trends—such as greater communication among racial groups in general, specific groups' cautious stances toward other groups, and an apparent need to search for another model other than that of national reconciliation based on a shared sense of "us"—call for a fresh evaluation of the TRC's work and impact. This IJR survey effectively illustrates the complex situation of post-TRC South Africa. Moreover, this is the only follow-up survey that has been conducted with chronological consistency around the TRC ideal of national reconciliation, as TJ organizations usually do not receive long-term evaluations, although longer-term impacts are arguably the only way to judge how a society has incorporated the legacy of TJ activities. Spontaneous involvement in such unfinished business is not officially controlled by an institutional TJ entity, yet that unplanned development is crucial from a longer-term perspective to positively interpret feedback on the TJ initiatives and advance new social policies.

Fambul Tok

Whereas Khulumani in South Africa has engaged in social matters such as lawsuits and funerals, Fambul Tok in Sierra Leone has pursued more culturally based symbolism to facilitate victims' healing. John Caulker, chairman of the Truth and Reconciliation Working Group from 1999 to 2008, advocated for the Special Fund for War Victims and the country's reparations program. After leaving the TRC in 2007, he launched a grassroots TJ initiative called Fambul Tok, in collaboration with the US-based organization Catalyst for Peace. Through this organization, he insisted on the need to develop more community-based traditional strategies than the TRC mechanisms to cope with local victimhood.[12] Like many other invented traditions in the contemporary age, Fambul Tok's tradition also changes form with greater flexibility than traditional models do. Although conventional chiefs play a central role in the program, women, youth, and other historically marginalized groups are also included as candidates for leadership.

One of the main activities of Sierra Leone's Fambul Tok is called the "reconciliation bonfire," based on the principle of "emergent design," which allows space for flexibly changing the agenda in the course of local interaction. By adopting an emergent design approach, the organization allots longer time than a general aid program for "drawing on local perspectives and responses to ongoing assessment and reflection, allowing each community to shape its own process."[13] As a result, Fambul Tok spends several months preparing for its implementation of this event (Iliff 2012:262–263). A bonfire ceremony is conducted that partly follows a cultural tradition, with several hours of singing and dancing, while former enemies face each other and listen to testimonies. The following morning brings a "cleansing ceremony" with sacrifice and purification rituals, aimed at calming people's hearts. After sharing in a bonfire ceremony, an affected community will proceed to the communal work of collective reconciliation. The products from a "peace garden" are shared among residents. Options at this stage also include building a guest house and a marketplace (Iliff 2012:263–264).

Former TJ staffers, who were well aware of the limitations and restrictions facing the official TJ institutions, constituted Fambul Tok and IJR as core founding members. But given their adoption of SAHA's understanding (namely, that a TJ program is a social phenomenon that entails a series of divergences and related products), these movements can be placed along a continuum relative to the official institutions. With regard to terminology in social-movement theory, the key figures possessing skill and knowledge on a certain issue, such as the founders of these organizations, can be described through a resource-mobilization framework rather than through propagation of repertoires. Yet those activities that have been deployed in the derivative organization might be viewed as repertoires that should have been implemented in the institutional TJ process but were not. Such should-have-been repertoires are thus realized by a spontaneous successor in an unplanned form.

Positive Government Divergence from a TJ Program

An actor in a movement that diverges from a TJ body can sometimes follow a somewhat twisted path. In South Africa, even though then president Nelson Mandela was a strong proponent of the TRC, other politicians younger than him within the ANC were skeptical and maintained a distance from the mainstream of the TRC. Those politicians, including the next president, Thabo Mbeki, were inclined toward more pragmatic positions in regard to redistribution of social resources and reparation policy. They continued to hold these positions until the end of the TRC and even boycotted the presentation ceremony of the TRC's official report in 1998. Looking back at these reactions by ANC politicians of Mbeki's generation, one gets the impression that they never cooperated with any TRC programs, even opposing and undermining their legitimacy. Yet some years after the end of the TRC, another governmental unit became an actor in an inquiry regarding missing persons. Jay D. Aronson (2011:262) traced these "efforts to account for missing persons from the apartheid era in South Africa by family members, civil society organizations and the current government's Missing Persons Task Team [MPTT], which emerged out of the Truth and Reconciliation Commission process." Curiously, this movement has not been supported by a local ANC branch.

In the case of the families of the Mamelodi Four (four ANC operatives who were tortured to death by apartheid security police), they first learned about their lost family members at the TRC amnesty hearings and then testified at the hearings of the Human Rights Violations Committee in 1996, "where they not only told their stories but also demanded information about their missing loved ones and return of the remains so that they could perform appropriate burial rituals" (Aronson 2011:270). But after their testimony, the TRC did not contact them. Instead, the MPTT started examining the suspected remains of the disappeared in the Winterveld cemetery and confirmed their identity with DNA tests. Following that, in 2005, the relatives received remains from the MPTT consisting of fragmented hip and leg bones. They reburied them at the local cemetery in Mamelodi (Aronson 2011:270). This is another story of victim empowerment that happened on a divergent track from the mainstream program of the TRC. It is interesting because the MPTT was on the side of the ANC government, which had been opposing the TRC for years on contentious issues, such as the responsibility of the liberation movement for civilian losses or reparations to victims. However, a space for political appeal and maneuvering remains. As we learned with regard to the term *ideal victims* in the previous chapter, Aronson pointed out that an empowerment process is complicated:

> These stories tend to be framed in terms of heroism, both of the missing, who are said to have died in service to their country, and of justice finally being served after decades without any resolution. Headlines like "Heroes 'Return' to Motherland," "ANC Hero Saved from an Unmarked Grave" and "Former MK [uMkhonto we Sizwe, ANC's armed unit] Cadres to Get a Hero's Welcome" illustrate this narrative device well. . . . Madeleine Fullard, head of the MPTT, openly acknowledges that the exhumations carried out by her team tend to be weighted in favor of ANC and MK figures. (Aronson 2011:272)

A government is not an innocent entity, and we should not overlook the question of political will. But such political bias and maneuvering is not really the essence of families' experience. Maria Ntuli, mother of Jeremiah, one of the Mamelodi Four victims, said that there were no remains with DNA matches to her children, but she was satisfied with the burial ceremony for others. Katherine Magagula thanked the team for its dedicated information sharing, even though no positive DNA results were found for her child, either. Photographs of the crime scene obtained from security police were provided to those families, and an opportunity to examine the mortuary records was also provided. Even a forensic anthropologist gave a presentation to the families at their request (Aronson 2011:274).

These reactions by the MPTT may not have been planned from the beginning. Yet when confronted by the fact that no valid DNA records were found for some participating families, the team created an agenda to meet those families' needs. Lizzie Selofo recalled the experience of witnessing the exhumation as a chance for the families to become part of the investigation process rather than being passive recipients of information (Aronson 2011:274).

A further complication is that the families that appreciated the MPTT's work criticized the responsibility or follow-up efforts of the local ANC branch that was in charge of memorialization and reburial. In other words, the MPTT, an ANC government agency, offered valued service to families on its own initiative, while local ANC bodies were rather reluctant and "did not even bother to inform the community that a reburial of formerly missing

MK comrades would be taking place at the cemetery" (Aronson 2011:278). This exhumation project resulted from the efforts of one unit within an ANC government that was opposed to the TRC's proceedings, while the local ANC bodies were largely unsupportive of the families or the ceremony. We see here that a positive divergence from a TJ program can emerge from a government agency, not just from a civil-society organization or social movement, although we must offer some reservations about the possible political utilization of such an event.

Divergence of Local Social Movements in Cambodian TJ

If we adopt the framework of a social movement when understanding the local influence of a TJ process, some aspects of TJ activities that have been criticized as evidence of failure become open to other interpretations of TJ influence, impact, and effectiveness. The propagation of movement repertoire can be one new standard for such an informal evaluation of TJ bodies, and we have seen examples of that dynamic in South Africa and Sierra Leone. In other words, a TJ body's function can be assessed by how it prepares the residual space for divergent movements that emerge from its programs and activities. The idea of TJ bodies as mechanisms to ensure that the greatest number of individuals might engage in the process based on their own initiative must be evaluated by observing such direct or indirect sequences of divergence.

However, such a sequence can still be challenged by the unique social and political conditions of a transitional society. In this last section of the present chapter, a case study from Cambodia serves to examine the emergence of spontaneous local initiatives that should have compensated for the deficiency of the official TJ project. Yet in a local political context, these initiatives were forced to deviate from their original motivation, being restricted from deploying their visions to their full potential. The following episodes demonstrate the unique restrictions that those movements have faced after their spontaneous divergence from the official process.

This section covers two Cambodian NGOs led by Cambodian diaspora returnees, exploring how these movements related to society, generated a unique communality, and changed the nature of their activities in the course of the judicial process of the Khmer Rouge Tribunals. Even though a clause about victim participation was contained in the law authorizing the ECCC, the court did not immediately establish a Victims Unit, which did not begin substantial outreach activities until 2009, had no budget, and, as we have seen previously, suffered high job turnover (Elander 2012:107–108). Amid these circumstances, local Cambodian NGOs have assumed the role of disseminating information on the court and mobilizing locals to participate in the various outreach programs. Youk Chhang, the director of the Documentation Center of Cambodia (DC-Cam), managed the organization's work in a way that he considered similar to the typical function of a truth commission. Theary Seng, the ex-director of the Center for Social Development, emphasized the significance of the ideal of reconciliation at the CSD's public forums. DC-Cam and CSD, both led by former exiles, have been the two most prominent civil actors engaged in the ECCC process.

From Independent Documentary Center to Authorized Institution: DC-Cam

Developing a database. Starting as a unique repository of historical materials on the Khmer Rouge era, DC-Cam, established in 1995 as the local branch of Yale University's Cambodian Genocide Program, was tasked with researching and documenting material relating to the Khmer Rouge regime. Chhang was the first local leader of the project and continued to run the center after its inception as an independent Cambodian NGO in 1997.[14] DC-Cam's main activities first involved identifying secret mass graves around the country and developing a database of written materials related to the Democratic Kampuchea (DK) regime. Even though the center was allocated only $25 a month in 1995 for its work, Chhang remained motivated to engage in this solitary task.[15] His sense of justice is evident in his insistence that DC-Cam would "distribute all documents it has to every institution for the sake of truth and justice," including the tribunal, media outlets, or other organizations (*Searching for the Truth [SFT]*, December 2003:3). At that time, acquiring historical material was like an intellectual arms buildup for him. However, his offer to distribute documents to other, more powerful entities itself illustrates the center's relative lack of influence at that time.

Arrangement of the gathering space; Chhang as victim. Bilateral communication has been key to the various activities undertaken at DC-Cam since 2003. In this regard, it changed its direction from gathering and keeping materials and evidence to preparing a space for new relationships. In 2003, it approached the Cham community, a Muslim ethnic group in Cambodia, with a suggestion that the group record its experiences as a religious minority. This community had not been addressed as a special minority that might have been treated differently from other victims during the DK era.

During this time, as DC-Cam extended its outreach not only to domestic minority groups but also to foreign human-rights experts, it maintained its position that DC-Cam itself and its staff members were victims as well. Although Chhang and his staff were certainly leading the project, they implied at the same time that their movement was driven by Cambodian victims of their own accord. In particular, Chhang repeatedly mentioned his experiences during and after the DK era:

> When I picked water grass for my sister, who was pregnant and starving, I was considered to be a criminal. . . . When Khmer Rouge soldiers accused her of stealing a small amount of food, she denied their charges. To test her veracity, they cut open her stomach. They found no food there, and she died soon after from her wounds. (SFT, March 2004:2)
>
> Thirty years later, our family is divided over whether putting the Khmer Rouge on trial would bring them justice for my sister's death. . . . I take a different view [from my family]: that the tribunal is important and that we need prosecution before we can ever reach the point of true forgiveness. (SFT, September 2007:4–6)

Chhang also let his young subordinates write their stories as family members of victims (*SFT*, June 2006:52).

While extending DC-Cam's programs from 2003 to 2008, Chhang directly demonstrated his perceptions of justice when he launched plans for a history textbook on DK for high school students. He stated with determination that "if the government doesn't agree to publish it, DC-Cam will print and distribute it free throughout the country" (*SFT*, September 2006:5). He also took a critical stance toward the ECCC when suspicions of corruption among Cambodian court officials were reported, pointing out that all the officials belonged to the ruling party (*SFT*, March 2008:5).

As of this writing, DC-Cam and Chhang continue to maintain their relative uniqueness and their independence from official government bodies. This view is confirmed by Chhang's statement that DC-Cam possessed critical information (such as archives and a history textbook that it could use independently at its own discretion). Through these processes, DC-Cam created a space for communication among various victims, one where minority groups could present themselves as unique entities with different historical experiences from other victim groups. DC-Cam thus allowed the various victims to speak out for themselves while fostering public discourse and creating a sense of victimhood among people who had formerly not been offered such support by any public entity.

Institutionalization and authorization; representation of Cambodian nationals (2009–present). The first change in DC-Cam's character occurred with its move to become a pseudo-governmental organization, cooperating closely with the ministries. This activity started with the official approval of DC-Cam's history textbook, which was released in 2007. In September 2006, he warned that the center could distribute the book on its own, contrary to the government's preferences. However, after its publication, DC-Cam started to emphasize collaboration with the government and its ministries.[16] This close relationship was deepened as DC-Cam developed an accompanying instruction manual for teachers using the textbook, followed by official teacher training (*SFT*, June 2009:1).[17]

Training in an authentic historical understanding of the Khmer Rouge era was further extended to civil servants. In July and November 2011, DC-Cam conducted sessions to educate police officers and university teachers.[18] Army officers participated in DC-Cam's educational campaign in July 2012.

By this time, DC-Cam had become an authentic organization in charge of history education. It was not just a body that encouraged the gathering of various views, but one that provided *legitimate* knowledge. This direction aided the process of obtaining government approval to establish a permanent genocide education center. In December 2008, DC-Cam explained its plan to establish such a center, which would be "the leading Asian institution focused on genocide studies, one that will be connected to leading scholars and other institutions throughout Asia and the wider world" (*SFT*, December 2008:1). In 2012, the Ministry of Education transferred a parcel of land to DC-Cam for the construction of its permanent center, called the Sleuk Rith Institute.

Through this process of institutionalization and authorization, Youk Chhang has become increasingly aligned with the political establishment. In 2010, after his return from a lecture trip to American universities in April, he wrote about the responsibility of Association of Southeast Asian Nations (ASEAN) member states to fund the Khmer Rouge Tribunal (*SFT*, December 2010:1). When a US delegation visited Cambodia in November 2011, Youk Chhang, rather than Cambodian government officials, was put in charge of guiding the delegation through the historic sites of the DK era.

The above impression was also confirmed in October and November 2011 when DC-Cam organized a conference with minority groups in Cambodia to gain understanding of their experiences during the DK era. The conference included a film screening, lecture, and discussion, as would be typical for a forum of this kind. However, a noticeable item was included on the schedule: "Memorializing the Minority Groups." In this session, Chhang and Andrew Cayley (an acting international prosecutor of the ECCC) presented memorials to representatives of the five minority groups in attendance (Cham Muslims, hill tribes, monks, Chinese, and Vietnamese). It was described as "a solemn and meaningful affair."[19]

Memorial plaques were inscribed for the groups. The one for the Cham Muslims read as follows:

> This commemorates the suffering and death of the Cham people of Cambodia from 1975 to 1979. It also expresses the solemn hope and resolve that justice will be done and that these events will never happen again—anywhere. To the young who read this in future years,

whoever you are, never forget what happened to the Cham people. Do your utmost every single day of your lives to respect and love one another. Genocide, Truth, Memory and Justice. Phnom Penh, 25 October 2010. (Andrew T. Cayley, ECCC International Co-Prosecutor)

Even though the person named on the plate as holding the authority to grant this symbolic item was a foreign prosecutor, Youk Chhang, who organized the event, was one who could authorize the experience of victimhood under the Khmer Rouge regime. This event illustrated the continued evolution of DC-Cam's activities and its stance toward the people it originally intended to reach. Along with gathering data, sharing, publishing, and networking, DC-Cam was adding a new element: acting as a patron. Chhang and DC-Cam's policy expressions reflected an increased sense of nationalism, as in this statement at the opening hearing of Duch's trial: "Today is a turning point for Cambodia. . . . This journey [to attain genocide justice] is essential for us to come together as a nation. The Khmer Rouge trials are not only about justice; they are also about the Memory of Our Nation" (*SFT*, March 2009:1).

The apex of Youk Chhang's nationalistic inclination was his announcement of plans to launch the *Preah Vihear Times*. Preah Vihear is a temple in northeast Cambodia, located very close to the Thai border, which has been the center of territorial disputes with Thailand that even led to brief armed conflict. Although the site was officially assigned to Cambodia by a decision of the International Court of Justice in November 2013, it has long been a symbol used to provoke Cambodian nationalism. Chhang stated that "as well as being a symbol of Cambodian heritage, *Preah Vihear* is an example of the types of regional conflicts on which the paper intends to focus."[20]

Although it received a publication license from the Ministry of Information in August 2010 and secured a well-known American journalist as its international editor,[21] as of January 2018, the *Preah Vihear Times* had still not been published. Regardless of this inability to actually launch the newspaper, DC-Cam under Chhang's leadership became strongly established as an authentic institution and as it did so, naturally, it departed from its previous course.

Radical Mobilizing and Dissolution: The Center for Social Development

Changing the image of human-rights activity; Theary Seng's American style (2006–2009). Another example is the rise and fall of a movement led by a Cambodian returnee named Theary Seng, a smart young lawyer who had survived the killing fields and grown up in the United States. She was the first civil party to be registered by the ECCC in 2008, and she was one of the most iconic survivors on the Cambodian scene until her withdrawal from civil party status in 2011. Born in 1969, she was thirty-seven years old when she became executive director of the Center for Social Development in April 2006. The CSD had been founded in 1995, and before Seng's arrival it had organized several programs, for example, the Parliamentary Watch Project and the Court Watch Project, both of which fell into the category of monitoring. These are standard activities for a human-rights organization, and paradoxically, they are safe for donors, too, because monitoring on its own does not mean directly challenging the ongoing political status quo. However, the atmosphere inside the CSD must have seemed, in Seng's eyes, insufficient to fulfill the ideals of a human-rights organization. In her first year in charge, she set out to reform behavioral rules inside the center, saying, "I knew that CSD must be run like a business enterprise. . . . We wanted to marry business efficiency, professionalism, and accountability with humanitarian goals" (Center for Social Development [CSD] 2007:1).

Upholding good business values may have impacted the younger generation, which might otherwise not have had an accurate image of the workings of a human-rights NGO, although many in this generation considered working at an NGO to be a desirable career path. In addition, Seng's career and sophisticated manner soon attracted foreign donors. The center received US$534,000 in the first year, double the center's budget for the previous year. This was quite impressive and a pleasant surprise for the center's staff.

The young high-performing leader soon started a radio program to promote dialogue on human-rights issues, broadcasting seven days a week and reaching nineteen provinces and municipalities. This type of activity might be typical in a democratic society, but it was new in Cambodia, "allowing everyone to be on the 'same page,' and [acting as] the foundation for other outreach efforts or reinforcements."[22]

In January 2007, Seng signed a contract with the German governmental aid agency Deutscher Entwicklungsdienst for a three-year, $300,000 grant to organize public forums around the country. The implementation of these events indicates the lively atmosphere of the CSD at that time. Twenty-one public forums entitled "Justice and National Reconciliation" were conducted around the country from 2006 to 2009. Forum participants were encouraged to express their "questions and doubt" or "hope[s], expectations, and benefits from the tribunal" and their opinions on "whether Khmer Rouge history should be taught to the next generations."[23] This description shows that the forums were organized as a space to supplement and utilize the ECCC process and deepen local people's own perception of their experiences. The forums differed from other events in that they allowed questioning, which was fundamental to their purpose but tended to detract from other official communications between locals and the authorities.

Some participants expressed straightforward comments about or criticisms of the ECCC, which one rarely hears in a politically sensitive social environment. It is unclear whether those who expressed themselves in such a manner were motivated to do so by Seng's own message, which directed the tone of communication at each forum venue; however, one cannot find similar diversity of expression in the openly accessible records of other NGOs. In this sense, Seng's engagement in outreach on the topic of the ECCC was unique among local movements.

Theary Seng's ability to attract the progressive younger generation was amplified through a television program, *Youth Leadership Challenge*, funded by the US Agency for International Development (USAID). The program was designed to promote civic activism among Cambodian youth through a format loosely modeled on American television shows such as *The Apprentice* and *American Idol*.[24] A former CSD staff member recalled Seng's popularity and influence among young students at that time, stating that the government must have been watching her actions closely because her political positions were substantially aligned with those of the opposition party.[25]

The collapse of the CSD and attempts to create a new space. In July 2009, representatives of the Phnom Penh Municipal Court visited the CSD office with a preservation warrant to suspend Theary Seng as executive director and replace her with Vi Houi. Court officials claimed that Seng had violated an internal rule (*Phnom Penh Post*, July 22, 2009).

Not to be stopped in such a manner, Seng immediately moved to establish another NGO in August 2009—namely, the Center for Justice and Reconciliation (CJR)—somehow obtaining permission to do so from the Ministry of the Interior. By October 2009, the CJR was giving tutorials to the ECCC staff on victim support. In December 2009, at Paññāsāstra University (a well-known private university), the CJR held a public forum with ECCC officials, continuing with the same program deployed at the former CSD. At that time, the general impression was that the former NGO had been taken over by people close to the ruling party; however, Seng was able to resume her prior activities in a new and freer space. By March 2010, CJR staffers were looking forward to expanding the center's outreach with a more community-oriented approach. When the Duch verdict was handed down in July 2010, Seng organized another conference at Paññāsāstra University, which was attended by several active court officials from the ECCC as well as famous foreign scholars. This collaboration showed that the CJR was maintaining its public status and reputation and developing its outreach efforts smoothly. But a new source of internal discord emerged during 2010, and some core Cambodian staff members left the CJR.

Perhaps partly due to this internal incident, Seng established yet another NGO, the Center for Cambodian Civic Education (CIVICUS). This entity presented the play *Speak Truth to Power: Voices from Beyond the Dark*, which was performed in Cambodia in February 2011. The play, written by Ariel Dorfman, featured people who were facing similar hardships to those experienced by Cambodian victims and searching for a way to connect with one another. The notion that foreign insights could enlighten Cambodia was clearly in the forefront. This idea was incorporated into a program to educate monks and teachers on human-rights issues that took place between October 2011 and May 2012. The program textbook, *Khmer Courage Curriculum*, was introduced as follows: "This is your book! . . . The drafting of the Khmer curriculum . . . is based on extensive discussions between CIVICUS Cambodia in Phnom Penh and RFK Center in Washington, D.C., with comments and ideas from Kerry Kennedy after her visit to Cambodia in February 2011."[26]

Seng had organized places for dialogue to provoke alternative views of justice with regard to the Khmer Rouge issue. Her background as a returnee from the United States and her outstanding character positioned her to spread these ideas effectively. However, this project differed from the previous one in that it delivered something directly from abroad to locals, requiring the locals simply to translate the text.

The return to a single activist; the vanishing of embryonic solidarity. On November 15, 2011, Theary Seng abruptly published a press release announcing her resignation as a civil party at the ECCC. It stated:

> Ms. Seng no longer wishes to have any legal association with this ECCC which is mocking the dead, her and other victims and embedding impunity. . . . She denounces this ECCC as a political farce, an irreversible sham of extraordinary perversion in denying justice to victims, exploiting their suffering, soiling the memories of their loved ones, and embedding cynicism in an already fragile population living in paranoia, mistrust, and distrust.

Explicitly denying the legitimacy and significance of the judiciary, Seng introduced an alternative way forward with the slogan "Poetic Justice." Media, particularly foreign media, favored her action, and she consequently set up press conferences, following a strategy of using the foreign media to communicate a critical view of Cambodian authorities, including the ECCC, through this channel. In the week following her resignation, Seng went to a riverside space in front of a café in Phnom Penh where foreign tourists gather and played a public game of darts on a dartboard superimposed with Nuon Chea's face. She planned to play this dart game again in 2012 when US president Barack Obama visited Cambodia, but a raid by twenty police officers interfered with her plans.[27]

Seng's experience clearly demonstrated the explosive political atmosphere in Cambodia at the time, and video footage of the dartboard game incident and the following police raid provoked cautious reactions from ordinary Cambodian locals. Her attitude was politically radical, but her behavior did not allow the locals, who were still afraid to express themselves, to act in the same way—namely, in Western-style protests for human rights. Foreign media favored her, but one former CSD staff member said that foreign donors might begin fearing that investing in her work was too risky because of her political clashes with the authorities.

Seng succeeded in constructing various activist movements around her actions based on her uniqueness as a returnee. She started her work among Cambodian locals as a fellow citizen returning from the United States. Her use of local media as channels for human-rights work, such as television programs for youth or radio shows featuring Cambodian DJs, must have been surprising for local students. Her emphasis on public relations and media activities and her inclusion of UN personnel in CSD events sought to motivate diverse expression among locals. The CSD was unique in adopting new approaches for communication among former victims.

However, by deepening her conflicts with the government and diverging from local staff members' perspectives and behaviors, Seng isolated herself. Ever since her resignation from her ECCC position in 2011, her activities have been performed mostly for foreign media and human-rights organizations. Her role as a human-rights activist is more like that of an artist, although this style does not eliminate the possibility of creating new supporters. Political or social circumstances may influence future responses by other people to her appeal.

Limits of Divergent Movements in Authoritarian Post-Conflict Societies

Both DC-Cam and the CSD expanded the space for communication and networking with local minorities who previously had not been treated as public actors in the justice arena. These groups were not included in a public context, even when the ECCC was active, until DC-Cam started its operations. The viewpoints of returnees played a significant role in the development of such opportunities. Yet in the authoritarian social context, DC-Cam underwent institutionalization and authorization to sustain its social influence, whereas the CSD collapsed. The two movements, both of which promoted American-style democracy, inevitably changed their course, being affected by different social circumstances, which also resulted in changes in their support base. For instance, the people participating as leaders in these new NGO initiatives needed some level of English competence to communicate with foreign donors, and thus the pool was largely limited to the younger generation, which had no experience of the Khmer Rouge era (for older people, the only foreign language taught at school had been French). Furthermore, young participants who could afford to go to university and master English were more likely to have rich parents whose sympathies lay with the ruling party. As a result, it was difficult for the type of Cambodians who could work as NGO staff to direct harsh criticisms at the current government, given their parents' position. Partly for this reason, the CSD would not have been able to retain the support of its young staff as it radicalized.

In sum, in social circumstances where various political ideas cannot be unconditionally disseminated, organizations and gatherings that encourage people to speak out about victimization and appeal for their rights as victims may be forced to change course, whether through institutionalization or by resorting to sporadic action.

Conclusion

Outreach and mobilization in institutional TJ programs have become gradually more significant. Where a strong and stable government maintains the power to control locals, mobilization means ordering people, "Come to a specific venue if you are a true, obedient citizen." Examples of such orders include conscription, court subpoenas, various qualification examinations, compulsory education, and observance of national holidays. In other words, mobilization is an appearance of political control that directly affects the subject citizen's body. However, as we have already seen in Chapter 3, many TJ programs have no such force to compel locals' participation. To rouse public interest and seek locals' cooperation and participation, a TJ project must make PR activity around the country one of its standard components.

There are examples of TJ programs, such as Rwandan gacaca and East Timor efforts, that have successfully mobilized local participants. Yet this chapter has cited testimonies that indicate a compulsory atmosphere in local contexts, where nonparticipation is perceived as the behavior of a disloyal citizen and where many participants fear being labeled negatively if they do not participate. Given the compulsory character of this mobilization, spontaneous participation might be added as a necessary condition to promote one of TJ's main ideals, the internalization of democratic subjectivity.

TJ bodies often claim that locals' perception of their participation can be verified through participants' direct comments. But the positive comments by locals require cautious interpretation because they are inevitably social constructs, produced in a specific social context. When asked by a foreign interviewer about his or her perception of TJ activities, possibly while in the presence of a more decisive factor such as a local TV camera, an individual's lips might automatically utter delighted words: "I have been waiting for this moment for a long time," or "I am glad to see justice realized."

Moreover, official mobilization can document its efforts by the objective number of people who have been mobilized. In a developing country where TJ is being implemented, official requests to local chiefs may generate a continually increasing degree of official mobilization. The program's legitimacy is based on the assumption that mobilized locals who directly experience any TJ activity will become positive supporters of the process. Further, such locals are even expected to promote the TJ project to their neighbors.

Some readers might be suspicious of the assumption that locals will become positive participants in such a manner, wondering if their feelings about extremely emotional past experiences can be changed dramatically in this way. More cautious considerations warn that locals who are given just a short time to prepare for or participate in the proceedings may derive a negative impression. Yet this possibility seems to have been excluded from the process of application, acceptance, and execution of a TJ project's official budget. Outreach and mobilization have been treated as indispensable options in recent TJ cases and are now seen as the means to objectively demonstrate an acceptable number of mobilized people over a relatively short period in circumstances where donor organizations and countries want to see a concrete influence on the society concerned.

On the one hand, given the difficulty of TJ to mobilize locals, which has compelled it to devise more effective methods of giving incentives to locals, the character of the TJ body can be better compared to a social movement rather than to a government organization such as a ministry or court. Just as a social movement may have cooperative relationships with other social movements, a TJ program can also be deemed successful when it develops positive networks with local NGOs. Because TJ is new and does not have enough mobilization competence, local NGOs that have already been accumulating social resources for mobilization might be helpful to it. But conversely, failure to develop such relationships may lead to a negative assessment by locals, as in the Kenyan TJ context.

On the other hand, comparing TJ to a social movement offers another analytical benefit. As arguments on the propagation of repertoires by social movements tell us, a certain repertoire may possibly be passed on to other actors working in a different time, space, and social context. As such, incorporating the idea of the propagation of TJ repertoire opens a path for further analysis of TJ's influence on local society beyond an assessment of the program's implementation.

This chapter has addressed instances in South Africa and Sierra Leone in terms of the above understanding. The characteristic nature of these activities is their spontaneous divergence from the main TJ bodies because they recognize the limits of TJ, and because other organizations can implement the TJ project's unfinished business while still affirming that the ideals and aims of TJ are themselves good. Such groups came into being with the establishment of the TJ body but became aware that they were replacing or supplementing TJ in terms of completing the tasks expected of a TJ program by victims.

Without a doubt, the appearance of these organizations was not planned in a TJ body's official mandate. The TJ entity cannot necessarily support the work of these organizations because sometimes they are critical of its insufficient implementation of expected tasks. On the other hand, these activities would not occur if the TJ body were perfect, because people who are already satisfied with TJ work will have no motivation to engage in unfinished business.

These circumstances indicate that the core actors in such movements are people who feel disappointed, have complaints, or are even angry with official programs while agreeing with TJ's official ideals. They may develop the repertoires that have been demonstrated in the TJ process. Given the possible shift of agenda items from TJ entities to other social-movement bodies, or even another governmental organization such as Missing Persons Task Team in South Africa, raising locals' expectations with highly promising ideals and goals should not simply be dismissed as unrealistic, even though such a strategy cannot always insist on its legitimacy as long as the official appeal may still leave space for the spontaneous engagement of locals who attempt to fill in the gap between official words and their expectations. Put another way, an evaluation of TJ can be implemented in a broader manner, incorporating the activities that diverge from official TJ programs.

A divergent movement outside an official TJ program is not always on the side being influenced by TJ. Cambodian cases have remarkably illustrated this reverse relationship between the TJ project and other related bodies. The DC-Cam has long been cultivating the voices of minorities to share their experiences under the Khmer Rouge regime. Their engagement with the collective memory of Cham Muslims was subsequently connected to the agenda of the ECCC. The form of the CSD's public forums has been directly adopted by the court's official outreach program. In a sense, these entities have shared the repertoires of outreach options. Yet a local movement in a transitional society might be affected by unforeseeable challenges. As a result, the Cambodian NGOs that were once active in catalyzing diverse local communication have changed course. These changes are not recorded in the official documents of the ECCC, but they have left crucial footprints permitting us to contemplate the threshold of influence of international judicial intervention in the Cambodian local context.

Such by-products and divergences are not necessarily perceived as positive symptoms, yet they provide a means of understanding TJ differently than through an authentic policy evaluation that scrutinizes its outcomes in light of the official objective announced at its inception. Considering the post-TJ elements of these divergent activities contributes to a more complete long-term assessment of a TJ project.

Notes

1. Timothy Longman, Phuong Pham, and Harvey Weinstein, "Rwandan Attitudes Toward the International Criminal Tribunal for Rwanda," presentation, Annual Meeting of the American Public Health Association, Philadelphia, PA, November 2002, cited in Alison Des Forges and Timothy Longman (2004:56).

2. Mills (1940:906) found earlier sociological insights on this issue in the works of Karl Mannheim and Max Weber. "Both motives and actions very often originate not from within but from the situation in which individuals find themselves" (Mannheim 1940:249). Motive is a complex of meaning, which appears to the actor or to the observer to be adequate grounds for the actor's conduct (Weber 1922:5).

3. International Criminal Court, *Strategic Plan for Outreach of the International Criminal Court*. ICC-ASP/5/12 (September 29, 2006). Available at https://www.icc-cpi.int/NR/rdonlyres/FB4C75CF-FD15-4B06-B1E3-E22618FB404C/185051/ICCASP512_English1.pdf, accessed April 21, 2018.

4. Suhrke (2001:10), quoted in Kent (2012:49).

5. Bates's work is based on the estimate of a total ECCC budget of $338 million, spread over ten years. According to his calculations, the cost per convicted defendant is $112.7 million if Case 002 is the ECCC's second and last trial. "To put this into perspective, the estimated cost per defendant at the Special Court for Sierra Leone is between $23 and $25 million, $21 million at the ICTR and $17.5 million at the ICTY. The ICC aside, the ECCC is the most expensive of all the international or internationalized courts" (Bates 2010:45). The ECCC listed its actual expenditures as of March 2016 as $261 million; therefore, Bates's estimate needs a slight revision. Even though the ongoing—but government-opposed—investigations into further cases (003 and 004) and the intention to try four more suspects have appeared on the court's schedule, the final judgment of these suspects may be rendered far later. Given that the convicted cadres so far still number only three, the cost per defendant is thus $87 million.

6. *Daily Maverick*, August 22, 2013, www.dailymaverick.co.za/article/2013-08-22-us-corporations-cant-be-sued-for-apartheid-court-rules/#.VhfzwnLotjp, accessed October 10, 2015.

7. See Sarah A. Altschuller, "Alien Tort Case Development: Second Circuit Affirms Dismissal of Claims Against Ford and IBM," July 31, 2015, accessed at www.csrandthelaw.com/2015/07/31/alien-tort-case-development-second-circuit-affirms-dismissal-of-claims-against-ford-and-ibm.

8. See the SAHA web page, www.saha.org.za/projects/trc_archive_project.htm, accessed October 9, 2015.

9. SABC News, March 1, 2013, http://www.themarketingsite.com/news/29559/sabc-truth-commission-special-report-now-on-the-web, accessed April 21, 2018.

10. The full records detail the following events and issues: the Helderberg disaster inquiry, after 159 people died when a South African Airways plane exploded in midair

near Mauritius in 1987; the Mandela United Football Club and Winnie Madikizela-Mandela's knowledge of its activities; the incrimination of Joe Mamasela, a notorious Vlakplaas askari (a secret agent of the apartheid security force who infiltrated the ANC), in the abduction of the Pebco Three; and the deaths of anti-apartheid activists such as Rick Turner and Griffiths Mxenge. See www.saha.org.za/news/2010/March/trcs_secret_hearing_transcripts_handed_over_to_saha.htm, accessed October 9, 2015.

11. Quoted from the IJR website, http://reconciliationbarometer.org/wp-content/uploads/2014/12/IJR-SA-Reconciliation-Barometer-Report-2014.pdf, accessed January 27, 2016.

12. See the Fambul Tok web page: http://www.fambultok.org/about-us/our-history, accessed January 30, 2017.

13. For a description of their practice, see http://www.fambultok.org/what-is-fambul-tok/our-process#consult, accessed January 30, 2017.

14. Information on Youk Chhang is available at http://d.dccam.org/Brief_Biography_of_Youk_Chhang.pdf, accessed April 21, 2018.

15. Youk Chhang recalled an episode in 2001 during an encounter with a former Khmer Rouge soldier who wanted to sell photos of Pol Pot and other Khmer Rouge leaders as well as a "confidential" videocassette of a meeting of Khmer Rouge leaders. Although the materials may have been valuable, his policy that justice could not be bought with money precluded accepting this offer (*Searching for the Truth* [*SFT*], May 17, 2001:1).

16. See, for example, p. 3 of a DC-Cam report from 2010 at www.d.dccam.org/Projects/Genocide/pdf/DC-Cam_Genocide_Education_Report_to%20Belgium—2010.pdf, accessed on January 12, 2018.

17. See a DC-Cam document for 2013 at www.d.dccam.org/Projects/Genocide/pdf/MOU_Between_DC-Cam_and_MOEYS_2011-2013_Eng.pdf, accessed on January 12, 2018.

18. This activity is described at www.d.dccam.org/Projects/Genocide/pdf/GENOCIDE_EDUCATION—Police_Academy_of_Cambodia.pdf, accessed on January 12, 2018.

19. The description can be found at www.d.dccam.org/Projects/Public_Info/pdf/Understanding_Genocide_Report_November_24_2010.pdf, accessed on January 12, 2018.

20. See Youk Chhang's statement at www.d.dccam.org/Projects/Preah_Vihear_Times/pdf/The_Preah_Vihear_Times.pdf, accessed on January 12, 2018.

21. Joel Brinkley, former editor at the *New York Times* and Pulitzer Prize winner, was designated as a foreign editor for the planned newspaper.

22. Accessed at Theary Seng's website, http://thearyseng.com/peace-builder/42/54, accessed on August 10, 2016. Seng explained her motivation for launching her radio program with that expression.

23. Seng's comment as a facilitator, CSD Forum, Kampot, June 14, 2006.

24. For a description, see https://partnerships.usaid.gov/partnership/youth-leadership-challenge, accessed April 21, 2018.

25. See http://www.civicus-cambodia.org/the-latest-from-civicus, accessed January 29, 2017.

26. See http://www.civicus-cambodia.org/speak-truth-to-power-courage-without-borders, accessed January 29, 2017.

27. For an account of this incident, see "Kissinger in Cambodia," http://latitude.blogs.nytimes.com/2012/11/20/protests-greet-obamas-visit-to-cambodia, accessed on January 12, 2018.

5

Challenging the Official Scenario

Instead of meekly accepting an official announcement by a TJ body, locals are often moved to provide dissident understandings of the past, sometimes accompanied by disparate new conflicts in discourses even among victims (see Chapter 3). Alongside such a critical response by locals, an institutional TJ program engages in a mobilizing mission (see Chapter 4). On the surface, the mobilization is justified and necessary to empower victims. Yet the mobilization organized by TJ authorities often entails a particular bias that contributes to a specific political purpose of the government. In theory, as not all nationals can be mobilized into a TJ venue, a selective mechanism for participants must be in operation. Maneuvering by authorities, political conflict, and negotiation among disparate social groups happen during the selection process. In addition, some seek to create a more suitable space outside TJ venues. Divergent collective actions are thus positively incorporated as a part of the sequence of propagated repertoires of mobilization stemming from a TJ project. Even at this stage, where a certain number of locals are deemed to have been derailed from an official track of a TJ effort, some people must be mobilized by and participate in TJ programs. This chapter focuses on such people. What does a TJ body expect them to do, and how do they actually behave?

Official Drama for Victim Healing

Identifying a truth commission with a drama is an understandable analogy, because a truth commission usually holds open public hearings as its main public function. But tribunals or courts have also been described in this fashion.

Maria Elander has noted that in the early 1990s, many scholars viewed war-crimes trials as having significance beyond just a finding of guilt or innocence (Elander 2012:99). The trials were also interpreted as providing a community with opportunities to shape collective memories and allowing victims to regain their self-respect. Even more direct benefits of the court, such as the healing of victims in the courtroom, were expected.[1] Mark Osiel (1997:3) uses a unique set of phrases to depict this function, stating that "moral entrepreneurs" and "activists of memory" have a responsibility to conduct "liberal show trials" in traumatized societies. Arguments along these lines about possible functions of the court are reflected in the framework of *expressivism*. Other scholars bring the classic term of *ritual* to their analyses of modern tribunals. Martti Koskenniemi (2002:10) indicates the symbolic function of the criminal trial as enabling the community ritually to become a workable "moral community." Inclined to anticipate the court's societal effectiveness, Mark Drumbl (2007:174) applies a classic Emile Durkheim theme—"by expressing condemnation, punishment in fact could strengthen social solidarity"—to his explanation of expressivism as embodied in the court process: punishment internalizes and even reinforces social norms. Also while discussing expressivism, Diane Amann (2002:119) stresses the function of naming, saying, "Naming something 'genocide' makes a difference." Doris Buss (2011:414) follows this neo-Durkheimian line, mentioning that naming and condemning serves as a "theatre of renewal" through which collectivity is reconstituted and order returned. Yet to what extent is this chorus of positive expressivism valid? An expressivist argument should also consider the potential negative influence of court processes, such as participants' disappointment because of the court's incompetence or biased agenda setting. I will address this issue later in this chapter.

The Psychological Need for Official Drama

Regardless of whether it is a truth commission or a tribunal, TJ is a social setting where testifying—by both perpetrators and victims—occupies a crucial role in creating the venue and legitimizing the program. As we saw in the previous two chapters, if locals never react to the governmental announcement or to the call for mobilization, TJ activities cannot substantially happen in the society concerned (for a government with dishonorable intentions that just wants to pretend to take action for the benefit of giving the international community a positive impression, such local indifference is rather convenient). However, if people appear at events, such as public forums and open court hearings but everyone remains silent, the space cannot function, either. For one thing, a *speech code* exists, so that people cannot express whatever they may want to say in a public setting. Moreover, not everyone is allowed to speak in this setting, particularly in a transitional social context.

With these restrictions, people who attend TJ events are encouraged to speak and to listen calmly to the testimony of other participants. The concept of the ideal victim is applicable in this situation. The official scenario requires the participants—many of them presumably victims—to be obedient subjects who act in a docile manner. Based on the unspoken but easily understandable preconditions of the space, testimony at such TJ venues is justified by the following combination of assumptions: (1) a traumatized individual achieves healing through testifying at or even by just participating in a TJ setting, and (2) a traumatized nation will attain collective healing by sharing the testimonies heard. These assumptions were expressed in a speech by UNTAET's (United Nations Transitional Administration in East Timor) transitional administrator, Sérgio Vieira de Mello, in January 2002: "It [the CAVR] will provide the East Timorese people with an official ear to listen to their grievances and acknowledge their past suffering. . . . It will bring together those who have been in conflict in the past and give them a way forward, an opportunity for grievances and long-lasting reconciliation" (Kent 2012:15).

This cause-effect understanding of testifying has provided the psychological rationale for TJ methodology, but scholars have criticized its practical application. For example, the victim-centered orientation of the South African TRC's program design was widely praised, yet victims normally had the chance to testify only once, and the witnesses selected for the public hearings did not receive sufficient attention to ensure that their opportunity to testify would indeed lead to psychological healing. Even worse, some indicated that the lack of sufficient attention or of a follow-up mechanism triggered the retraumatization of witnesses.[2] At the collective level, this phenomenon was described as an "after-circus syndrome," because South African locals were once reported as having said, "The circus comes to town and the circus leaves—and then what?" (Hayner 2001:142).

Others have cast doubt on these assumptions in the expression of therapeutic discourses. Their criticism is theoretically based on the Foucauldian understanding of a pastoral power to provide people with a space and a position to be protected and nurtured in exchange for their acceptance of the official mode of speech and becoming a docile subject. That criticism also contains a warning about expanding the idea of personal recovery from trauma to the scale of whole nations. After all, the realization of psychological recovery through sharing testimony at the collective or national level is, in a strict sense, not provable in any empirical manner. It should at most be called a discourse of expectation.

With more careful consideration, we can see that evaluating the outcomes of these two assumptions about healing from trauma depends on how the related terms and conditions are defined. For example, when one reads a description of narrative therapy (White and Epston 1990), which teaches that narrating and being listened to rather than accepting a diagnosis by a professional doctor play a central role for therapeutic outcomes, we can see a persuasive explanation of the first assumption. A more general and empirical version of recovery from mental damage is presented from the perspective that working together, or sharing of meaning, changes one's image of opponents and promotes mutual understanding. When we consider the transformation of one's self-image or identity, that social-psychological explanation may underpin the assumption that talk-oriented therapy can produce self-enlightenment. The question of whether a TJ space should be considered as consistent with such a therapeutic method is left for further inquiry. Rather, this chapter focuses on the justification given for TJ venues and programs based on the two assumptions of healing from trauma—that is, the concept of an *official drama*.

The Rupture of an Official Drama

David Apter's (2006:250) concept of *political theater* is well suited for a transitional situation where the founding of a new society is required and an alternative has not yet emerged. Politics in such a stage becomes more dramatic, and drama is expected in politics.

Also germane, a theoretical position in sociology uses the notion of drama in a broader sense. Scholars of interactionism, typically espousing the theory of Erving Goffman, argue that all social phenomena are composed of endless repetitions of human behaviors, constituting performance and symbolic exchange. Each individual at first glance is pursuing his or her own purpose, yet the legitimacy or meaning of such a purpose is ultimately accorded socially, so the behavior can be construed as public actions in that sense. The possible range of variation in performance is restricted by social norms.[3] If one deviates from the range, then one's behavior is sanctionable.[4]

Role Expectation and Performance

A social norm that roughly orients one's behavior appears as a *role expectation* to each person, and people usually perform within the possible range of such role expectations. The range can be inferred to be wider in moments of political and moral rupture because of their anomic condition. In a social transition, as old orders transgress and purifying alternatives come into being, many role expectations in an old regime are no longer functioning as a compass to secure smooth communication in a public arena, but alternative codes and modes of conduct have not yet been fixed. A typical example is the dysfunction of a legal norm. Put differently, such anomic status means that people do not know what their proper role is or how they are expected to behave.

Generally, at least in Western societies, a person called (or calling oneself) an artist has been allowed to test the limits and expand the borders of possible behavior in a modern society. Yet in an anomic context, an ordinary person may reach such a position without realizing what he or she is doing.

The framework of dramaturgy used in the interactionist approach is helpful in critically examining an official drama of TJ. Let us first consider the likely proponents of that official drama, the TJ project's official staff. They must collect and exhibit positive comments uttered by local participants. Comments such as "I am satisfied with this TJ program because it heals my wounded memory" are gathered and programmed for that purpose. If you become a PR staff member for a TJ body, one of your occupational duties is to collect such discourse. Some truth must lie in such comments. We do not need to dismiss them with an overly critical stance. For some victims, a TJ body can be legitimately helpful, giving their lives a positive direction and offering a sense of redemption. People speak out, recover psychologically, and are healed. Thus, national reconciliation is then expected as a next step in this direction, cultivating the soil for the prevention of future recurrences of violence.

However, the concept of role expectation or performance in a dramaturgical framework and the argument that a vocabulary of motive is present lead to reservations in relation to the above scenario. As we saw in Chapter 4, locals' textbook-style responses can create a sense that these statements demonstrate compliance with a specific role expectation in a certain social context with a façade of acceptable vocabulary. As for the reason underlying such statements by actors in the TJ drama, no one, not even the speaker, is thought to know what the true motivation for the utterance is, or if the utterance genuinely reflects the actor's will. Yet we can point out certain trends:

1. Locals' textbook-style replies tend to fall within a certain pattern of expression, and some of them are excessively abstract and universal.
2. There remains a troubling gap between two images: traumatized victims who tend to be suspicious about the legitimacy of TJ and subjects who applaud a TJ program in a politically or socially correct manner.
3. Textbook replies are convenient for a TJ authority that aims to reach out to locals through mobilization tactics and wants evidence of the positive impact of its outreach.

Reasons for Rupture of an Official Drama

If an official TJ drama goes as the scenario writer expected, this chapter could end here. Unfortunately, past TJ studies based on long-term field research have reported many episodes that deviate from the expectation.

The rupture of an official drama, actors' deviant performances, authorized players' attempts to maintain consistency with that theater, and the creation of an unintended script are all parts of the real-life enactment of a TJ program. These episodes involve a surprising range of deviants and shatter the superficial expectation of TJ salvation. They compel us to reconsider the complex reality of TJ experiences.

But before moving on to study cases of the generation of divergent dramas in a TJ space, let us consider the reasons for ruptures in the staging of an official drama. Why does it encounter deviance?

First, an official drama loses its legitimacy when the neutrality and qualifications of core staff members such as commissioners or legal experts of a body are put in doubt. As we saw in the Kenyan case in the previous chapter, this sometimes happens in a TJ event's political context.

Second, when TJ staffers demonstrate an institutional priority such as maintaining the authority of the judiciary over participants' needs and dignity, an official drama becomes reduced to a political routine and loses local support. A typical example of this pattern ensues when a judge behaves arrogantly and a victim feels alienated from the process. Although maintaining authority in a TJ space is certainly necessary, the slogan of victim empowerment comes to be seen as merely the specious word of officials.

For instance, the ECCC judge Nil Nonn repeatedly reproved survivors (Chum Mey and Nong Chan Phal) on June 30, 2009, when they could not continue their testimonies because they became agitated. When Chum Mey, a survivor from the S-21 torture center, broke into tears, Judge Nonn said, "Mr. Mey, please recompose yourself. We are conducting our trial at this time." As Mey's voice was still trembling, the judge added in a reproving manner, "You should recompose yourself as this is your chance to describe your story to the Chamber." There was even an irritated tone in the judge's voice, probably because he was mindful of delaying the procedure. On another occasion (July 9, 2009), when civil party lawyer Silke Studzinski asked judges if witnesses could have time to express their emotions and feelings, Judge Silvia Cartwright answered that all judges were highly experienced and needed no advice from the civil party lawyers. However, none of the judges in the ECCC trial chamber had prior experience in any other international tribunal or court, and some locals complained about their weak backgrounds.[5] Judges have spoken to and ordered the victims at the court based on specific authority; however, this episode illustrates that some locals have also questioned whether the qualifications of authorized experts were proper enough. An exclusive game only for the advancement of the political elite delivers a sense of empty political symbolism as well as a waste of precious resources.

Third, a rupture occurs when a TJ entity is revealed to be a closed game among top political elites—that is, government decision makers, international legal experts, and UN-related personnel. This situation arises, for example, when locals get the impression (perhaps accurately) that foreign legal experts came to a country where a TJ body is operating because of their interest in their own career advancement. This critical comment is more serious than the previous point in terms of locals' distrust of a TJ body, because the arrogant judge does not destroy, at least, the stage's authority, although such behavior erodes the court's legitimacy. Working as a TJ staff member entails many unpredictable restrictions and challenges, so it is unreasonable to expect such personnel to fulfill flawlessly the altruistic expectations of outsiders. However, the failure to maintain the image (the *front*) of the stage as neutral and victim-empowering naturally produces a sense of detachment and alienation among locals. Fourth, particularly in the case of tribunals, the foregrounding of a prearranged scenario, or a put-up job in the audience's mind, immediately diminishes the stage to a routine policy, alienating many nationals. Even though an international or internationalized tribunal does not take the form of a war-crimes tribunal, and even though the UN supplies defense lawyers, when some accused receive sentences that are too light, then the performance is deemed to have been derailed from a prearranged scenario. If an international tribunal has ended with no substantial sentences because of professionally elaborated legal examinations, no party other than legal experts would admire the tribunal's strict obedience to due process and professional ethics. There is no doubt that very few people in a local society, besides legal experts, ever read the full text of a sentence, so the persuasiveness of legal logic is unlikely to be shared among the affected people.[6]

For these reasons, international justice in a TJ body cannot have any acceptable result other than sentences for the accused. The presupposed logic of the argument is similar to one in theology. A goal is determined (though not in too clear a manner), and discussants are required to follow the *officially legitimatized bias* of the scenario, into which the culpability of the accused is correctly inserted. It is an open secret with broadly shared anxiety at the beginning of the process, as people wonder if the process will properly follow the scenario. Some wonder if unexpected disclosure of new findings will emerge from the process, and others want to resolve their cognitive dissonance between desiring punishment for the accused and recognizing the unfairness of a predetermined process. A person holding the latter position would come to reconsider his or her own expectation as improper in this context. The legal actors on such a stage must display their stage skills as well as their deployment of legal logic so as not to reveal to local audiences the backstage scene or expose the prearrangements. However, high-ranking actors (judges and other experts) sometimes fail to maintain the front projected by the court proceedings and thus lose audiences' motivation to engage in the process.

Fifth, as in the case of the South African TRC, if a TJ program is accepted as a policy inclined to a certain political position, the official drama loses its effectiveness for some social members. In this case, the outcome of TJ is not as predetermined as in the previous case. Rather, several conflicting parties are competing to acquire hegemony in the representation of legitimate positions.

Sixth, institutionally unwelcome behavior by participants also affects the healthy processing of an official drama. Crucial factors that may challenge all the above situations are participants' silence and lies. A TJ body is a space and program constituted by the presupposition that participants will speak the truth. Yet some participants maintain silence even when they appear in TJ venues. Others intentionally put on a performance and even give false testimony. The legitimacy, or the sense of authenticity, of a stage is damaged by these acts. If such acts are relatively few and can be dismissed just as noise, there may be no problem in proceeding. But when these acts happen often, or when few acts generate a certain critical impact, a TJ stage is obliged to repair the open seam.

These negative patterns of discoloring or disillusioning an official drama's legitimacy and authenticity are latently engendered by pervasive distrust in a transitional society. Such distrust can be amplified by the inadequate behavior of actors in the TJ process. An underlying distrust of an official institution and its public servants is waiting for a moment of ignition. In this sense, TJ organizations and staff are forced to engage in "expectation management." This expression may remind us of the condition and atmosphere observed in postmodern Western societies, in which constituencies are fragmented and lack shared values or ideals to the extent that their reactions to a certain stage cannot be anticipated in any unified manner.

Referring to the work of Elaine Aston and George Savona (1991:120), Jeffrey Alexander (2011:75) offers a starting ground for postmodern theatrical analysts in the awareness that "theatre is attended by the 'non-innocent' spectator whose worldview, cultural understanding or placement, class and gender condition and shape her/his response." The expression "non-innocent spectator" is reframed in other expressions: "fragmentation of the citizenry" (Alexander 2011:76), conflictive publics (Eley 1992:306), and "multiple publics" (Fraser 1990:67–68). These expressions represent the different interests forming disparate orthogonal subcultures, along with social constituents' awareness of that fragmented situation. Participants in TJ programs may display similar fragmentation in any politically scripted drama on a public stage because they, too, have been disunified into disparate positions through a conflicting past.

However, the following explanation from Alexander suggests the limits of identifying a postmodern society with a post-conflict transitional society:

> Audience interpretation is a process, not an automatic result . . . every performance is compared to an idealized or "remembered" model available from earlier experience. In other words, audience interpretation does not respond to the quality of the performative elements per se. . . . Scripts, whether written or attributed, are compared to the great and convincing plots of earlier times. (Alexander 2011:76)

In terms of the negative recognition of circumstances where a certain social norm is no longer shared unconditionally, both postmodern and post-conflict situations might have commonalities. Yet in the former society, other comparable norms exist. Alternative norms, or the larger social stock of norms, are functioning. If desired, people can change a norm that they use to legitimize themselves. However, a transitional/post-conflict society, which is largely characterized by dysfunctional legal norms, lacks an established stock of norms on which people can draw. The pressure of role expectation is sometimes reduced to the fear of simple physical revenge. People in post-conflict societies tend not to be actors who can compare and calculate several standardized meanings in public. A social norm applied through the setting of an official drama may be abandoned by these people, not because it compares unfavorably to other alternative norms but because establishing a predominant or prominent norm is difficult among social actors. In fact, in post-conflict societies, the probability of results being attributable to unknown, unanticipated, and unintended factors can be higher than in other societies.

Talcott Parsons (1951) introduces the term *double contingency* in his social system theory. He explains that fundamental contingency logically exists in all relationships between actions and reactions, because the first action initially expects the other's reaction. Yet the reaction can never be foreseen with certainty. On the other hand, the reaction follows the action, yet it is theoretically open to various possibilities. Therefore, the reaction occurs within contingent conditions. In Parsons's social-system theory, individuals rely on social norms when they make logical attempts to remedy this unstable condition. Social norms enable people to avoid becoming trapped in endless vacillations before they take action.

A TJ body's position, as well as individuals' reactions to that body, can be elucidated with this double contingency argument. TJ programs are conducted based on the anticipated achievement of results in the same manner as other policies. However, from the outset, expectations contain contingencies (more properly, false logic) that cause individuals to fail to consider TJ realistically; for instance, they may have placed too much hope in it. False logic arises from the expectation that TJ might possibly occur in circumstances in which sufficient resources, sufficient conditions such as the rule of law and social norms, and public service functions are secured. On the other hand, for local people who must react to this policy, no shared codes or standards are available to moderate their reactions, because the TJ body is a new institution. Applying Parsons's framework, no stable social norms are available that can unconditionally guide individuals' reactions to the TJ body and its ideals or goals. Consequently, each receiver can react based on his or her own subjective interests. An individual who expects monetary reparations could be disappointed. Other individuals who believed the program should have publicly addressed their victimization experience may feel alienated. Victims who expected that perpetrators would show remorse might feel betrayed. These explanations all center on the difficulty involved in managing the hidden agenda within the TJ body as staff members (and citizens as well) attempt to maintain the supreme fiction of an official drama. It is thus vulnerable and has faced various patterns of rupture.

Utilitarian Players

Nevertheless, the framework of dramaturgy brings us another new lens to examine the TJ bodies' rupture of, or other local participants' divergence from, an official script. Some participants come to a TJ space with the understanding that, in principle, the space will not offer the desired positive outcome. Some even appear on the stage with a different script in mind, seeking to have it reflected in the ongoing process. These motivations resonate with the strategic engagement in TJ of Serbian politicians and Sierra Leonean generals in the course of international tribunals, as shown in Chapter 3. Whereas those previously illustrated episodes refer mainly to state-level politics, the following episodes will demonstrate strategic and divergent involvement of various stakeholders in more ordinary TJ processes, such as public hearings and other outreach programs held by a TJ entity.

A theoretical cornerstone of adopting the dramaturgical approach to a TJ program comes from Leigh Payne's *Unsettling Accounts: Neither Truth nor Reconciliation in Confessions of State Violence* (2008). Focusing on perpetrators' confessions at official accountability events after regime change from a former authoritarian state, Payne methodologically pursues how each public testimony, as well as the session itself, is unsettling, provoking and involving tactics, cover-ups, and challenges to the dramatizing efforts by various stakeholders. Through incorporating the concepts of stage, script, player, audience, and performance into the recognition of TJ settings, events such as public sessions for perpetrators' confessions vividly acquire meaning and function in the local context.

Payne posits categories such as heroic confessions, denial, silence, fiction, lies, and amnesia to grasp the pattern of perpetrators' tactical maneuvering around the stage and the political drama as a whole. Repentance and remorse are not always driving factors causing people to appear on a public stage. The perpetrators predict the script and prepare their performance. The former Argentine naval captain Alfredo Astiz, who had infiltrated the Mothers of the Plaza de Mayo and organized the raid on the Santa Cruz church[7] and several kidnapping cases, presented himself as a heroic figure:

> Every day, at every moment, I know that someone could kill me. My legs shook in every shootout, your whole body hurts, I go through so much fear, I went through a lot of fear. I died of this shit. And next day you have to go out again. . . . I don't regret anything. I am not perfect. . . . But in the big picture I do not repent anything . . . there is one thing that I learned from my mother and it is the only advice I can give: watch out for traitors. He who betrays will always betray. (Payne 2008:81)

Brazil's former military president, General Ernesto Geisel, used a strategy that "avoided either denial or admission" (Payne 2008:173) in terms of the military's responsibility for past violence during its authoritarian regime, particularly in 1969–1974:

> Many accuse the [military] government of torture. I don't know if there was, but it's probable that it happened, principally in São Paulo. It is really difficult for someone like me, who didn't participate in, nor live directly with, these events to judge what happened. On the other hand, it seems to me that when you are directly involved in the problem of subversion, in the middle of the struggle, you cannot, in general, limit your action. (Payne 2008:173)

When Payne refers to the confession with "graphic details about the event" provided by Joe Mamasela, a former collaborator with the South African apartheid police, the political drama can be understood as a space where "the temptation to tell a good and convincing story leads to confessional lies" (Payne 2008:215). Lies in a political drama might be attributable to a desire for material benefits, security protection, or a reduced sentence; however, more complicated motivations can also be inferred. Payne recalls the case of a dancer, dying of AIDS, who choreographed and performed a dance based on his front-line experiences in the Vietnam War; the dance "recounted the trauma and horror of participating in senseless acts of violence." However, after the man died, it was discovered that he had spent the war at a desk job in the United States (Payne 2008:222). The false confession, which on the surface makes a confessor's position more vulnerable, can function for the performer in a different way from the norm of public confession: "Confessing to violence he did not commit made his life appear more dramatic and interesting than it truly was. He performed a fictional confession to violence on a media stage to gain attention he would not otherwise have received for his unremarkable life" (Payne 2008:222).

The above episodes, interpreted through dramaturgical analysis, suggest that TJ venues provide a space for the public exposure of hidden motivations, expectations, and contestation rather being simply the solemn demonstration of governmental authority and pure motivations to achieve justice. Under the surface of the formal slogan of mutual understanding and healing through dialogue, players on the TJ stage attempt to reorient the course of drama, thus painting the public knowledge of the past with new meanings.

In some critiques, past TJ projects have been negatively viewed partly because of these attempts by participants with dissident motivations to rewrite the script and recreate the stage. Their engagement has inevitably moved the outcome of TJ activities away from the one originally planned. However, dissenting effort of this kind should not be dismissed, for two reasons: it reflects local perceptions of the past conflict and of TJ itself more than the formal, surface-level TJ objectives, and it could be a significant clue to infer what local impact and influence the TJ process is generating. Payne offers the notion of contentious coexistence for the status of players on the above-cited public stage and suggests that it embodies the beginning of substantial democracy, which must be contrasted with formal democracy as observed in the implementation of national elections or the existence of a multiparty system. The following episodes explore the complex context of local digestion of TJ, to understand what results TJ programs have brought to the societies concerned beyond the TJ organizations' official terminology and intentions.

Gamble and Fail

Phil Clark observed a former perpetrator who intentionally gave false testimony at a gacaca hearing. Doing that is, of course, a gamble because the risk of being punished doubles when the truth is exposed. But the desire to engage in plea bargaining for a minimal sentence made the bet worthwhile.

In 2006, in the Bugesera district of Kigali Ngali Province, the suspect attended a gacaca and confessed to looting some property from "a house on the edge of the community, near the main road leading to Nyamata" (Clark 2010:209). With these details, the judges were about to classify his action as a Category 3 crime, which was not a serious crime and therefore required the suspect only to provide compensation for the price of the goods stolen or perform some community service. When the judges asked whether the audience had any questions, there was silence initially.

Then one elderly woman stood up and said, "This man is lying and you judges are not doing your job because you should know that he is lying." The judges were visibly shocked and asked the woman to explain herself.

She said that she knew the suspect was lying because the house from which he claimed to have looted property was her house, and the judges should have known this because, six months earlier, they had convicted a different man of these same crimes (Clark 2010:209).

After the judges' deliberation, the woman's objection was considered valid and the suspect was sentenced to two more years in prison for perjury. To complicate the episode further, it turned out that the suspect was innocent of all genocide crimes but had been imprisoned before this incident on a false charge of genocide: "After spending many years in prison, however, he had deemed it preferable to fabricate a confession to a low category of genocide crime, which would bring a minimal sentence, rather than spend further years in jail, with no immediate prospect of release" (Clark 2010:209–210).

His tactics failed as his case and the lie he told was officially recorded, but this episode allows us to infer that many others have doubtless gambled and won by presenting false testimony.

Utilize Material Within Limitations

Lia Kent describes the tactical participation in a hearing by a victim's family in order to pursue a personal agenda where, on the surface, a TJ venue could not offer any help. Kent's observations of the Community Reconciliation Process (CRP) in East Timor caused her to recognize that "individuals who were not necessarily committed to the official goals of the CRP sometimes viewed the hearings as useful arenas for furthering their efforts to gain 'facts' that might be relevant to the recovery of bodies, or future prosecutions, or as a means to clear their family's name in relation to a preexisting dispute" (Kent 2012:158). For example, one widow whom she interviewed could positively identify witnesses to her husband's killing, although the CRP could neither prosecute the perpetrators nor provide any material assistance to her. She told Kent that she expected this information to prove useful in a future prosecution (Kent 2012:158).

This modification of TJ space to suit the participants' own agenda also occurred in cooperation among locals. Kent describes the case of a CPR hearing in the village of Aldeia in Lautem that was initially proposed by the villagers and their chief, "who wanted to 'clarify' facts surrounding the 1999 murder of a father of seven, 'Gil,' allegedly by . . . militia members from a neighbouring Aldeia" (Kent 2012:159). The CAVR commissioners were unwilling to hear this case because they wanted to focus on less serious crimes such as the burning of a house or minor assaults. Therefore, the CAVR arranged a hearing for these less serious cases from the agreed deponents, while knowing that they had a murder case as well. At the hearing venue, a tug-of-war ensued between the CAVR commissioners, who wanted to confine the discussion to less serious crimes, and Gil's family, backed by the local community, which tried to pursue their own agenda. The latter's challenge was successful, resulting in "the public shaming of perpetrators and the restoration of the reputation of the victim's family" because it matched the "customary understandings of justice" (Kent 2012:159). Kent explains this divergence from the official TJ stage as a translation into the vernacular. Participants do not necessarily remain a docile audience. Even when they recognize the limitations of the official script, they seek useful signs from the process in the way of bricolage (constructing something from a diverse range of available things).

Spontaneous Arrangement of Testimony

A TJ body, as an official drama, remains a space for *derivative work*, particularly in a venue where interactions between stage actors and audiences are generously allowed. The following newspaper article offers a typical description of how locals perceived the agenda of the South African TRC:

> Seated in the truth commission boardroom, MP and former member of the Soweto Committee of Ten, Ellen Khuzwayo closed her eyes and started speaking. In her usual soft, calculating voice . . . Ma Khuzwayo . . . took us through the June 16, 1976, scholar's march. Before she could finish her story, Sophie Tema, the *World* newspaper journalist, took it up. Then the *Rand Daily Mail* photographer Peter Magubane spoke, followed by Leonard Mosala, a member of the Committee of Ten who had also been a member of the urban Bantu council. Then it was my turn. We had been assembled as witnesses to give evidence of what happened in Soweto on June 16 and in subsequent months. As we were going through the motions of compiling our testimony, it suddenly dawned on me that we were trying to piece together events that had taken place twenty years ago. Information gushed out. . . . As we came from different parts of Soweto, there was little danger of repeating what someone had already said or of duplicating information. But, then again, if there was repetition it could only enhance a particular viewpoint, thus making it even more credible. (*Business Day*, July 23, 1996)

Testifying in an officially designated space is neither solely for individual catharsis nor just for participation in authoritative discourse. The public hearings unintentionally allowed participants to create their own views of collective history. Here is a vivid example:

> I cried on Wednesday morning. This happened as I listened to SAFM's reporter at the Truth Commission hearings in East London as she reported on the wailing of victims of apartheid atrocities. Mrs Nomonde Calata had broken down and cried uncontrollably as she

recalled the death of her husband, Fort Calata.... Then came ex-MK fighter Mr Singqokwana Malgas, who also cried as he recalled the torture that he had to endure at the hands of the brutes who called themselves police officers.... As the reporter played the sound bites of this sequence, tears welled up in my eyes, for as I listened to Malgas I was taken back to a room on the third floor of the police building in Krugersdorp, where I was tortured in 1982. As Malgas spoke of the electricity torture and the "helicopter" experience, where a detainee is suspended in mid-air and beaten so that he rolls around a pole inserted between legs, I saw myself lying naked that winter night on a floor full of water.... I cried on Wednesday because I felt the pain again, as I also remembered other comrades who were there with me in detention. (*Sowetan*, April 19, 1996)

How can these reactions be understood? These are not the outcomes that the TRC had planned for or expected, because the primary purpose of setting up the TRC public hearings was to share the truth, just as is the case with court hearings. However, the TRC public hearings did not involve executing the strict investigation and interrogation that are necessary for criminal justice. At the TRC hearings, information that was not strictly objective from a judicial viewpoint could also be shared. The proceedings were sometimes halted because of the reactions of audience members or witnesses. Yet these deviations, which provided the symbolic character of the hearings, prepared spaces where memory could be collectively and safely recalled by both witnesses and the audience. The vague definition of the terms *truth* and *reconciliation* left the TRC open to the aforementioned divergences. By not tightly defining the type of truth to be legitimized, the TRC enabled such unplanned truth sharing. If the mandate of the TRC had been limited to pursuing judicial punishment or historical truth, such a flexible arrangement may not have been possible.

Unexpected Steering of Dramas in Interaction

Derivative work in a TJ space may also take a harsher form in the course of actors' conflict during staging. Jeffrey Alexander (2011:165) argues that this divergence is inherently embedded in a script of social drama and that "performative failures allow the law of unintended consequences to enter into the cultural sphere." He explains the concept of performative failures as follows:

Even if the means of symbolic production are sufficient, the script powerfully written, and the mise-en-scène skilfully set in place, there is no guarantee that a performance will succeed. There remains the extraordinary challenge of acting it out.... In social dramas, actors perform a role they often do occupy, but their ability to maintain their role incumbency is always in doubt; their legitimacy is subject to continuous scrutiny; and their feeling for the role is often marked by unfamiliarity. (Alexander 2011:70–71)

The following case, from a public hearing of the South African TRC (November 19, 1996, East London),[8] demonstrates that the suspected person performed too correctly in a legal manner, which was not fitting for the hidden norm of the space. In unexpected interactions with the audience, he was pushed to the point where he had to change his strategy.

Oupa Gqozo, formerly head of the Ciskei Defence Force, testified about the Bisho Massacre with regard to his responsibility for the killing of civilian protesters. He started his testimony with a cautious and well-prepared expression of remorse. He denied his own responsibility, claiming that the ANC should take more of the blame. Even though the audience cried out, Gqozo's logic was consistent and seemed to secure his innocence at first.

> BRIGADIER GQOZO: I am aware that many people have and still do blame me for what happened on that unfortunate day. My reaction to that day was and still is one of great remorse and distress. . . . As far as I am concerned the ANC alliance needed to return to the negotiating table and stop using the lives of innocent people for their own political gain.
>
> MR POTGIETER (Chairperson): Order please, order. We won't proceed until we have got order . . .
>
> BRIGADIER GQOZO: I know that the question on everybody's lips is whether I am going to say that I am sorry for what happened on that day. I feel that I am not personally to be blamed for what happened on that day.

The testimony moved to the question of whether the soldiers of the Ciskei Defence Force had started shooting first or not. The process stopped several times because of the audience's outcries, drawing the chairperson's calls for order and discipline. During testimony, which indicated that a soldier had fired the first shot, Gqozo stressed that he was not in the exact location of the massacre and was just receiving reports from the front lines inside his office. He defended himself using technical matters brought up by his lawyer while the audience members, displeased by his resorting to tactical communication, escalated their expressions of discontent. The transcript records the tension at the hearing:

> BRIGADIER GQOZO: I find it very difficult to accept that. Because Mr Chairman let me put it this way . . . (Interruption by screaming of woman in the audience)

REV FINCA: Please keep quiet. We know that you are all frustrated, please bear with us.

MR POTGIETER: Thank you very much. We appreciate your cooperation . . .

BRIGADIER GQOZO: Mr Chairman if one of the soldiers was shot by one of the soldiers, it may have meant one thing, the soldiers hated each other, how else would they shoot . . . (intervention)

Finally, one commissioner asked Gqozo to answer her question without consulting with his lawyer and to pay attention to the audience members in the front rows, one of whom had already left the room screaming and breaking down. She continued to ask if Gqozo had ever sent any messages to the families of the deceased and the injured. Gqozo still tried to protect himself by relying on logical argument, but again, a woman's screams from the floor interrupted the communication. Then the commissioner asked Gqozo to talk to these people "from the heart," and the audience outcries against Gqozo, who continued to defend himself, reached their apex. The following excerpt vividly shows the interactions among the participants.

MR POTGIETER: Order please, silence, silence, thank you!

BRIGADIER GQOZO: I also didn't want to justify myself in anything that I did, because I know that it is not necessary. . . . Perceptions are around people and I am a skunk. . . . I am aware of that. . . . I want them to know that I regret that it ever happened and if anything can be done to replace their loss then I pray God a plan be found to do it. And I would like to look at them and say please forgive me. I know that I don't deserve your forgiveness under the circumstances. . . . And I want to tell you from my heart that I never willed and I never wanted your people to be killed.

MR POTGIETER: Thank you, order please, order.

What interaction is noted in the record of Gqozo's testimony? His status was sufficiently protected by legal logic, but he was forced to change his stance in the informal interaction with the audience.

If their performances are successful, we are persuaded. Whether we become convinced is less a matter of rightness in a moral or cognitive sense than of aesthetic power, of whether a political performance has "felicity." Is it structured in a manner that evokes our concerns, builds pictures in our minds, allows us to share their worldly visions? (Alexander 2011:102)

According to Alexander, even though the official script of TRC amnesty hearings indicated that perpetrators were allowed to behave with legal logic, which may guarantee a testifier the granting of amnesty, too much legally protected communication loses "felicity," thus causing the testifier to dig his or her own grave.

Challenging an Official Script

One of the outstanding interactions between former victims and perpetrators in the South African TRC is without doubt the case of Jeffrey Benzien (July 14, 1997, Cape Town).[9] In it, we can recognize the appearance of accidental truth drawn from an interaction that was not planned by the TRC. A public forum focusing on the testimony of Benzien—a former intelligence officer who had tortured anti-apartheid activists—accidentally facilitated an encounter between former torturer and victim. Like Gqozo, Benzien also showed remorse in the form of elaborately developed self-justifications to build a foundation for interrogation under conditions that would be advantageous to him:

> MR BENZIEN: I cooperated with the Truth Commission from the outset. On the 8th of April of this year, I met members of the Truth Commission and I approached them of my own free will and I wasn't subpoenaed to attend proceedings. . . . In letters to the Truth Commission, I declared myself willing to, should I be provided with the necessary information, to further assist the Committee. . . . To conclude, I would once again like to say to the family and all the men and women whom I harmed, I would like to apologise to them. . . . My purpose was to arrest him and not to kill him. Although his death was a tragedy for his family, I am very, very sorry that he had to die, but the tables could very easily have been turned on that day, the outcome could have easily been very different and it could have left myself and Sergeant Abels being wounded or killed. And once again, I apologise to the family for his death and I thank God that I, who also have children, also a daughter who is twenty-two years old, that I was not the person who was killed on that day.

This carefully constructed, politically correct apology combined with tactical self-justification was interrupted by an unplanned agenda. Victims of Benzien's torture were present at the hearing and applied to testify without any official registration. Their appeal to testify before the commission surprised the chairperson. However, the appeal was finally accepted as an exception, and the following communication ensued.

> CROSS-EXAMINATION BY MR YENGENI: The first question I want to pose to you, Mr Benzien, is: Can you tell the Commission the circumstances surrounding my arrest and subsequent transportation to Culemborg? . . . Why did the Security Branch choose you specifically to apply this [wet bag] method on MK guerilas?

MR BENZIEN: Mr Yengeni, today in a new South Africa I can sit here and tell you in all honesty, that I was used by the then Security Branch. . . . Mr Yengeni, with my absolutely unorthodox methods and by removing your weaponry from you, I am wholly convinced that I prevented you and any of your colleagues and any one of them that ever had an explosive device in Cape Town, I may have prevented you from being branded murderer nowadays. . . . But in the spirit of reconciliation, we lived in a different era, we were enemies then. I have not fled the country, run away from the Police Force, I am still a policeman and trying to serve my community to the best of my ability. . . . Yes, Mr Yengeni, I did terrible things, I did terrible things to members of the ANC, but as God as my witness, believe me, I have also suffered. I may not call myself a victim of Apartheid, but yes Sir, I have also been a victim.

Benzien's statement was logical and consistent, and there seemed to be no falsehoods in his explanation of the political (or occupational) reasons for his conduct. He apologized, calling for understanding of the era of apartheid and referring to the ideal of reconciliation. The purpose of the interrogator, Yengeni, however, was not to examine the judicial facts. Accordingly, he posed a question to Benzien that required an answer based on values, not logic:

MR YENGENI: What kind of man that uses a method like this one of the wet bag, to people, to other human beings, repeatedly and listening to those moans and cries and groans and taking each of those people very near to their deaths, what kind of man are you? What kind of man is that, that can do that kind of, what kind of human being is that Mr Benzien? . . . When you do those things, what happens to you as a human being? What goes through your head, your mind? You know, what effect does that torture activity [have on] you as a human being?

MR BENZIEN: Mr Yengeni, not only you have asked me that question. I, I, Jeff Benzien, have asked myself that question to such an extent that I voluntarily, and it is not easy for me to say this in a full court with a lot of people who do not know me. I approached psychiatrists to have myself evaluated, to find out what type of person am I. . . . I did not either through my own stupidity or ignorance as long as I was one of the Whites, the privileged Whites who had an education, who had a house, I couldn't see it being taken away. If you ask me what type of person is it that can do that, I ask myself the same question.

The unplanned interaction between Benzien and Yengeni did not end there. Having deviated from usual judicial discourse, Yengeni next produced a black cloth bag and demanded that Benzien demonstrate the "wet bag" method of torture for the commissioners and the audience.

Finally, Yengeni's atypical interrogation of Benzien came to the point of eliciting Benzien's expression of his political values. The previous relationship between Benzien and Yengeni became reversed. Now Yengeni was the interrogator, trying to compel Benzien to disclose not a factual confession but an admission of his values.

> MR YENGENI: Now, so if now with the benefit of hindsight, you believe that you were wrong, so in other words you are then saying that not only were you wrong, but that everything that you stood for, was wrong?
>
> MR BENZIEN: Mr Yengeni, yes.
>
> MR YENGENI: Can you, Mr Benzien, look me straight in the eye and say to me that you now as you are sitting there, believe that the Apartheid system was evil and was wrong?
>
> MR BENZIEN: Yes, Sir.

The dialogical truth drawn out in this interaction is not a final answer, nor a complete consensus between contesting parties. The two parties maintained their own justifications. Yet each person's idea, which previously had never appeared in a public space, was elicited by an unexpected conversation that could never have occurred in a judicial cross-examination. This is a riveting example of the many events and outcomes not planned for in the formal agenda. The TRC never intended to become the venue for such encounters, but the vague and loose definition of such basic terms as *truth* and *reconciliation* may have prepared a space where such incidents could occur. The participants discussed these incidents as part of their strategic engagement in the official program. The structural *residual space* that developed owing to the lack of an official definition, but with a normative form, allowed participants to act with greater freedom to pursue their own interests.

Many observers noted the powerful visual impact of that scene, which was repeatedly aired on television so that the image of the inverted relationship between a former perpetrator and a victim could be widely consumed as a symbol of South Africa's new social conditions. At the same time, it still went along with the official script in that the weight of justice had moved from apartheid's side (Benzien) to that of the liberation movement (Yengeni).

Actors may perform a hidden script that is often not clear to observers who do not share the symbolic context. Foreign researchers of TJ have tended to presuppose a sense of sincere exchange among actors performing an official script or have otherwise resisted abandoning the idea that such exchange should be promoted as an ideal goal of justice and reconciliation. Yet actors, while posing as sincere, docile testifiers, are often pursuing consequences other than justice, such as specific social recognition and symbolic re-identification. They aim to alter how the surrounding people see them, as a creative artist seeks to change how an audience perceives reality. In both cases, the goal requires the existence of an audience.

Uncontrollable Drama

In examining cases from the South African TRC, we have seen situations in which actors bring to the surface a strategic script that underlies the official drama of justice and reconciliation to try to change, derail, or redirect the scenario. This multilayered type of performance, challenging the official TJ agenda, may appear in a less visible manner. If it is too subtle or highly elaborated, even the other actors in a TJ program struggle to decipher the actors' behavior. And sometimes even their best attempts at deciphering fail. The cases reported from the Sierra Leone Special Tribunal in Tim Kelsall's detailed work vividly demonstrate the dazzling plexus of meaning-making and misunderstanding. The sequence of inserting and decoding informal scripts in the official drama of an international judiciary produced rather surreal encounters between the rules and norms of international justice and local cultural and social meanings. In the following section, we will trace three remarkable topics emerging from Kelsall's documentation: (1) strategy for hedging discourse, (2) unexpected consequences of locals' cautious cooperation, and (3) possible reasons for witnesses to produce fictional information in the course of an official drama.

Hedging Bets or Compliance in Communication

Kelsall deeply explored the court transcripts and detected strange and unexpected results of the actors' communication. This divergence from the official drama did not result from a certain party's aggressive maneuver or conscious intervention. Rather, it came from the actors' miscommunication, as each party misunderstood each other's interpretation of how to read an official script.

First, Kelsall (2013:180) explained how locals under Sierra Leone's culture of secrecy cautiously distanced themselves from the legal discourse, which inevitably led to "a clash between a Western-style technology of truth recovery and a local culture in which guarding secrets and dissimulating the truth was a well practised skill." In that cultural context, testimony tended to be ambiguous, which is fatal to legal judgment. The Civil Defense Forces (CDF) trial was full of such ambiguous testimony, with lack of clear indications about time and space (Kelsall 2013:183). The lack of specificity can easily be attributed to trauma and memory lapses, and it is usually reasonable to assume that the "ideal victim" will exhibit this tendency. But when that tendency becomes generalized, as when virtually all the witnesses in the CDF trial were unable to indicate "details that could anchor an event in space and time" (Kelsall 2013:189), sympathetic understanding gives way to suspicion. Because specifying the date and place of events is one of the basic requirements for legal reasoning, judges and lawyers were compelled to seek other ways of eliciting this information. Some witnesses could at least remember days of the month or years, but others could not testify to any chronological information with reliability.[10]

Contrary to the legal experts' labeling of them as unsophisticated persons, by adamantly not adopting the court's code of communication, witnesses could perform their duties while not running any risk of facing accusations by other locals after the court session. The officials' laborious efforts to decipher the details continually ran up against the witnesses' strict obedience to "a non-committal conditional tense" (Kelsall 2013:194). Even if a witness had been at the same place as a suspected person and there was other evidence, the witness could protect his or her position by saying, "I didn't see it." Here is one typical example:

> Q. But was [Kosseh Hindowa] present at the Barri in the meeting we discussed this morning after the taking of Koribundu?
>
> A. I did not see him there.
>
> Q. And Joe Tamidey?
>
> A. I know him very well.
>
> Q. Was he at the Barri?
>
> A. Even if he was there, I did not see him, because you would meet with people, but if you did not see the person, you can't say he was there. (Kelsall 2013:194–195)

Surely, no one can confirm whether the testifier was speaking truthfully, because lack of visual memory, in theory, can be applied to everything. Officials tried to endure this irritating exchange, but nothing positive resulted from their examination. Kelsall (2013:195–96) provides many more similar exchanges, as if they were ubiquitous in the court transcripts. Sometimes officials reached the limit of their patience with the twisted way in which witnesses answered. The following extreme yet illustrative example merits an extended quotation:

> MR KOPPE: My question, Witness, is: Is your father buried at the cemetery of the town?
>
> WITNESS: I have told you just now that when he was killed, I didn't know whether—[interpretation interrupted]

PRESIDING JUDGE: Answer the question. Was your father buried in the cemetery in the village? Simple question. We have heard your explanations, but answer that question. It is very simple.

WITNESS: I didn't know whether he was buried there.

PRESIDING JUDGE: You don't know. I mean, stop answering questions in a twisted manner. You have a cemetery in your village which is what counsel is referring to. You have said that when somebody dies in the village, he's buried in the cemetery. Was your father buried in that cemetery?

WITNESS: I didn't see him being buried there.

PRESIDING JUDGE: You didn't see him being buried there, but was he buried there?

WITNESS: Whether they buried him there, I didn't see it happen. . . .

Q. Mr Witness, I'm putting it to you that you're not speaking the truth. You are not speaking the truth.

WITNESS: What am I—what I saw is what I talk about. What I didn't see, I wouldn't talk about . . .

MR WILLIAMS: You know that these people were killed in [Bo]. Is that correct? You know they were killed in [Bo]?

WITNESS: Yes.

MR WILLIAMS: And your father, you know very well that your father was in [Bo] at the time? You know very well?

WITNESS: I heard that he was in [Bo]. But I didn't know whether he was in [Bo] Town because we didn't see each other. Where he was, I didn't go there.

MR WILLIAMS: I'm putting it to you, Mr Witness, that you know very well that it was your father who orchestrated for the killing of those people. You know very well.

WITNESS: Even if he did it, I didn't see. What I saw is what I'm talking about.

MR WILLIAMS: Mr Witness, I'm not saying that you were in [Bo]. I'm saying that you were told, you were informed subsequently—you could not have been present in [Bo]. My question is this: That you were informed, you knew, through some other means, secondary means or whatever it is, that it was your father who orchestrated for the killing of those people.

WITNESS: Now, who told me? (Kelsall 2013:196–198)

In spite of the pressure applied by judges, local witnesses would not deviate from their path of couching their replies in vagueness, probably in order to protect their position within the community after the court hearings (Kelsall 2013:201–202). An alternative possible interpretation is that the witnesses made their best effort to comply with the rules of communication in the courtroom even though the exchange seemed evasive on the surface. I am reminded of researchers who have used the ethnomethodological approach to patiently ascertain, through repeated questioning, the meaning and definition of individual words, the correctness of background knowledge, and the presuppositions underlying the use of each expression, trying to elicit the invisible code of communication in a society.

In reading the transcripts, the readers, who are immersed in a context where legal norms and judicial legitimacy are established and accepted as natural, are inclined to side with the court officials and feel irritated with the witnesses' answers. But for those who are not familiar with the implicit rules or norms of communication in a courtroom, the minute and confirmatory focus on the definition, meaning, and usage of words may appear to be following a specific set of rules or procedures that their own utterances are also expected to observe. Therefore, the locals' perspective is the flip side of these skeptical comments from one judge regarding a citizen's utterances: "Probably you should advise your witness that the sort of responses we are having may well persuade an imaginary judge from space, perhaps, to think that he is trying to hide something" (Kelsall 2013:203–4). In other words, the locals may feel that they are complying seriously and sincerely with the script (rules) of legal examination, but they do not realize that the script (rules) is asymmetrically applied and that only the type of communication on which legal experts can act is acceptable. Lacking any clear instruction, the locals may have responded in the best way that they knew to their recognition that the legal experts' mode of communication, one designed to pursue the utmost objectivity, is the proper procedure for an official script. Witnesses may have thus tried to cooperate with keeping the official drama going properly, but without understanding the unspoken (meta-)script that only legal experts can scrutinize the objectivity of an utterance.

Unexpected Results of Cautious Cooperation

An assumption that local witnesses tried to cooperate with foreign court officials but with different understandings of the official script becomes more credible when one considers that testimony brought financial rewards. Witnesses were given up to 20,000 Leones ($8 in currency rate in 2004 and $3 in 2018) a day in compensation for their lost work time, as well as medical treatment and other perks—for example, gifts of official clothes in which they could stand before the court. They also received accommodation fees in Freetown and financial support for their family. The duration of their stay in Freetown was often around a month (Kelsall 2013:208). The

United Nations Development Program's Human Development Report estimated Sierra Leone's annual GDP per capita in 2004 as $520, which would be converted to 1.3 million Leones—3,500 Leones per day—in the local currency.[11] Some witnesses received more than enough, in view of the Sierra Leonean economic context: "John Wesley Hall established that [witness] TF2-162 had received Le 833,000. . . . Quincy Whitaker told the witness (TF2-032) that the Court had given him more than 1 million Leones. TF2-140 had received over Le 1.5 million. . . . TF2-021, another child soldier, received over 2 million Leones" (Kelsall 2013:209).

Becoming a witness can be good business, but witnesses are reluctant to admit to receiving payments when questioned in a courtroom. Under cross-examination, they usually admitted that they would be eligible to take such rewards and perks, but rarely did they testify to actual payments. Why did they behave in this manner? In addition to their too strict and circumspect obedience to the rules of communication in the courtroom, the witnesses seem to have treated their payments as something improper that should be kept secret. The witness perhaps perceives the fact of payment as unfavorable to securing his or her legitimacy, because a paid witness's answers can be expected to vindicate whoever paid the witness. The defense raised the possibility that "the witnesses had a financial incentive to testify, plus an incentive to massage their stories to fit the theory of the prosecution, on whom they were dependent in a patron-client type of way" (Kelsall 2013:211). One accused person even observed, "Every time the witness has come to give evidence to [a local] chief, they are not difficult. But when [we] question, then they become non-understanding, noneducated" (Kelsall 2013:211). Perhaps, in the guise of being ignorant and unsophisticated, witnesses were rewarding the prosecutors who had guaranteed them payments as large as five times the nation's average daily income per person.

Reasons for Producing Fictional Information

The interpretation that witnesses might be cooperating with the prosecutors' scenario in return for payment leads to another suspicion. Some witnesses presumably figured out that the longer the drama lasted, the more they would be rewarded. This suspicion of actors' divergence might help to explain the interesting fact that "some witnesses had met with the prosecution several times, changing their statement more than once" (Kelsall 2013:212). These changes could be due to the recording errors that commonly occur in translation, or to memory loss, traumatic symptoms, or instruction or intimidation by other agents. We will never know.

In one case, a witness provided a written statement on an order received from his superior and on the name of the person who attended a particular meeting. However, later, in his oral testimony, he changed his stance and the inconsistency was pointed out. The judge tried to confirm whether he agreed with the contents of the written statement he had made earlier:

> JUDGE BOUTET: When they were finished with writing something on a piece of paper, did they read to you what was written on that piece of paper and did they do so in Mende?
>
> WITNESS: No. They would just ask me and I'd answer; they would ask me and I answer; they would ask me and I'd answer, and when I finished asking [sic] the questions, they thanked me. And that's the end. (Kelsall 2013:212–213)

Other legal officers were more straightforward in suspecting that locals' motivation to testify was related to personal grudges or to money paid by prosecutors and the Victim Support Unit. Kelsall recalled the view of one lawyer:

> "There's no doubt that witnesses change their stories in response to payments and perks. Look at what they know two years before the trial, then as they get closer to the Court their memories improve. And I saw that with Defence witnesses also." In Jordash's experience, "Very few failed to understand that the more valuable they became in terms of testimony, the more money they stood to make." (Kelsall 2013:235)

Witnesses change their testimony. The reason for this has been inferred as misunderstanding. However, doubts have crept in about prosecutors' monetary offers giving the witnesses a motivation to extend the process. If they want to be on stage for as long as possible, they have to sow a seed of mystery or give other information that pushes the official drama to the point where it needs to be scrutinized further.

Another explanation as to why witnesses changed their testimony was fear, which was sometimes admitted in a naïve manner. A former member of CDF's death squad, Tucker, stood before the court as an insider witness. His testimony was crucial for prosecutors to support their theory of the command responsibility of the big three cadres—namely, Hinga Norman, Moinina Fofana, and Allieu Kondewa. Several other indictments would be affected by Tucker's information. Nevertheless, his earlier statement and his court testimony did not line up. In particular, he changed his story about who was the "ultimate source of authority on the battlefield":

> A. I used to say those words to the investigators. But during the time that I made those statements I was in deep fear, because I knew that I myself was somebody who took part in the war. . . . All the other statements I made were under fear. I was really afraid.
>
> Q. So you admit to lying to the investigators then to protect yourself?

> A. I was not telling lies. I was really afraid and when you are scared you do not know how to position yourself. (Kelsall 2013:214–215)

Here is another extreme example of changed testimony allegedly due to fear:

> Albert Nallo, the prosecution's star witness . . . provided seventeen separate statements to the prosecution, his story growing more elaborate over time. Pressed on this, Nallo explained to the Court that he did not tell the full truth to the prosecution in his first encounters since he was afraid that he himself would be apprehended. (Kelsall 2013:215)

Given the social context of a post-conflict society, whether attributing these false statements to fear constitutes dissembling remains unclear. However, this can still be used as a last resort in a (potentially) fake performance. One prosecutor adopted an enlightened standpoint toward the locals and interpreted changes in testimony in a positive way, saying that witnesses need time to deepen their confidence in their security, and therefore statement taking is required several times to follow the changing course of their testimony (Kelsall 2013:215–216). Yet at the same time, this explanation justifies the prosecutor's methodology of payment for repetitive and lengthy statement taking. A discourse that seems to be based on goodwill can also be utilized as a tactical maneuver. The principle of pursuing truth through courts of law has perhaps brought the stakeholders to the point where an image of a traumatized, vulnerable victim and the motive of imparting Western legal norms to locals become intermingled, leading to the creation of lengthy, unpredictable dramas. The method is regarded suspiciously by many, but it might be beneficial to certain positions. Here the contents of a scenario, which are surely a leading concern for legal experts, no longer represent a central concern for local performers. Instead, a strategic dramaturgy based on the principle that "longer is better" can supplant an official script. Witnesses could be moving further from the truth as they became aware of the material benefits that this strategy would bring.

In this situation, images of innocence, cultural norms, calculation and tactics, and justification of foreign intervention are indistinguishably mixed, and disentangling these factors is almost impossible. An official script as a judicial stage is ongoing, yet substantial drama among performers becomes largely self-referential justification.

One witness, when shown inconsistencies between his prior recorded statement and his current oral testimony, insisted that the recorded testimonies were not his. Responding to this situation, Michiel Pestman, counsel for one of the accused, lamented, "Either the investigators made up a statement, or the witness is lying, so it's quite interesting" (Kelsall 2013:217). Yes, it is quite interesting, particularly when one is considering a dramatic meta-scenario as we are doing here, that speech should be examined in this context not by its contents but by its function. Local witnesses resolutely kept to their own tracks. How did the chamber finally react to this impasse? In some instances, the officials played along:

> MR TAVENER. Q: You've spoken about the War Council and they made recommendations. To whom did the War Council make recommendations?
>
> NALLO. A. To the national coordinator of CDF Chief Hinga Norman.
>
> Q. You've spoken about Allieu Kondewa. To whom did he report to?
>
> At this point Nallo utters a long "Errrr."
>
> A. There were three persons. I wouldn't know who was reporting to whom. When this one speaks it will go to the other one. It's like the Son and the Holy Spirit.
>
> Visibly chortling, Judge Itoe intervenes at this junction to put words into Nallo's mouth:
>
> PRESIDING JUDGE: The Holy Trinity.
>
> WITNESS: Yes, My Lord. It's the trinity.
>
> Chuckling a little himself, Tavener gratefully seizes on this:
>
> MR TAVENER: Who were in the trinity?
>
> PRESIDING JUDGE: Please, hold on. Wait, Mr Witness. Wait. Yes.
>
> MR TAVENER: Who were the persons in the trinity?
>
> WITNESS: Well, Chief Hinga Norman was the boss—God. Chief Hinga Norman was the God, sorry. Moinina Fofana the Son.
>
> Again, unable to contain his enthusiasm, Itoe interjects:
>
> PRESIDING JUDGE: And Kondewa the Holy Spirit.
>
> WITNESS: And the high priest is the Holy Spirit. (Kelsall 2013:220)

In the final judgment, this metaphorical and metaphysical notion of command responsibility appears without commentary: "Norman, Fofana and Kondewa were regarded as the 'Holy Trinity.' 'Norman was the God, . . . Fofana was the Son, and [Kondewa] was the Holy Spirit.' The three of them were the key and essential components of the leadership structure of the organization and were the executives of the Kamajor society" (Kelsall 2013:219–221). The stage curtain was drawn in a mundane way. The authentic judicial settings needed to be maintained safely.

Covert Secession and Creation of Parallel Dramas

Religious Experience on the Justice Stage

An invisible script in an official drama performed by locals can also take a more covert guise. The case in Rwandan gacaca analyzed by Phil Clark also displays a twisted meaning shared by participants. Gacaca, as already described in the previous chapters, has been publicized and understood as an inventory institution created by applying a mechanism of local justice to a nationwide judiciary. But according to Clark's observation, the unique reality among local participants is not framed in gacaca practice in terms of justice, but in terms of the people's religious perceptions of space and opportunity. One remarkable feature of the locals' interpretation of gacaca was that they found a potential linkage between its objectives and Christianity in pursuing healing and forgiveness (Clark 2010:257). Here is a contrast between an official script of gacaca as a legal program and an informal script as a religious opportunity. In Clark's observation, many suspects said that their Christian faith motivated them to confess:

> "It is not an easy thing to confess unless you are pushed by the Bible," said Maurice, a detainee in the ingando at Kigali Ville. "I was converted while I was in prison. Because I wanted to live in peace with myself, I decided to confess to being part of a group that killed a man during the genocide. . . . Now I have nothing to fear at gacaca. Gacaca is only a threat to those who have not yet confessed." (Clark 2010:268)

In keeping with these religious influences, when discussing healing at gacaca, suspects often employ highly metaphorical, theological language to describe the forms that they believe healing will take. Many suspects employ the metaphor of the body and express a desire for "cleansing" through confession. They express their sense that their crimes had polluted their souls and that they therefore required some form of purification:

> "I was forced to kill during the genocide, against my will. . . . Before I confessed to what I did . . . I felt dirty and needed cleansing. Being a Christian, I knew that I needed to confess to feel clean again. I have confessed to assisting in the killing of a man. . . . Now I will tell the truth about my crimes at gacaca. Confessing is important for the truth, for my faith and for my own cleanness." (Clark 2010:268–269)

For others, confession at gacaca is like medicine to cure the soul, or a means to be reborn, to become a new person. It is curious that such comments were not elicited from the participants of the South African TRC, where the ideal of reconciliation had begun with Archbishop Tutu, but from participants in a gacaca *court*, an organization where justice is the main priority. Even though these comments that related people's confessions to their Christian faith could function as a proper vocabulary of motive in Rwandan society, the religious connotation appears not to have been simply pretense. Clark recalled how people have often used gacaca as opportunities for "communal mourning":

> In Nyarufonzo district of Kigali Ville province, several women brought to a gacaca hearing framed photographs of loved ones who died during the genocide. They clutched these photographs tightly throughout the hearing and pointed to them [suspects] when they stood and gave evidence. When the women sat down again, many of them cried and hugged each other. . . . The women holding the photographs appeared to gain solace and strength from those who showed them concern. . . . The solidarity displayed by those around them affirmed them as members of the community and acknowledged their traumatic experiences. (Clark 2010:264–265)

When reading this passage, one might think that a government could set up a mourning ceremony as a TJ program from the beginning. It might be a valid option in addition to a standard program of seeking justice. The South African case of exhumation as a symbolic funeral, referred to in Chapter 4, also addressed that concern. In some places it may work well, whereas in other places another cultural option may be required. Yet observing the cases related in this chapter leaves the strong feeling that any TJ options that come from the top may trigger opposite or divergent movements from the locals.

An Honor Game in Court Outreach

The covert performance of an invisible script could appear multilayered. In the case of Rwandan gacaca, we have seen two layers of meaning: an official drama of local justice and a religious opportunity in the context of local Christian faith. In this section, we will turn to engagement in Cambodia, analyzing three layers of meaning in the ECCC and related events—international justice, domestic politics, and the local context of interaction. The story starts with the paradox that many locals disagree with the legitimacy of the ECCC but still join in outreach opportunities. Their deep distrust of the judiciary has been reinforced by their suspicion of corruption among local ECCC staff members and the tensions and disputes between national and foreign legal staff inside the court (see Chapter 3). However, many people still indicate enthusiasm about the chance to participate in outreach programs. Why do they attend these programs even though they seem not to support the purpose and legitimacy of the ECCC? Or is there a more complicated motivation for them to take part?

One possible inference is that being selected to participate at an outreach venue functions as a social token that confers enhanced social status. In the Cambodian villages, receiving an invitation to participate from an NGO makes a positive impression on one's friends and neighbors: "Wow! You were invited by them? You are honored. You must be doing something good to be asked to join in the NGO program." This statement implies, conversely, that you must have done something wrong if only your neighbors were invited. In this way, the NGO can actually instigate tension and frustration among villagers through its outreach activities. Such instances of "honor competition" are reflected in Alexander Hinton's observation of Cambodian locals' performance of the concept of *ketteyuos* (good reputation and honor). Hinton notes that the term *face* is used as a "metaphor for relative social standing," which is "strategically negotiated and at times competitively structured, particularly insofar as it is bound up with *ketteyuos*. . . . *Ketteyuos* may be gained through proper moral behaviour, but it is largely focused on external recognition and evaluation" (Hinton 2005:252, 257).

For example, one episode on civil party participation took place as follows.[12] In one commune, twenty people were admitted to a civil party, some by the Transcultural Psychosocial Organization (TPO) and others by DC-Cam. Then the Cambodian Human Rights and Development Association (ADHOC) came and held a local forum with the "clients." Other people, who were affiliated with other NGOs, were naturally not invited and subsequently complained.

Even within a single NGO, this problem can occur. Let us assume that one NGO has 1,000 civil party applicants. The NGO divides the members into six groups according to its budget. Then the NGO holds six forums, with 100 people attending on each occasion. The people not included on any list complain, charging that the NGOs have "their own people." If you are selected as a representative of a certain area, you may be invited to or choose to travel to Phnom Penh, securing *ketteyuos* among related locals and community members. The honor competition thus continues in the circumstances created by the ECCC and related NGOs. The circumstances are not intended by the ECCC and provide evidence of the deviant usage of ECCC outreach by locals.

For instance, the ECCC's pamphlet for visitors, "An Introduction to the Khmer Rouge Trials," contains a picture in which survivors from the Khmer Rouge period are raising the Full Appeal Judgment Books with satisfaction.[13] In the local newspapers, they were reported as having commented that they were satisfied with the books and thought that the ECCC had brought justice to the nationals (*KT,* May 22, 2012). The picture seems to capture their spontaneous expression of happiness at the verdicts. But is that true? This question becomes more meaningful when the backstage of the picture, which shows jostling journalists pointing cameras at the victims, is presented in parallel.[14]

Clearly, there was an element of performance and staging in front of the court officials, microphones, and TV cameras. Indeed, can anybody with no background of political activism express negative or critical remarks regarding the court under such circumstances? When ordinary local people are required to comment within the public space in front of a camera, there is no option but to join the chorus of "justice has finally been brought to us." This is the only *truth* permitted within this context. The chorus of ECCC self-congratulation and local acquiescence is well choreographed. Similarly, the ECCC has also used images of a group of school students cheering while displaying copies of ECCC publications and expressing their approval of the verdict. What we view in these images cannot be locals' spontaneous expression of satisfaction but a directed performance at an official setting.

This dynamic can arise at any place in any society, but the pressure to make participants behave in a certain way at a public, staged event in Cambodia calls for particular consideration. Alexander Hinton's remarks on Cambodian cultural norms are suggestive:

> The stereotype of Cambodians as "gentle" people emerged in part because most foreigners interacted with Cambodians in more formal situations, in which politeness and smiles are the expected norm . . . there is an expectation that people will act in accordance with pre-existing rules of etiquette and respect. Therefore, as mentioned, when two non-intimates interact in a formal situation, the subordinate person is expected to honor his or her social superior by employing the appropriate speech registers, assuming the proper body position and mannerisms, and generally acting in a polite and reverent manner. The subordinate person receives honor by behaving in this way and through his or her superior's positive response. When two people interact in this orderly manner, social relations remain smooth and friendly, and no one loses face. (Hinton 2005:253–254)

Normative behavior is performed not only for the performer's benefit but also for the superiors (including court staffs and politicians), the organization (the ECCC), the audience (including the foreign media), and the Cambodian citizens (perhaps including the silent dead). The performers are embedded in a context where good citizens must show their support for the authoritative expectations present in the social context. This requirement entails the delimitation of all official and unofficial public relations.

One question remains with regard to this situation: Is there a script for this drama? The answer, based on prevailing critiques of the present government found in human-rights and activist circles, is yes, for the political explanation is visible as a restriction and determination of this story. This, however, assumes that a predetermined result of the ECCC process folds neatly into broad consensual public approval of the ECCC. The empirical argument in this chapter requires more cautious understanding on this matter, taking into account several factors, such as people's deep distrust of the legal system, the cultural value of *ketteyuos*, and social norms for conscious performers as active agents in maintaining social order.

This drama is held at ordinary locals' discretion, not only to prevent making a mockery of the experts' effort, or out of their fear of disrupting the predetermined orientation endorsed by the government, but also because of their spontaneous preference for maintaining stage settings, even though the several scenarios are not actually compatible in their contents. It seems that because of the aforementioned background conditions, which become visible through contradictions displayed in the attitudes of locals, this drama cannot be altered by outsiders' enlightening criticism.

Conclusion

Richard Wilson, who conducted extensive field research in South African township areas during the years when the TRC was active, once wrote, "People may pragmatically perform roles and take part in HRV [Human Rights Violation] hearings and reparations procedures, but did not necessarily accept the core human rights assumptions of the institution" (Wilson 2001:152).

People who gather at a specific venue or participate in a certain event may attribute different meanings to events than the official or public ones, and they may even share such impressions covertly with others. People participating in a TJ event use dual meanings to rebuild their sense of their world. According to the framing of this chapter, public hearings of international tribunals and truth commissions, regardless of their formal objectives, are perceived as a social stage that purports to represent the past using a specific scenario. In the tribunals, the curtain falls as the accused are declared guilty. Truth commissions, on the other hand, arrange the stage to build toward an officially expected goal of healing and mutual recognition among former adversaries.

As these happenings are publicized as official events, elaborate political scenarios must be prepared beforehand. In these scenarios, local participants are required to behave in certain patterns according to the situation of the official drama. Victims need to behave in accordance with the role of victim in the local societal context; they are sometimes pressured to behave as ideal victims. Accused persons are subject to stricter rules than others regarding their role in the process. All need to respect the TJ experts as organizers and conveners of the drama.

However, as shown in the aforementioned examples, experiences of dual meaning seem to often take the form of challenging official, formal scenarios, attempting to change the scenario or appropriating, utilizing, or misunderstanding it. These challenges may occur when the actors on the stage acknowledge their inaccurate expectations to others, or when the actors negatively view their positions as passive, alienated, and submissive. Actors appearing in the TJ venues may perform different roles from those required, demand rewriting of the official scenario, or play their roles in a way that is outside the expected behavior. Others might try to be actors despite their role as audience.

Why have such happenings occurred? Primarily, they occur when the official drama that a TJ body provides does not match the needs of local participants. The locals demand a different experience from the officially planned one supplied by the TJ scenario. As some scholars have already indicated, the needs of local stakeholders vary too much for a TJ body to sufficiently address all of them with its limited resources. Therefore, TJ projects have started and continued their activity without accommodating some stakeholders' requests. A mismatch between an institutional TJ program and local needs is inevitable and intrinsic, yet what matters is how it appears in a real context. That is, although an official scenario cannot match the one borne in locals' mind, it must be not too far from what they demand, while leaving space for challenging, interpreting, and deviation.

Actors who acknowledge such limitations of TJ projects may dare to enter the public space of TJ with their own strategies. People who agree with the significance, purpose, and practicality of the TJ stage but disagree with the scenarios provided by TJ are likely to take on the task of changing the official drama. If TJ's scenario and stage-setting function as a good rhetoric consistent with locals' expectations or values, those official forms may still work to elicit further actions. In other words, scenarios with specific inadequacies may induce actors to become involved in changing the drama.

This is a worthwhile topic for further discussion. Undoubtedly, an inadequate stage lacking elaborate preparation would be boring and would elicit no engagement, either by actors or by audiences. Specific conditions are needed to produce actors' divergent engagement. Conversely, a perfect scenario—if such is possible—might not produce enough participant motivation to lead to a change in the drama (as indicated in Chapter 4). Thus, the idea that actors' motivation becomes concretely molded when the stage is attractive to them but the scenario remains inadequate can be offered as a working postulate. The change in the official drama itself does not need to be evaluated positively or negatively, yet it clearly must be understood as an unintended consequence of TJ. Our remaining agenda is therefore to explore what stage settings, including the character of the drama's script or the social conditions surrounding the stage, might stimulate actors' motivation for engagement and how their needs might be embodied in the course of divergent performances.

Notes

1. See also Cassesse (1998), Danieli (2004), War Crimes Research Office (2007), de Hemptinne (2010), Holness and Ramji-Nogales (2011), and Victims' Rights Working Group (2010).

2. However, Thulani Grenville-Gray, a South African psychologist, insisted that the retraumatization itself is not necessarily fatal or contrary to mental recovery (Hayner 2001:144).

3. Many scholars in interactionism locate the source of symbolism in a social context, but more radical researchers in ethnomethodology stoically restrict themselves to the ongoing situation.

4. As a remarkable instance, Marcel Duchamp's *Fountain* (1917) invaded the border that demarcated artworks in that era, with the result that the piece was not accepted by the Society of Independent Artists for an exhibition at the Grand Central Palace in New York City. However, the social norm for sanction has changed and the piece is now given a legitimate position in the field of contemporary art.

5. Personal interview at the court, August 2009.

6. Robins (2012:100) and Kent (2012:144) reported the case in the context of East Timor.

7. In this case, known as Grupo Santa Cruz, twelve human-rights activists were kidnapped at the church and later executed by Astiz and other naval officers on December 8–10, 1977.

8. The record of the hearing is available at www.justice.gov.za/trc/hrvtrans/bisho2/gqozo.htm, accessed on January 12, 2018.

9. The following record is available at www.justice.gov.za/trc/amntrans/capetown/capetown_benzien.htm, accessed on January 12, 2018.

10. Kelsall (2013:191–192) offered these colorful details: "'I'm a Mende person. I don't count months,' said one. Counsel would often try and locate stories in time by reference to other well-established events, such as the election, overthrow or restoration of the Kabbah regime, but they were not always successful. . . . When they could not get temporal details, prosecution and judges often resorted to describing witnesses as 'illiterate,' 'unsophisticated' or 'relatively unsophisticated.'"

11. Sierra Leone's GDP per capita in 2016 was $577.

12. This anecdote is based on my interviews with a local NGO staff person in August 2013 and July 2014.

13. The picture is available at https://www.eccc.gov.kh/en/gallery/photo/distribution-appeal-judgement-s-21-survivors-and-civil-parties-3, accessed on January 20, 2018.

14. These pictures can be found at https://www.eccc.gov.kh/en/gallery/photo/distribution-appeal-judgement-s-21-survivors-and-civil-parties-14, accessed on January 20, 2018.

6

From Nation Building to Achieving a Dynamic Equilibrium

Regardless of its options, institutional TJ's official slogan contains an expression of national reconciliation. We can see examples in South Africa, East Timor, Sierra Leone, and Cambodia. Thus, the concern for reconciliation is not limited to truth commissions. TJ is expected, at least in theory, to "close the book," or to collectively promote forgetting (or at least pretending to forget) the past in a public space, by re-presenting past negative experiences through the correct channel. It is assumed that a series of TJ experiences—that is, public announcements, collective mobilization, and staging of official dramas—will bring about a state of social integration often called national reconciliation. Nationalistic discourse, as an expression of national reconciliation, is rhetoric aimed at preventing future occurrences of past atrocities.

This assumption is demonstrated, for example, in the symbolic banner of "healing our nation" and in the typical type of commissioner's comment: "Your sacrifice provided the basis for the rebuilding of our country." These are without doubt discourses for nation building. An institutional TJ program may thus be understood as a type of nationalistic state project in a post-conflict or transitional society.

However, these nationalistic utterances or discourses regarding TJ activities have not escaped critical analysis by scholars, who see them as a simplifying lens applied to various forms of victimhood and as being used by governments to justify and manipulate the past for their own political aims (see Chapter 3 on the pastoral power of TJ authority in Foucauldian analysis).

As shown in the previous chapters, the basic three steps of institutional TJ programs have not succeeded in controlling locals' behavior. It is logically difficult to imagine that the last step can be reached by a fortunate jump, and the case studies demonstrate that indeed this jump does not occur. But a TJ system can influence its society in different ways than those suggested by the official slogans. This chapter references the concepts of "contentious coexistence" (Leigh Payne), "substate nationalism" (Will Kymlicka), and "mimetic desire" (René Girard) as alternative ways of understanding how locals relate to the developing collective bond, as I consider what forms of social cohesion may appear in a transitional society through unexpected interaction among locals. The South African case in the years following that country's Truth and Reconciliation Commission period is examined as an example.

Institutional TJ as a Nation-Building Project

In his famous 1882 lecture "*Qu'est-ce qu'une nation?*" (What Is a Nation?), French historian Ernest Renan pointed out that a nation is defined as much by what it chooses to forget as by what it chooses to remember. Remembering everything, he said, could present a threat to national cohesion and self-image; therefore, forgetting the violence and unity-threatening events while remembering the heroes and the glory days is required (Renan 1990:11). Eric Hobsbawm has traced the use of national symbols and images, such as flags and anthems, invented in the modern era for the purpose of nation building. "They are highly relevant," he stated, "to that comparatively recent historical innovation, the 'nation,' with its associated phenomena: nationalism, the nation-state, national symbols, histories and the rest" (Hobsbawm 1983:13). His observation illuminates the fact that an attempt at nation building is always accompanied by the selection of a few symbolic objects and agents.

Victims, or a few victims officially selected by a TJ body, are presented as emblematic agents for national reconciliation in the course of "transformation of private, individual memory into shared public knowledge" (Humphrey 2003:172). The image of *ideal victims* is utilized as an agent for nation building. "Therapeutic ethics" (Colvin 2003), which assumes personal as well as collective healing through truth-telling, endorses the procedure.

These amalgams of the grammar of nationalism in a political transition, nation-building policy, and therapeutic ethics have been embodied in the context of East Timor by placing "ordinary people at the centre of the national debate on healing, reconciliation and justice" (Commission for Reception, Truth, and Reconciliation in East Timor 2005:33). The chairperson of CAVR said at the public hearing on women and conflict, "In telling your stories, sharing them with all the people in our nation, you are helping to create a new culture of peace in our new land so that this violence will never be repeated" (Kent 2012:90).

Close the Book and Forget the Past, or Remember Selectively

A state mechanism of nation building under the banner of national reconciliation sets in advance the boundaries as to who should be represented in the public arena of truth demonstration and what can be mentioned for the collective good, as we have seen in Chapter 3 (whereas an excessively controlled speech code has been criticized, such as in the Rwandan case described in Chapter 4). Often in this sort of reconciliation schema, a position on what constitutes proper victimhood excludes certain social groups, such as former Khmer Rouge victims in Cambodia, residents in former Shining Path strongholds in Peru, and Hutu victims in Rwanda.

The grammar of nationalism is designed to encourage a nation to follow a model of *ideal victims as heroes* via the concept of survivors. The South African TRC demonstrated such a grammar in the concluding remark made by the chairperson at the hearing for each victim. Following is an example:

> Moloko and the family, we would like you to note that the death of Maki was a national shame. . . . Maki and the family have emerged, after all these disclosures, as heroes. I would say the people in this hall who have heard this testimony are witnesses of how noble Maki was and I will, without shame, request this house to stand and observe a moment of silence. Can we all rise. Thank you.[1]

Another survivor was blessed in the following manner: "You've lost a great deal, but now after all of that time, we have come to a new society, a new democracy and we hope that in some way you will feel that the things that you experienced were part of the process of transformation of our country and in that way you have made a contribution."[2]

In East Timor, the grammar appeared as follows: "CAVR has sought to construct the Indonesian period as a story of heroic endurance, unity, national liberation, and sacrifice, and to write individuals' painful experiences of suffering and death into the wider story of the march towards freedom" (Kent 2012:119).

A former president of East Timor stated in his book, *A Hero's Journey*, "Many people complain and accuse myself and the State of forgetting the suffering of the past, forgetting the sentiments of the victims. I always say that during a liberation struggle we cannot use the term 'victims'; they are all heroes."[3] Major Mau Buti, a prominent FALINTIL (the military wing of the opposition in East Timor) veteran, is reported to have said: "We should not talk about victims of war in Timor-Leste. Those who died are not victims of war, but heroes because they won."[4] Kent backed this public norm of discourse by citing this clause from the Constitution of the Democratic Republic of Timor-Leste: "The Democratic Republic of

East Timor acknowledges and values the secular resistance of the Maubere people against foreign domination and the contribution of all those who fought for national independence."[5]

Although "heroic stories were viewed as a means of binding together 'the people' based on a shared past and perceived solidarity, and imagining a new postcolonial national identity," Kent warns that they also generate a hierarchy among victims and that, in implicitly downgrading "those perceived not to have made sacrifices for the resistance, among them traitors, collaborators, returned diaspora, women and young people, the resistance narrative holds the capacity to divide as much as unite" (Kent 2012:137).

Other, more expansive critiques of TJ's nationalistic inclination have linked the presumed influence of TJ to the succeeding xenophobic disturbances in South Africa, arguing that the TRC's nationalism fostered an exclusive sentiment among South Africans toward other foreign African migrants. Drawing on the TRC as the site of the founding myth of the "rainbow nation," Nahla Valji (2003) connects the notion of all South Africans being victims—healing the wounded nation—to the sense of exclusionist identity.

But there should be at least two objections to this alleged connection between TRC programs and xenophobic exclusionism. First, no program or discourse of the TRC promoted or supported any exclusivism toward foreign Africans who had been the main target of xenophobic attacks in recent South Africa. Both African victimhood and the perpetration of crimes by secret missions of the apartheid government in other countries on the African continent were simply dropped off the official agenda. Second, we have seen few positive signs of national solidarity or integral identity shared in South Africa as a whole. For instance, in the very early stage of political transition, the 1995 Rugby World Cup, which was hosted and won by South Africa, was analyzed as contributing to the promotion of a sense of pride in being "we South Africans." President Mandela wore the Springbok jersey, having been the symbol of the oppressor's sport, and gave the championship trophy to the Afrikaner captain. The scene was repeatedly circulated on television and generally accepted by many South Africans as a symbol of racial reconciliation. Yet it was surely a temporal event with no sustainability, and it occurred before the TRC's work had even begun. We can again refer to the attitudinal survey conducted by the Institute for Justice and Reconciliation, which was introduced in Chapter 4, that illustrated no substantial progress among racial groups toward national solidarity during the post-TRC period. Others, such as Clark, have raised similar doubts about the achievement of this ideal in TJ contexts elsewhere. Clark stated, "The greater problem with the government's view, however, concerns its expected outcomes of popular participation in gacaca. The government's discourse concerning a lost sense of national unity that must be regained through gacaca is highly unconvincing" (Clark 2010:146).

Looking back to the politics of victimhood, or the politics of entitlement—which suggests those who suffered more should be rewarded more—it becomes clear that TJ as a nationalistic project faces destabilizing factors even though it appeals to the notion that we are all victims.

In light of such data and stories, this chapter proposes the following questions. Can these nationalistic discourses that have appeared in a TJ program be assessed as valid in a post-TJ context? And is the analytical framework of nationalism fit to assess the effectiveness, impact, and influence of TJ in the concerned society?

Sociology of Nationalism and TJ

Scholarship on nationalism in the contemporary social sciences has been inclined to deploy arguments on its causation and grounding mechanisms. The basic question is why an irrational sense of nationalism has been aggressively accepted and passionately supported through the modern era, and even in highly scientific, late-capitalist societies. In response to this question, Anthony Smith posited the notion of primordial ethos (*ethnie*), whereas Ernest Gellner proposed an instrumentalist approach, according to which the political elites have used nationalism to acclimatize citizens to an industrialized society. In a different approach, Benedict Anderson coined the now popular phrase "imagined community" to suggest that nationalism is a historical phenomenon that arises from the people's shared experience of printed scripts—such as newspapers, novels, bureaucratic documents, and religious scriptures—in a national language within a state territory.

In the context of transitional society, TJ as a nationalistic policy seems to be explained mainly by an instrumentalist approach, which says that TJ programs, or the political elites who set them up, use past victimhood to implement a nation-building agenda as well as to pursue social stabilization. More straightforward critiques indicate bluntly that they use victims for political purposes. Moderate but compelling criticisms refer to a Foucauldian viewpoint on the power of knowledge production in any specific framing of the past. Anderson's argument supplements this orientation with the existence of official records, such as a truth commission report or court verdicts, that should be shared by a new nation as legitimate text. The "founding myth" (Christie 2000) of a new nation is thus materialized by a TJ program. However, these criticisms also imply suspicion or reservations regarding its validity. There is no doubt that official TJ records are read by few locals in a transitional post-conflict society where few people are interested in reading voluminous, detailed professional reports. Ordinary people never read them. Anderson noted that newspapers were "one-day best-sellers" (Anderson 1983:35). For reports, that is less true; for the most part, only foreign experts read them.

Robins (2012:100) described this pattern in the context of East Timor: "[CAVR's] report remains largely inaccessible to ordinary Timorese, both physically and as a result of widespread illiteracy." Kent agreed: "During my fieldwork, in mid-2007 and again in mid-2008, very few respondents had actually seen the truth commission report, or heard about it, let alone read it. Their views, then, were based on the 'idea' of an official history, rather than *Chega!* ['Stop, No More!'] itself" (Kent 2012:144). Indeed, the document was 2,000 pages long, making wide distribution unfeasible.

The reports and court verdicts of truth commissions must understandably be as professional as possible to secure their legitimacy. However, being more legitimate in that sense means that fewer readers can substantially access or understand the contents. Recent developments in information technology have enabled easier access to TJ data online; however, this seems not to have changed the number of people who actually read the official records, which are rather perceived only as symbolic materials reflecting the authority that the TJ projects embody.

Regarding Anderson's argument on imagined community, Nicola Palmer provided an ironic new application of the concept in an interesting observation on the ICTR:

> As one judge, who has dedicated a significant part of her career to international criminal law, articulated in relation to the ICTR and ICTY cases, "something concrete has been done." . . . Just as Anderson argued that newspapers and novels provided the images and symbols of the imagined community of a nation, so the case law of the ICTR provides solidity to the illusive notion of the "international community," reinforcing this community's ability to respond to the Rwandan genocide. In doing so, the case law contributes to the broader building of an international consciousness. (Palmer 2015:62)

Something concrete—this expression reminds us that *something has been constantly increasing* (see Chapter 4) through a TJ setting, and that it can contribute to reinforcing the imagined community among international societies, or perhaps more of an international judicial circle. Not only the verdict but the court itself might function to produce such a community. In the Rwanda case, "Many see it as a 'fig leaf' covering the international community's shameful failure to intervene at the time of the genocide" (Sloane 2012:281).

At first glance, applying the framework of nationalism in analyzing TJ policy is suitable because a post-conflict transitional government publicizes the need to integrate its people. Even though there should be reservations about the extent of the validity of TJ as a nationalistic project, descriptions of nationalistic policy using Foucauldian concepts are still persuasive in articulating the mechanism of diminishing victims' various experiences and memories into a unified version of a past story.

On the other hand, we can recognize that the mainstream theoretical settings of scholarship on nationalism have tended to adopt the logic that social constituents share a core idea or other specific material or symbol. That space has been occupied by a national identity, a primordial ethos that becomes the soil in which nationalism grows, a national tradition is creatively located in the near past, or a discourse pretending that the people have adopted nationalistic sentiments takes hold. Anderson's argument about the significant role of national print-languages in unifying people can be developed in a more abstract way to claim that the use of a specific series of symbols creates and reproduces a sense of "us"—that is, an imagined community.

From Nationalism to Living Together in Conflict

We can also ask whether this framework of nationalism with the basic idea of a shared status is suitable for an analysis of a TJ program and a transitional society. Even if we set aside the assumption that a legal norm is dysfunctional in a transitional society, the perception of TJ among a country's people as revealed in the previous chapters presents further reservations with regard to applying the framework of nationalism to understand TJ.

One auxiliary line of inquiry worth pursuing is the relationship between the two concepts of nation and state in a post-conflict setting. Shu-Yun Ma questioned the perception that nation-states are pervasive in the contemporary world. According to Ma, there are many "state-nations," particularly in the Third World, and their nationhood does not fit the conventional understanding of a nation-state: "The difference between nation-state and state-nation is that the states in the former are formed after nations, whereas in the latter the sequence is just the reverse. Geographically, nation-states are those [where] boundaries of states and nations are more or less coterminous" (Ma 1992:295).

In referring to the post-colonial governments that have gained independence after World War II, Ma maintained, "They inherited a state structure from the colonial power, but with no nation to fill it. Many of the leaders of these new states thus charged themselves with the duty of using the state to build a nation" (Ma 1992:296). When thinking about the availability of conventional arguments on nationalism to transitional post-conflict social settings, Ma's indication of state-nation-ness is suggestive, because it provides an interpretation of statehood that does not need to presuppose any sort of unconditionally shared norms, values, or collective image (which would represent metaphysical forces or influences on behavior) among a society's constituents.

Keeping this relationship between nation and state in mind, we can then turn to Will Kymlicka's work on "substate nationalism" to search for a possible incorporation of arguments on nationalism into TJ contexts. Kymlicka identifies TJ's main official purpose as the nation-building dimension; however, that aim is acknowledged as difficult to realize, particularly in a society where collective identities were the very source of conflict. Another option alternatively proposed is "to acknowledge and legitimize the political mobilization of ethnicity, but to channel this mobilization in peaceful and democratic ways"; this option is explained as "to regularize and normalize ethnic politics, to treat it as an accepted and everyday part of democratic political life, subject to the same rules and conditions as any other form of democratic participation and claims making" (Kymlicka 2010:305).

Normalizing ethnic politics through a multicultural conception of "citizenization" is called a model of accommodating "substate nationalism." The reconciliation framework in Guatemala is understood to be such a case, as it "is promoting a different sort of nation building" (Kymlicka 2010:307). Guatemala's Commission for Historical Clarification, known as CEH (Comisión para el Esclarecimiento Histórico), adopted a "pluricultural" approach to nationhood, giving explicit public recognition to indigenous ethnic identities "in the form of language rights, customary law, [and] legal protections of Mayan sacred sites or dress" (Kymlicka 2010:304–305). This model surely cannot "guarantee that ethnic politics will stay peaceful and democratic," and "the risk that ethnic politics will degenerate into violence may simply be too high" (Kymlicka 2010:306). Moreover, one might worry that it will generate "parallel societies" where social groups stay "side-by-side in relative peace, but unable or unwilling to work together, not feeling any sense of shared purpose or solidarity" (Kymlicka 2010:306–307). The negative possibility of essentializing or fixating on ethnic identity is also indicated. Yet Kymlicka indicates:

> The reality is that all political processes in a multination state (including TJ) inevitably become filtered through the lens of competing nation-building projects. . . . TJ could provide one of the first lessons for citizens in a newly democratic multination state in how to learn to live with the ambiguities of contested nationhood. (Kymlicka 2010:318)

Reflecting on Kymlicka's argument on substate nationalism within a frame of constitutional democracy opens a way forward that departs from the shared model of nationalism. This leads to another question: How can such a divergent argument be deployed in the context of a nation-building policy that presupposes the unified status of dissident people? This chapter proposes a way to make the necessary conversion, focusing on the status of people's coexistence or social cohesion.

Dynamic Equilibrium

Leigh Payne has proposed the concept of "contentious coexistence" in grappling with people's relationships and social conditions in a transitional society. Within this notion, which she further describes as "a conflictual dialogic approach to democracy in deeply divided societies," she stresses the need to realize "the reality and importance of competition over ideas and conflict over values and goals" (Payne 2008:3).

The requisite conversion of viewpoint appears when we consider the status of social cohesiveness as a model of dynamic equilibrium across a certain range of interactions, including conflictive ones, instead of a collective model of subjects who share the common marker of "us." The term *dynamic* indicates change over time in a particular relation, rather than a static configuration of some elements at a certain time. The two concepts of period/duration and change are incorporated into a sustainable relation—social cohesion. The notion of contentious coexistence contains a latent danger that a society in such circumstances may be plagued by unbroken tensions, serious conflict, or even a complete rupture of social integration. However, interactions within the framework of contentious coexistence are presumed to be sustainable in a specific context.

From Coser to Girard via Deliberative Democracy

In sociological thinking, we can go back to Lewis Coser, or Georg Simmel through Coser's work, to find a basis for the notion of dynamic equilibrium. For Coser, the term *adversary* contains a clue for further negotiation: "Conflict is seen as a binding element between parties that may previously have stood in no relation to each other. . . . By definition, engaging in conflict with another party means that a relationship with that party has been established" (Coser 1956:121–122). The existence of a conflict is understood as evidence that two parties share some form of communication, because "the very outbreak of conflict usually denotes that there exists a common object of contention" (Coser 1956:123). Coser offered this example:

> A conflict over the ownership of a piece of land implies that both parties to the conflict accept the idea of property rights and the general rules regarding the exercise of those rights. What they are fighting about is not the principle, but its application in the specific case. . . . Property laws, accepted in common by the parties, constitute a unifying bond between them. (Coser 1956:123)

This explanation suggests that the conflicting parties can at least share a specific value or meaning despite their conflict. Furthermore, Coser suggests that in the course of lasting conflict, the meta-rule of conflict may change and create a new rule within the conflicting process: "By bringing about new situations, which are partly or totally undefined by rules and norms, conflict acts as a stimulus for the establishment of new rules and norms" (Coser 1956:124).

In Kymlicka's argument on substate nationalism within the frame of constitutionalism, a new rule that requires a balance between admitting a certain group's ethnic identity and remaining vigilant against state instability replaces the old rule of nation building with a unified national identity in the course of conflicting transition. Thus, Coser's consideration helps us to assume the compatibility of continuing conflict between parties, on the one hand, and, at the same time, the existence and growth of negotiation around the meaning of any public matter. This status can be subsumed under the frame of dynamic equilibrium.

Yet we need to pursue a condition, in the context of a transitional society, that makes conflict "a stimulus for the establishment of new rules and norms" for conflicting parties. Even though Coser's proposition might indicate that any conflict is inherently rooted in the presence of stakeholders whose views of each other may change, giving more consideration to the triggering conditions that could push conflicting parties to the point of violence is required in a transitional context.

Our task here is a paradoxical one. Based on Coser's argument, conflict should be viewed as a social opportunity that enables an explicit binding effect between conflicting parties, or a continuing relationship. Yet presupposing a situation where conflicting parties will converge to a united status with a shared identity should be avoided, because sharing such a symbol in a sustainable fashion requires a prior common ground among the conflicting parties that is not present here. Further, a mechanism not to let parties revert to armed conflict is better suited to the present discussion.

A hint comes from the following questions: "How can separation become a principle of union? And how can hatred keep the very ones who hate bound together?" (Girard 1976:213). If we focus, particularly in Coser's works, on such elements as the sustainability of conflicting relationships and norm-creating functions, arguments around deliberative democracy should be added to the picture. Weighing the sustainability of conflicting relationships corresponds to a process-oriented approach and a norm-creating function, which connotes the transformation of conflicting subjects in the course of conflict. This expectation of a deliberative-democracy approach, the transformation of conflicting subjects, has been remarkably exhibited in the TJ context, especially when it is adopted to deepen the function of reconciliation discourse.

Unintended Consequences of Nation Building in Post-TRC South Africa

What the Politics of Reconciliation Creates

In discussing the meaning and social function of the South African TRC, scholars of deliberative democracy and related fields have established a unique perspective in which contestation, expressions of disagreement or discontent, and lingering negotiation are interpreted as symptoms of positive social change after the implementation of TJ policies. Amy Gutmann and Dennis Thompson (2000:38) explain the significance of deliberation with the term "democratic reciprocity," especially in light of "the economy of moral disagreement." In the context of democratic reciprocity, they argue, consensus among contesting parties is not necessarily essential. They insist that such a perspective is not only realistic but also desirable in a deeply divided society such as South Africa.[6]

Erik Doxtader (2009:288–289) also spoke positively about the scenario in which words of reconciliation served as a trigger to change the character of a relationship of conflict: "Appeals for reconciliation employed speech to create a time for speaking . . . a process of rhetorical invention that turned justifications for enmity into the potential for productive opposition." Thus, disagreement, discontent, distrust, and resilience—all expressed not only among the conflicting parties but even toward the TRC itself—are transformed into meaningful signs of the "power of political rhetoric" (Doxtader 2009), "deliberative democracy" (Gutmann and Thompson 2004), "aversive democracy"[7] (Norval 2007), and "agonism"[8] (Schaap 2005) that weighs the significance of constant struggle in politics rather than reaching a point of consensus. In a profound sense, these signs prove the existence and pervasiveness of democratic circumstances or a democratic ethos (Norval 2007:213).

The fact that the South African TRC and its predecessors and successors in other countries have not officially established a core definition of reconciliation during their work lays the foundation for a productive opposition to emerge discursively. In other words, the lack of a legitimized definition is expected to elicit diverse and constant debate over the meaning or possibility of reconciliation. When Doxtader (2009:286) says that "calls for reconciliation set language into the motion of speech," he is pointing out that even the lack of a shared understanding of reconciliation can create an accommodation for "individual and collective (inter)action and productive (dis)agreements" (p. 20). Moreover, in such an accommodation, "reconciliation provides a common vocabulary within which citizens may contest the terms and possibility of their political association" (Schaap 2005:13). Here, we can recognize an inversion of the ordinary usage of the term. Doxtader

(2009:24) sums up this position simply: "I do not answer the question of whether reconciliation in South Africa 'worked.' . . . I suggest that this persistent question is very much the wrong question."

Many people tend toward a tacit understanding that reconciliation is or can be an ultimate goal; thus, they may negatively assess scenarios in which the word is not officially defined (Van der Merwe and Chapman 2008:254). They consider the lack of a definition of reconciliation as an official omission that fails to provide adequate direction and goals for a public program (Duffy 2010:34). On the contrary, the insights of Erik Doxtader and Andrew Schaap show that words and works of reconciliation without any public definition generate unique social phenomena, which are clearly distinguishable from the standpoints that explore the fundamental conditions that bring about true reconciliation.

However, one important concern remains. Did the people who did not accept the officially provided understanding of reconciliation—one that requires forgiveness of or sympathetic dialogue with the former enemy through the TRC process and advocates these actions as essential steps toward national healing—did these people truly behave as democratic subjects? Charles Villa-Vicencio, who worked as the head of the South African TRC's research unit, once noted the people's dilemma: "Most South Africans are ambivalent about reconciliation, finding themselves pushed and pulled between recognizing the need for reconciliation and complete indifference toward it" (Villa-Vicencio 2003:33–34). The theorists of deliberative democracy and agonistic politics dare to assume a rational subject who (explicitly or implicitly) approves the establishment of accommodations where opponents are also guaranteed opportunities to express an adversarial remark in a transitional society in which abiding animosity among the groups remains. They assume that the TRC helped to forge such a specific accommodation. However, considering the "pragmatic and resistant" subjects that Richard Wilson (2001) observed at TRC venues and the internal discord that describes, does the assumption of a "democratic subject" actually fit with the people's attitude under the circumstances? One can also assume that ordinary people may decline to use force in the face of severe discontent with opponents—not because they approved of their opposition's political rights, but only because they realized that force would not effectively resolve the situation. They may not have started debating spontaneously on the contents of reconciliation; instead, the politics of reconciliation had already started when they were themselves embroiled in the accommodation of contestation. Rather, as Villa-Vicencio remarks, the dilemma and discord in which they might be caught needs to be articulated.

In discussions of the effects of pursuing reconciliation (not just political coexistence) at a social level, irrational factors and deviations from rational attitudes, which are induced by the ambiguous ideal of reconciliation, are considered essential. Paying attention to a specific tendency of people's attitudes when they disagree, the following argument will diverge from the theory of deliberation or agonism to address a factor that sustains the enduring contestation. The notion of desire is applied to the discussion—invoking René Girard's argument—to understand both the factor that sustains the contestation and its outcome.

Sustainable Relationship in Animosity and Competence

Disagreement may be expressed publicly in various ways, but with a definite overarching theme. Schaap indicates the specific relationship between the concept of reconciliation and how South African people disagree with it as follows: "Actors may disagree over what form reconciliation should take or how it should be realized. However, even the most conservative supporter and the most radical opponent of the old regime are likely to agree that reconciliation is a desirable social good in the changed political circumstances in which they find themselves" (Schaap 2005:12).

This dilemma involved in undertaking the ideal of reconciliation is widely witnessed in post-TRC South Africa. Some people supported the idea of reconciliation but were critical of the TRC (Foster, Haupt, and de Beer 2005:238). A number of reservations emerged in political discourse: There will be no reconciliation until our movement or political demand is appropriately admitted;[9] reconciliation is itself an adequate idea but is not acceptable in our present relation with opponents;[10] reconciliation is agreeable, but truth-finding should be regarded as the priority (Jeffery 1999); and reparation to the victims, for reconciliation, shall be paid, but by the present (ANC) government, because we were in "just war" circumstances.[11] These discourses bring to mind a newspaper cartoon drawn by Zapiro that characterized the criticisms of the TRC (Figure 6.1).

In the cartoon, Archbishop Tutu, the chairperson of the TRC, manages to execute a truth-gathering mission and reach Mandela, the symbol of reconciliation. Tutu is attacked with arrows by various political positions but is not fatally wounded. The message is that the South African people did not reject all matters related to reconciliation and accepted the significance of reconciliation as a direction, but rejected the unified condition in which the ideal of reconciliation was embodied. The lack of public definition of reconciliation and the TRC's weak institutional legitimacy laid the groundwork for the emergence of this dilemma.

Whereas the aforementioned scholars infer that this reconciliation dilemma brings about democratic reciprocity or perpetual agonism, the argument I present here focuses on a more irrational factor—desire—and incorporates René Girard's (1976:2) argument on the triangular structure of desire. When "the TRC opened up areas of contestation around the character

Figure 6.1 The TRC chair was attacked by all the political parties.
Cartoon by Zapiro, Sowetan © 1998. All rights reserved.

of nationhood, national identity, history, truth and justice" (Norval 2007:206), such contestation required the participants to develop superior and comprehensive remarks on these subjects. My further inference proceeds from that point to the stage where the conflicting parties each come to want to assert and possess such a superior and comprehensive understanding of the character of nationhood, national identity, history, truth, and justice. The notion of desire might offer us a different understanding of the potential relationships among dissidents in the course of TJ, as opposed to the former normative tone of deliberative democracy.

According to Girard (1976:2, 7), desire "can always be portrayed by a simple straight line which joins subject and object," but an ordinary perceived "spontaneous" desire is thought to be an outcome of imitating a desire "by another person whom he admires."[12] A desire appears in a person's mind because a person "admires" someone, or views someone as a model, who has owned that specific desire to the object. A desire is not intrinsically borne in one's subjectivity: "Rivalry does not arise because of the fortuitous convergence of two desires on a single object; rather, the subject desires the object because the rival desires it" (Girard 1977:145). When the desire is consciously held by the subject, then the mediator, or a model, appears as a rival. A subject, an object, and a mediator or model constitute the triangular structure. In interactions between the subject and the mediator, "each imitates the other while claiming that his own desire is prior and previous" (Girard 1976:99). Girard states that a mediator and an object can be imaginary or metaphysical, and a subject's desire always entails an ambivalent emotion toward a mediator. Further, an object can never be possessed in a stable manner (Girard 1976:4, 40, 88–89).

The sociological significance of Girard's conception of *mimetic desire* to the present argument can be summarized in the following two points: (1) desire, which is deemed to be one of the strong and uncontrollable factors that drive human behavior, is explained as a product of the behavior of imitation, and (2) people's lasting concern for and interaction with one another can be imagined without referring to mutual recognition in a positive manner or rational acceptance of a social norm such as rights and values. The second point is crucial in exploring feasible social cohesion or coexistence in a post-conflict society, considering the dysfunction of legal norms and the mutual distrust that remains following a conflict. Formation of the rivalry and the triangular structure among the participants of contestation brings about a situation in which the participants cannot leave behind the agonistic accommodation. In this argument, people pursue reconciliation neither positively nor spontaneously. The participants cannot deny the principal character or normative aspect of reconciliation, but they are not necessarily passive and subordinate in interpreting the meaning of the term. The object of this triangular structure should be a superior and comprehensive understanding of the character of nationhood, national identity, history, truth, and justice. The desire for a legitimate collective identity or a superior understanding of history is forged in the course of contestation. The parties involved in the triangular structure face a dilemma: they have to elicit the opponent's agreement in the end while maintaining their own position. This task is demanding and suggests the appearance of an abiding relationship with respect to reconciliation. The people are literally involved in a relationship that they did not ask for, and stuck within it, they still hold enmity or distrust toward opponents. Nevertheless, they cannot abandon the relationship, which binds them with an irrational factor: desire.

In view of this dilemma and the strain shared by the contesting parties, as Girard notes,[13] the result could be disastrous: a violent clash. However, the concept of mimetic rivalry still offers the possibility of an orientation toward a durable balance. How does this argument for reconciliation based on the rivalry scheme differ from those of agonistic politics and deliberative democracy? Schaap proposes "a community that is not yet" to be shared by participants in the agon (the struggle). Participants may hold different interpretations of that image; however, the community is perpetually in a fictional position that can be described, according to Mouffe's (2005:149) account, as "a good that exists as good only as long as it cannot be reached." This insight encapsulates the dual aspects of reconciliation that people have to grapple with in a contradictory manner. Yet this account does not suggest the factor or drive that makes the relationship among participants in the agon, or the motivation for participation in the agon, durable. What, then, is the crucial factor that can prevent the participants' attitude from retrogressing to a "benign indifference" (Schaap 2005:5)? Does the internalization of the democratic ethos in a profound sense fit the collective consciousness of a post-conflict society? The argument invoked for a rivalry between a model and a subject, on the other hand, presupposes the people's internal discord arising from the fact that their animosity toward former enemies and their trauma linger even while they are required to coexist with each other. In the newly formed accommodation for contestation, according to Girard's terms, they behave as if they desire a superior and comprehensive frame for the character of nationhood, national identity, history, truth, and justice. Thus, in effect, they create a new conflict, one in which they irrationally desire to imitate the adversary who is deemed to desire the same object(s). What is the essential factor for transforming the adversary into the substantial yet hidden object of desire? First, the adversarial party has been the specific source of the other side's hardships and is now the neighbor with whom the other side has not willingly chosen to coexist. Second, the contesting participants—including the adversarial party—have to explain comprehensively the context in which they have been involved. The dilemma here—that each side has to elicit the agreement of its most specific adversary while maintaining its unique and superior position—prepares the ground for forging the rivalry. In terms of social cohesion, this relationship ensures that a durable and intense balance is maintained, even though a risk of regression to a less stable condition remains. The theoretical pivot of this argument is the function of the paradoxical condition that promotes cohesion. The argument focuses on cohesion as attained through a rivalry that might be developed through the course of contestation over the condition for reconciliation.

Lingering distrust among former enemies and toward the political authority and legal norms makes it difficult to drive the positive changes or outstanding features in people's behavior that would lead to or increase trust in society. On the other hand, in terms of the mechanisms that support lasting social cohesion, Robert Putnam's assertion regarding the virtual world is significant: "If entry and exit are too easy, commitment, trustworthiness, and reciprocity will not develop" (Putnam 2000:177). Zygmunt Bauman (2001:96–97) offers a similar insight in referring to "really existing communalism" and the "resilience of community" among people such as those belonging to ethnic minorities: the former (really existing communalism) is "naturally" generated among those who are "denied the right to assimilation," and the latter "gives it [the ethnic minority community] a survivalist edge over [other types of] communities" instead of a restriction "in the freedom of community members." Both arguments lend themselves greatly to thinking about the possibility of substantially lasting cohesion in a contemporary society where any relationships can easily be thrown away in favor of a new association, because both these arguments pay attention to the functional role of restrictive factors outside the actor's rational choice in making and keeping cohesion.

Contested Interpretations of "Rainbow Nation" and "Blackness"

What is the merit of adopting this approach in a more general analysis of TJ? Not using the framework of nationalism for TJ allows us to incorporate two external factors that are presumably both essential and critical to the perception and influences of TJ in a given society: namely, the other policies and social conditions that may affect the people's perception of post-conflict transitional policy in general and the post-TJ phase. The former are synchronically external to TJ programs and the latter are diachronically external to TJ activities. If we do not view TJ as a nationalistic program, a methodological focus on the nature of social cohesion opens a space for a more flexible analysis of its influence.

As one such attempt, the following section will address the case of interracial relationships in post-TRC South Africa. The expectation of complete reconciliation or social integration has been abandoned in the face of resistance, disputes, indifference, and autonomous divergences. However, through such divergences, actors can create their own social space and communication network. Through the process, actors who were formerly separated are able to compete with each other; thus, a triangular form of model-rival, subject, and object functions in such a context.

Looking back to the period of political transition in South Africa, we recall that President Nelson Mandela advocated the idea of a *rainbow nation*, a metaphor for a national unity that would absorb several ethnic and racial groups after the severe and long-lasting conflict among them. One facet of this policy of multiculturalism was embodied in the establishment of eleven national official languages. However, as Bronwyn Harris (2004:3) indicated, the next ANC government, led by Thabo Mbeki (1999–2008), was characterized by a "return to race," tackling more directly the heritage of economic inequality that stemmed from the apartheid regime. The policy of affirmative action, which was applied mainly to the recruitment of public-sector personnel starting in 1994, was not backed by any law or official guideline. Pushed partially by criticism of conventional affirmative action and partially by the need to engage the private sector more substantially in the reallocation of social and economic resources to formerly disadvantaged (non-white) social groups, the Parliament established the Black Economic Empowerment Commission (BEE-Com) in 2001.

The BEE-Com subsequently published a report that directed how companies should address affirmative action in the business field. This institutionalization of affirmative action reflects the legitimated story of the new nation, which called for greater recognition of the historical role played by the people categorized as "black"[14] (i.e., non-whites) in bringing about the present society, one that would be fairer and more united than that under apartheid. For instance, we can refer to the following comment by one of the policy's supporters: "The idea [of the BEE] is to integrate the value of Ubuntu ("I am because you are") into the economic psyche of our country . . . the values that should underpin BEE are firstly integrity and Ubuntu . . . it is the sense of a shared destiny and a shared understanding" (Luhabe 2007:19).

Even though there is no straightforward legitimation of a certain social group in the citation, Ubuntu is recognizable as a word used by black South Africans. BEE is also justified from a historical perspective, particularly invoking the former political enemy, Afrikaners:

> It was on the basis of such clear thinking that the Afrikaners mobilized capital to launch Afrikaner businesses that were capable of rescuing the Afrikaner from British imperial domination. The reddingsdaad (act of rescue) campaign, and the spirit it embodied, foreshadowed the BEE movement, although it was not based on the transfer of capital with the kind of favorable financing schemes or share options we have now. (Luhabe 2007:20)

More aggressive justification of present policies compared with those of the prior Afrikaner government can be read in the following explanation:

> The period of Afrikaner affirmative action first emerged as an idea in the 1930s as the ekonomiese beweging (economic movement), and found expression in the late 1940s with the association of the National Party (NP) to power. . . . The period of the 1950s and 1960s was one of aggressive Afrikaner affirmative action. . . . Without affirmative action and pointed political intervention it is doubtful whether this community could have made the impressive business achievements that are apparent today. (Mafuna 2007:35)

How can we recognize the practice of *imitation*, which I argued for in the previous section, in these expressions of justifying the current affirmative action policy? One of the most notable attitudes displayed by supporters of the BEE policy is that they justify it on the basis that their political rivals, the Afrikaners, implemented the same policy in the past during another time of political transition. Nevertheless, as one black journalist reflects, the promotion of BEE and affirmative action has been implemented without giving sufficient consideration to existing internal tensions among the people categorized as black:

> While SA [South Africa] remains obsessed with the black-white divide, it appears that we are not addressing the colored-black issue or the Indian-black one.... Affirmative action has always been seen in the context of black-white. As a result, the government is seen to have failed to give direction with regard to the colored-black and Indian-black contexts. (Jimmy Seepe, City Press, July 6, 2003)

Although the BEE Act defines the term *black* as including Colored and Indian people, the term as applied in the actual social context is said not to guarantee the same empowerment to each social group. Franklin Sonn, president of the University of Free State, indicates a mentality that white and African businessmen tend to share: "If you empower with coloreds, it is not real empowerment" (*Sunday Times*, May 13, 2007). One notable episode illustrating this distinction is the Eskom[15] lawsuit, which ensued after a Colored employee applied for a promotion and initially received it, but then had the offer withdrawn because "he [was] too white to benefit from the company's affirmative action programme" (*Fin 24* online, April 13, 2006).

Situations such as this one trigger the Colored people's lament, "First we are not white enough and now we are not black enough" (Adhikari 2005:176). According to Mohamed Adhikari, "Expressions of Colored identity have undergone rapid transformation in the post-apartheid environment" (Adhikari 2005:175). And to some extent, this transformation is said to reflect the way affirmative action and BEE have been implemented. Political struggles inside the ruling party are also invoked: "'Blacks' were once united in their opposition to apartheid. Some Coloured political activists remember these times, too. But now some bitterly say that they've been part of a freedom struggle to liberate Africans and enshrine their own second-class citizenship status" (Dennis Cruywagen, *Cape Argus*, February 7, 2011).

These frustrations may well be summed up in an article titled, "ANC Ignores Coloured Contribution to Struggle" (Democratic Alliance councillor Nico du Plessis, *Herald*, April 30, 2010). Such objections have been lodged since the ANC policy was implemented in 1994, particularly regarding the redistribution of social and political resources. The essence of the Colored population's objection is that the historical understanding of the concept of black should be corrected and accurately reflected in the present policy. The affirmative action and BEE initiatives were led mainly by Bantu-speaking black people, who argued that black people's contribution to current society should be officially recognized in the form of concrete redistribution of resources. In contrast, in requiring the legitimate interpretation of the term *black*, the Colored people have adopted the basic strategy that their political rival, the Bantu-speaking black South Africans, used against the Afrikaner. Since the end of apartheid, many Colored people have begun dismissing the category of Colored, insisting instead on the name Khoisan, an umbrella category including the Griqua, Nama, Cape Khoi, San, Korana, and other indigenous groups. Their self-identification as Khoisan marks an effort to claim that they are more legitimate than Bantu-speaking black Africans with regard to authentic indigenous status, because the latter came to present-day South Africa from East Africa after the Khoisan people were already settled. This appeal to indigenous status is crucial on issues concerning ownership of social and political resources because the black South African politicians have grounded their arguments on redistribution policy in their historical claim that they existed in South Africa before the European colonizers arrived. The "newcomer" had historically promoted a wide-ranging apartheid system, they argue, so the new nation needs to balance that unfair and unjust ownership condition. But what happens when this principle is applied to the ethnic differences and disparities among the former non-white peoples, who were unified then and opposed to each other now? In 2014, President Jacob Zuma declared that the government would examine Colored appeals on redistribution policy on indigenous land. The fundamental and open-ended questions of who made what historical contributions to the birth of new South Africa and indeed of who constitutes a South African thus continue to germinate at the core of post-TRC politics in South Africa. Skimming the surface of these movements, it seems that Bantu-speaking African and Colored people have both repeated their predecessors' politics. However, they are not simply pursuing a redeployment of social resources under the banner of affirmative action; rather, they are proposing a logic for reconfiguring their political legitimacy on the new map of a rainbow nation, or a new sense of South African-ness.

The policy introduced by the ANC government was intended to construct a fairer society aimed at pursuing social justice toward a goal of eventual reconciliation. Just as African people promoted their political rights to collective identity and economic and social opportunity against the Europeans, Colored people now began to express dissent from the identity that their African rivals were constructing. The African and Colored arguments do not deny the fundamental framework of the rainbow nation; however, in imitating their political rivals, each group has deployed its contestation about just what the rainbow should be, particularly in terms of the meaning of blackness in South African history. The rainbow nation is the ideal understanding of how reconciliation should move forward. Based on this orientation, stakeholders dispute issues such as a comprehensive national identity and what constitutes a legitimate understanding of history.

Conclusion

Through the course of its activities, an institutional TJ program is publicly expected to realize its function as a medium for nation building. National reconciliation, a slogan espoused by various TJ bodies, points directly toward this formal goal. However, the term *nation building*, when understood under the authentic framing of nationalism based on a model of social constituents sharing a certain collective marker of "us," has been criticized by many scholars as an exclusionary discourse because it cannot respond to the various needs of the many categories of victims.

Further, the expectation that a TJ program can contribute to nation building has not been realized. As such, the following causal inference is suspect: local people in a transitional society promote mutual understanding through the TJ process; collective reconciliation, including its emotional dimensions, is embodied; and a unified national identity is established. In view of this skepticism, can the notion that TJ is a social device for nation building then just be dismissed?

This chapter has tried to answer that question through both a theoretical and empirical approach. Theoretically, it has offered a different view of social cohesiveness, presenting a model of dynamic equilibrium across a certain range of interactions, including conflictual ones, instead of as a collective model of subjects who share the common marker of "us." It focused on continuous communication in the context of persisting contentious, conflicting, or irrational situations. Intentional engagement in such communication was explained with reference to Lewis Coser's interpretation of the function of social conflict, Will Kymlicka's substate nationalism, Leigh Payne's concept of contentious coexistence, and debates around deliberative democracy. René Girard's theme of a rivalry between a model, who is admired by a subject, and a subject who imitates a desire of model-rival with regard to human desire, was viewed as conducive to thinking about the unintentional, durable dimensions of such communication. Thus, this chapter has argued that TJ does not necessarily function as a social device by which nation building can be realized, but that TJ may promote social cohesion as dynamic equilibrium, as a derivative of the official process.

An empirical case study was provided to substantiate this theoretical argument, addressing the relationship between the Khoisan (Colored) and black Africans in South Africa. Current South African society is an arena for newly developed identity politics among people formerly classified as non-white. In this context, tension has been rising around the concept of legitimate South African-ness. A political movement in South Africa since 1994 has required the redistribution of social and political resources in favor of formerly oppressed people, in parallel to the TJ initiative. The ANC government has been implementing such affirmative-action policies based on the logic that the special conditions of national reconciliation call for establishing a new South African collective self, and that this process should include the proper redistribution of social resources to the social groups that have contributed most to the birth of the new political regime. The ANC has adopted this stance as a representative of non-colonialist locals, yet ethnic inclination to favor black South Africans in the actual distribution has caused tension. This affirmative-action policy has been reinforced in political discourse since the Mbeki government, using a logic rooted in the policies of the Afrikaner apartheid government that was established in 1948. The resulting tensions between the Khoisan (Colored) and black people have again problematized the notion of "us," particularly regarding the proper way to redistribute social resources.

In this sense, post-TRC South Africa is still engaged in a dynamic negotiation in the process of its realization of a collective self. Retrospectively, the South African TRC was evaluated as not having functioned as a social device that made the harmonious image of "us" real. Yet it started a new negotiation among hidden rivals on the possibility of a collective identity. This negotiation is not free from political deals, maneuvering, and domestic political influence, and it is not necessarily perceived as a positive sign. But the continuation of questions such as "What can we be?" or "How can we define 'us'?" can function to prevent exclusionary political stances, such as those exhibited by sects of black supremacists, from becoming firmly fixed in the political landscape.

These circumstances point toward the following more abstract understanding of TJ. TJ started its work as a steward of the ideal of national reconciliation and was expected to be a social device to promote nation building; however, that direction has not necessarily been realized, leaving space for further negotiation or conflict among stakeholders regarding the correct definition of "us," or the ideal collective image. Nevertheless, these consequences can be perceived as bringing about the mechanism by which former adversaries—who cannot recognize the opposite party's legitimacy via rational dialogue because of various obstacles, including the influence of psychological trauma—maintain their relationship through conflicting communication. This mechanism can be counted as one of the many unintended consequences of an institutional TJ process.

Notes

1. Human Rights Violation Hearing (Case No. JB0289), February 4, 1997, Duduza, South Africa.

2. Human Rights Violation Hearing (testimony by Beauty Tantsi), October 7, 1996, De Aar (Karoo), South Africa.

3. Gusmão, *A Hero's Journey* (2006), cited in Kent (2012:119).

4. Mau Buti, cited in World Bank (2008:4).

5. Section 11(1), cited by Kent (2012:119).

6. It could be inferred, for instance, that even if societal contestation did not result in consensus, NGOs would attempt to make up for the deficiencies of government programs, and the internal networks of civil society would thus be enriched. This can be counted as a positive outcome that may be derived from deliberation without official resolution.

7. For Norval, "Democracy . . . should be thought of as a form of life rather than a regime" and the emphasis is on the role of disagreement, dissatisfaction, and "separateness of positions." The TRC is evaluated as a site where all the contestation, including objections to the site itself, is provided in the context of "problematization of the given, of prevailing opinion" (Norval 2007:185).

8. Referring to the work of Hannah Arendt, Schaap (2005:67) explains that "the affirmation of agonism requires an openness and ongoing responsiveness to others and to the world, a willingness to share the world with different others."

9. This position was held by the ANC and the Pan Africanist Congress (Krog 1998:379–381).

10. Taken from a participant's comment at a public TRC hearing at Duduza, personal interview, February 4, 1997.

11. A position taken by the former National Party and reported in the *Saturday Star*, August 31, 1996.

12. This point is similar to the concept of *reference individuals* (Merton 1957:302); however, the concept does not contain any paradoxical dimension where a subject possessing a desire and a mediator occupying a model position for a subject share the rivalry and the tension stemming from the relationship. The insight that a subject of desire in Girard's argument imitates a mediator without self-awareness should also be noted.

13. Girard once (1977:148) described "mimetic desire" as a catalyst that "would destroy the entire community if the surrogate victim were not at hand to halt the process." However, he later adopted the more modest standpoint that mimetic desire is not inherently harmful unless it becomes aggravated along a wrong orientation, and that because such desire is part of human nature, we cannot abandon mimetic acts any more than we could give up food and sleep (Girard and Treguer 1994:70). Because Girard considers preservation of tradition as a positive effect of imitation, mimetic desire also applies at a collective level.

14. The Broad Based BEE Act (No. 53 of 2003) defines a black person as an African, Colored, or Indian South African. See https://www.environment.gov.za/sites/default/files/legislations/bbbee_act.pdf, accessed April 21, 2018.

15. Eskom is the largest electricity company in South Africa. The judgment of the Cape arbitration court was published in April 2006, supporting Eskom's position.

7

Planning for Unplanned Social Recovery

In the episodes described in Chapters 3 to 6, the common theme is the successive divergence and derivation from the official plans of institutional TJ, with various ramifications. An official institution announces a new social direction with a national ideal, yet people's reactions might be skeptical. A call for mobilization to a public venue for an official event may be reluctantly accepted by locals because of its obligatory character, or the locals may listen attentively but not agree with the official message. Another opportunity different from the official program may instead attract locals' participation. People who appear formally compliant by attending an official theater with political drama may often challenge a planned scenario or simply misunderstand it, bringing about other actors' unexpected involvement that makes the stage even more complicated.

A series of formal steps is generally required for the institutional design of contemporary TJ because it is expected to contribute to a stable national identity, so as to protect a post-conflict transitional society against the recurrence of conflict or of undemocratic forms of social control. However, considerable animosity and grudges may remain, causing the social objectives of TJ (such as mutual respect and acceptance among former enemies) to be negatively assessed. Clearly, the local reactions and post-TJ realities demonstrate that the operations of institutional TJ produce unintended consequences, which appear as derailments from four expectations (examined in Chapters 3 to 6) that normatively support establishment of a TJ program: people's agreement with TJ's objectives, forming motivation to participate in the process, meekly experiencing an official drama played out in public events, and molding a collective identity based on a unified memory and official documents. It is understandable that many critics evaluate such TJ programs as failed projects. When one skims the surface of the local chaos that frequently appears to represent the empirical influence of TJ on a local society, one might plausibly view the situation as a malfunction. Weinstein's (2011:3) description of the "buzzwords" of justice and reconciliation, which "have no consistent definition or conceptual clarity and promote mechanisms to achieve these obscure outcomes with little evidence," might be appropriate in this context.

This chapter analyzes the nature and ramifications of these local responses to formal TJ projects as types of unintended consequences. Actual forms of social recovery are not necessarily consistent with those planned by any institutional project, but they can be interpreted as a type of unexpected meaning-making within a residual space of official failure—that is, where the planned program has somehow proved inadequate. Locals in a social context of multiple distrust often struggle to autonomously express and pursue their own political agenda in the same way that social movements do in the global North. On the other hand, their self-recovery cannot be ensured by an official court process, as international judicial experts expect. A paradox is involved here. A TJ project is assessed positively in this volume if the project's stated goals have been substantially achieved, even if that achievement comes mainly through the unintended consequence of stimulating other forms of meaning-making within the society.

Beyond the Success-Failure Debate on TJ Implementation

In Chapter 2, we saw why it is not appropriate to conclude that a TJ program is destined to fail. Given the circumstances of the transitional society where a TJ program is initiated, being beset by various criticisms is a natural consequence of any TJ attempt. Typically, a transitional society faces pervasive and multidirectional distrust among locals. In such a circumstance, an institution hindered by insufficient preparation time, a shortage of resources, and a limited mandate will be forced to end its activities at an incomplete stage. The four expectations of contemporary TJ at the normalized stage will be evaluated in this context.

Thus, an institutional TJ process encompasses a fundamental dilemma from the outset. On the one hand, a TJ design that rationally assesses the difficulties ahead and warns in advance of the uncertain results would lose sympathy and support both within and outside the country, worsening the conditions that should contribute to the realization of institutional objectives. Too sincere and realistic a blueprint might induce a negative result, in the form of a self-fulfilling prophecy. A TJ program, which should contribute to promoting democratization, formally requires democratic means of deliberation and communication, such as logical explanations of policy. Yet it will inevitably entail a degree of uncertainty and risk.

A TJ program offers a positive vision along the following lines: although a shortage of resources and a large amount of anxiety remain among the people in charge of implementing the plan, by stimulating people's emotions, increasing the number of project supporters through discursive engagement of the people concerned, and channeling people's interactions in the public space in a positive direction, the final objective, such as realization of a new national identity, in the appearance of national reconciliation, may be achievable. This is just an expectation until any action based on it is taken. For this prediction to be fulfilled, the publication of too-sincere calculations and simulations must be avoided from a strategic viewpoint. In such a sense, a TJ program needs to begin its work in an insincere way. In contrast to these rosy projections, the truth that gambling has a statistically high probability of ending in failure seems to have been applied to this field in scholarly assessments.

Recently, the term *spin* has appeared in political journalism to describe debates in highly democratized countries that are strongly influenced by the mass media. Classic political propaganda in a new guise, incorporating advanced information technologies and advertising techniques, has crystallized into a form that arouses collective interest and emotional sympathy by offering an appealing political objective without any realistic description of the process needed to achieve it. For an actor who adopts spin tactics, the word *failure* never exists. Even if the gap between the real data and his or her words is questioned, such carefully prepared explanations as the following will spew forth: the previous expression has reflected only an imperfect understanding of the issue concerned, or the words may have contained slight exaggerations. This problem will then be immediately solved by updating the expression with new information.

Needless to say, this is one of the newest defense mechanisms for a political actor who has to tackle the contingent nature of messaging in public space; the method of aggressively controlling such contingencies is to skillfully exploit various forms of public media. The strategy of spin aims at the audience's reflective reaction, roused by the surface of stimulating messages, while the message covertly indicates that its literal content is not very important.[1] Yet its strategy, which shares common characteristics with contemporary advertising techniques, also has a point that could be applied to the "insincere way" of designing an institutional TJ: by increasing the number of project supporters, the final objective may be realized; in order for the blueprint to be realized, the overly sincere calculations and simulations would need to be hidden from public view.

One of the reasons that past TJ projects have always been critically assessed shows up here, and research works have not successfully grasped the implications stemming from such an analytical trend. The cases in Chapter 2 illustrate the basic condition of a transitional society, in which a project based on normative objection cannot be guaranteed its normative status in society. Under such a condition, in order to have increasing positive perception among local recipients about the future, a TJ project needs a strategic action, such as the one taken in the advertising field. The strategic action of the current institutional TJ takes place along with this scenario, which, in this volume, is identified in four formal steps. This scenario is formed based on the expectations of policy makers and supporters, including outside donors, but whether the expectations generated by the four steps of TJ design fit for the local society cannot be assured. On the surface of implementation of the project, the more locals' positive comments, as well as the more people participating in the project that are counted in public, the more the scenario would seem to be legitimate when publicly demonstrated. A social reaction follows the implementation of any public action. However, according to the various derivatives and deviations drawn in the previous chapters, even when seemingly positive reactions are found in a local context in the TJ process, we should be cautious about the "black box" between the TJ's official objective and local reactions. Put differently, understanding a TJ project as a social construction based on the expected scenario demands that we search for another avenue for assessment rather than attempting to use cause–effect logic to find the internal reason for local reactions in the TJ process.

Meaning-Making in the Transitional Justice Process

We will now look back at the local divergences described in the previous chapters with these considerations in mind.

In Chapter 4, we observed that the Khulumani Support Group in South Africa represents an unplanned derivative of the TRC, changing its stance from supplementing the TRC's victim-oriented policy to spontaneously developing ways to cope with victims' needs. Its meaning-making activities included securing a space for sharing experiences among victims, constructing its own stages at various venues, and pursuing legal justice. The group never would have formed without the truth commission, but it has now taken on a life of its own.

The South African History Archive (SAHA) has adopted the idea that the truth commission is a social phenomenon. Based on that idea, its archives on the process of finding, recording, and sharing the truth have expanded beyond the TRC's institutional limitations. SAHA has also focused on the politically sensitive and therefore hidden information contained in the TRC's closed-door hearings. After more than ten years of negotiation with the Department of Justice, the government has revealed information from secret files, illuminating the truth about the truth commission.

By monitoring research on the relationship among formerly conflicting parties in South Africa, the Institute for Justice and Reconciliation has been dealing with the perpetually unfinished business of TJ. Even though the IJR's research shows the complex and lingering difficulties involved in improving racial relationships, its insights on these interactions can be critically applied to further policy implementation. Although one cannot define the term *transitional* in a way that is valid for everyone, a TJ body cannot continue its work forever. A local spontaneous offshoot like the IJR fills the gap between the people's need for transition and institutional limitations in dealing with a political transition. As explained in the prior section, a TJ project needs to attract locals' pervasive attention to its program, and for that purpose, the organization also needs to provide an appealing societal slogan that contains ethical, moral, and aspirational dimensions, as well as an urgently required collective status, such as mutual trust with former enemies. However, these elements are all difficult to realize in just a few years of TJ operation. If it were to only check the reaction to an official TJ program, an assessment would almost certainly be destined to be negative.

In the same vein, Fambul Tok in Sierra Leone was established by a former TRC staffer who was not satisfied with the program but recognized the potential of the TRC's basic idea. Cultural elements were arranged and incorporated into the organization's newly invented ceremonies. Foreign observers might view such a retreat to a more local method of meaning-making as negative, as they rather anticipate the realization of a universal rule of law or democratic political system. Yet the efforts pursued here might actually produce longer-term self-recovery. The Sierra Leone TRC, introduced by a foreign consultant, was not culturally relevant enough to elicit the locals' imagination to cope with that society's extraordinary disorder. However, if we adopt a position that pays attention to how a TJ has been connected to other local movements/initiatives/collective actions, the Sierra Leone TRC could be counted as having a positive function for the local society.

The episodes in Chapter 5 illustrate that divergent meaning-making can even happen concurrently within TJ programs. We saw locals as well as foreign experts trying to understand and reconstruct the victims' fragmented world in the context of pervasive distrust and malfunctioning of legal norms. Sierra Leoneans' struggles in the court, as depicted by Kelsall, involved impressive persistence in fair communication in the pursuit of truth and justice. Unquestionably, court officials have played the international judiciary game, which not only gave them legitimacy within their professional society but also caused them to believe that the game would benefit locals and the local society. Yet for those local participants seeking justice, the standardized methods of communication did not offer the material they needed to recover their sense of the world. Instead, local participants again had to attempt to digest such extraordinary and stressful circumstances to establish their own intellectual consistency among wars, absurd sacrifices, totalitarian fears, international justice, and distrust. Although the Sierra Leonean episodes in Chapter 5 focus on the activities of local participants, the reactions and perplexing responses of the court experts might be assessed as having functioned to allow locals' challenges—or their *sincere* responses—to the court stage, as compared to the more authoritative court process of the Khmer Rouge Tribunals.

Clark's insight into the local people's understanding of gacaca illustrates their spontaneous divergence even from a well-controlled TJ program. In this context, many locals were aware that the ongoing process was a highly politicized exercise, yet they were not completely detached from the official call to overcome the past. The basic orientation of the policy—gathering and confession—still offered a space for their intellectual maneuvering. Consistent with Wilson's description of a South African TRC hearing, they used the stage, behaved as they were required, and quietly played out their own scenario of meaning-making. The gap between the society's religious background and the formal judicial surface of the gacaca process, such as the lack of religious figures and a religious stage setting in gacaca, might paradoxically have functioned to induce locals' interpretations.

As we saw, the CAVR arranged a hearing for less serious cases from the agreed deponents, while knowing that it had a murder case to deal with as well. At the hearing venue, a tug of war ensued between the CAVR commissioners, who wanted to confine the discussion to less serious crimes, and the murder victim's family, backed by the local community, which tried to pursue their own agenda. The latter's challenge was successful, resulting in "the public shaming of perpetrators and the restoration of the reputation of the victim's family" because it matched the "customary understandings of justice" (Kent 2012:159). Kent calls this divergence from the official TJ stage a translation into the vernacular. The participants did not necessarily stay within the role of meek audience. Even when they recognized the limitations of the official script, they sought to make something new out of the process by means of bricolage.

Catalyzing Locals' Own Meaning-Making

How can we assess these episodes? Researchers who conduct their analyses from the perspective of the official objectives of an institutional TJ program will assess these instances as unintended consequences, specifically, as malfunctions. In contrast, this volume, while paying keen attention to the concept of unintended consequences, has adopted the position that the influence of TJ can occur even in latent ways. In such a view, these deviations and divergences are interpreted as showing that local participants in TJ programs have spontaneously supplemented the ideals and objectives of TJ, which could not be fully realized through the course of official activities. By merely focusing on the official process, this aspect cannot be ascertained. The term *latent function* would be applied to such an occurrence. According to this argument, insufficient implementation of institutional TJ has been remedied by locals' divergence or deviation. But those actors who have been engaging in meaning-making separate from any official request to do so may have no intention of contributing to the realization of the official objectives of TJ for TJ's sake. As has already been illustrated, some of their works have clear roots in the TJ programs. Some of them consciously pay tribute to the TRC for its unintended role in catalyzing their work. However, their ongoing activities have developed their own reference points to maintain their internal drive and motivation, as well as to revise their own behavior in the flow and accumulation of their activities. The principle and grammar of their work no longer involve supporting an institutional TJ process but instead are about deepening their unique agenda in the process of self-referencing meaning-making.[2] This volume suggests that this type of unintended consequence of the institutional TJ process can be counted as an indirect but positive influence of TJ on a local society, although it is neither planned nor expected by the TJ body itself.

Let's look at a criticism of the Rwandan gacaca. Gacaca has, on the one hand, had the positive, if unintentional, function of encouraging locals in their remaking of the official drama, as Clark indicated. But on the other hand, overly strict controls in certain areas or certain time periods have provoked many criticisms. Locals have tended to participate reluctantly, mostly out of a sense of obligation rather than out of their internal need and desire for justice. Some even testified that being absent from the public events would cause them to be labeled as potential separatists (betrayer to the nation) and become targets of official sanction.

The term *meaning-making* in this volume contrasts with the phrase *meaning-supplied*. The latter designates the usual socialization that reflects the process of accepting public meaning supplied by a social norm or official entity and internalizing the meaning by naturalizing it in oneself. Becoming a social subject is, in an ordinary sense, a process of becoming subject to norms and authority. A meaning backed by political control in the public space, such as the one reported from gacaca, is, thus, closely linked to the *meaning-supplied* level.

In contrast, *meaning-making* in this argument connotes the production of a series of meanings through digesting one's experiences. For such meaning to be developed stably in one's life, a social form that guarantees continuous communication with others is helpful. Meaning-making as social behavior—in a political movement, a social movement, an art expression in public space, or a religious movement—has usually entailed attempting to gather as many participants and supporters as possible to share and exchange the new values and ideas. The movement is proposing these new meanings to the public because its supporters were not satisfied with the de facto supplied meanings. Particularly, for those who have faced successive absurdities during and after political conflict and oppression, a desire to engage in meaning-making for one's own recovery might appear naturally when people realize that an institutional TJ cannot meet their expectations.

Villa-Vicencio's observation of the dilemma of many South Africans (that most of them vacillate between agreement with the need for national reconciliation and total indifference to the idea) infers the condition by which locals are channeled into their exploration of meaning-making. This dilemma was also noted by Schaap (2005:12), who commented that "even the most conservative supporter and the most radical opponent of the old regime are likely to agree that reconciliation is a desirable social good in the changed political circumstances," even though "actors may disagree over what form reconciliation should take or how it should be realized."

The remarks of one prominent Cambodian survivor who conducted long-term investigations on his own initiative have shed light on the dimension of recovery through meaning-making. Youk Chhang, the director of DC-Cam, wrote about the process of successive inquiry itself, which has produced an unexpected change in him personally:

> People often ask me why, after living through Democratic Kampuchea, I would want to return to Cambodia and document the Khmer Rouge regime. To be honest, at first, I was driven by anger and a desire to seek revenge on those who killed so many members of my family. A few years after I began my research, I visited the village chief who was responsible for the death of my sister.... Although he was older, his life was much the same. He still lived in a stilt house in a small village, and tended two scrawny cows. He really wasn't any better off than he was before the revolution.... I visited him several times and to my surprise, found that he was actually not a bad man; he was simply a man who did bad things because the revolution had promised him a better life and society.... Today, the challenges of doing research and seeking answers make me happy and give me strength. Research sets me free when I suddenly discover a piece of truth, no matter how small. (Chhang 2005:5)

Youk Chhang wrote these comments during the prolonged negotiation stage between the RGC and the UN on how to establish and manage hybrid tribunals—in other words, during a blank period when the victims' expectations of justice had been derailed for several years. The DC-Cam organized intensive research projects for local victims in a relatively short time with no official support from the Cambodian government during such politically barren years. Even though the nature of DC-Cam's activities has changed over the course of its interaction with the ECCC, the RGC, and local citizens, Chhang's remarks illustrate that the unsatisfactory circumstances pushed him and DC-Cam to engage in continuous and intensive meaning-making. His explanation demonstrates how meaning-making as a type of public enterprise could affect one's identity in a fragile social context that itself cannot supply a model of identification.[3] Being an actor or a player in a game of meaning-making in a public space would allow the people who have been affected by a totalitarian society, an authoritarian government, and extreme surveillance circumstances to recover a consistent flow of time and direction in their lives. Those actors in meaning-making are to be "positive deviants" (Duggan) who would cope with absurdity in a fragmented society plagued by multidirectional distrust. It is still possible to think of a person's own internal drive to open the door of meaning-making, yet we may need to consider the social context of the actor who can deploy such a public enterprise, because a context of strict political control rarely allows such events to happen. In the meantime, such intensive autonomy may also not appear in a setting where a similar initiative has already been systematically organized by any official entity.

Meaning-making cannot be a panacea in any transitional context. It is not empirically clear how many people have faced their past through meaning-making, achieved healing or obtained internal consistency through the process, and proposed a new framework on how to recognize the past. It is not even certain whether any proper criterion to judge that question could be established. It is still conceivable that many people may be healed and attain recovery through the meanings supplied by the formal judiciary. Meaning-making cannot be officially guaranteed to last as long as other governmental institutions and cannot guarantee by itself that the products of the activities will steadily increase as industrial products do.

However, it is significant that such meaning-making has been observed in a social context where local expectations and various meanings of victim-hood have not been reflected in the official rules, or where negative experiences have not been explained persuasively. Therefore, the autonomous drive for continuous meaning-making should be acknowledged as a positive symptom of change in a local society, rather than just being dismissed as negative deviance from the official process. Put differently, a TJ program, or a latent function of a TJ program, can be accepted as a catalyst for locals' unplanned but autonomous pursuit of meaning-making. A TJ process is a unique policy and official entity in comparison to other related or similar enterprises in the political field, insofar as it catalyzes such divergence in an unintended manner. Thus, this volume suggests a framework to assess the influence and significance of a TJ program on an affected local society, with regard to how and what meaning-making has been catalyzed through the process.

Functional Blank Space or Strategic Ambiguity

One still unresolved issue related to meaning-making in a transitional society concerns what can actually catalyze or encourage those positive divergences and ramifications. How can we infer a mechanism that prepares for such a latent function to appear?

The concept of a political-opportunity structure of social-movement theory would basically suggest the context in which those positive divergences might be possible. A political circumstance surely limits the threshold at which such collective action can be realized, yet, it merely suggests the context. A factor that functions as a trigger, or, a device, in a more practical sense, for realizing such meaning-making needs to be further explored.

We can find a hint at an answer in *Seeing Like a State*. In his search for an institution, social form, or enterprise that permits and even promotes people's diverse and creative reactions, James Scott proposes the example of the Vietnam War Memorial in Washington, DC:

> What is most remarkable . . . is the way that the Vietnam Memorial works for those who visit it, particularly those who come to pay their respects to the memory of a comrade or loved one. They touch the names incised on the wall, make rubbings, and leave artifacts and mementos of their own—everything from poems and a woman's high-heeled shoe to a glass of champagne and a poker hand of a full house, aces high. So many of these tributes have been left, in fact, that a museum has been created to house them. . . . I believe that a great part of the memorial's symbolic power is its capacity to honor the dead with an openness that allows visitors to impress upon it their own meanings, their own histories, their own memories. The memorial virtually requires participation in order to complete its meaning. (Scott 1998:355)[4]

This nature of this memorial—that it "requires participation in order to complete its meaning"—is presented in opposition to most war memorials that are more "symbolically self-sufficient" (Scott 1998:356). What is missing here is a strict rule for visitors to follow when they are at the Vietnam Memorial. But the memorial is not actually open to just any deeds, because it still retains the basic meaning of the venue. So we can identify a loose balance at this venue between ambiguity and a clear reference to a specific historical event.

In the sociological literature, the social function of ambiguous expression, or a tactical blank space to induce participants' behaviors, was discussed in Daniel Boorstin's classic work *The Image: A Guide to Pseudo-Events in America* (1961). Boorstin argued that the most necessary characteristic of company symbols is that they must be ambiguous in an extremely proper manner. Being properly ambiguous opens a space for consumers to project their own varied desires onto that blank context. Of course, a totally ambiguous symbol that has no points of convergence with various images cannot function effectively. On the other hand, however, a symbol that is too narrow cannot induce consumers to sympathize with it. A symbol that is too narrow would be close to the character demonstrated in propaganda, narrowing the space for autonomous participation. Boorstin (1961:184–185) referred to Mack Hanan's opinion regarding effective advertising, which should be open-ended to allow "the various corporate publics to be drawn into the corporate picture." Surely, ambiguity by itself induces no connection with consumer behavior. However, when provided with a certain proper code, it can spark people who can change perceptions to take subsequent action.

Boorstin's insights also appear in his scintillating analysis of the "backstage" of image making:

> We are all interested in watching a skillful feat of magic; we are still more interested in looking behind the scenes and seeing precisely how it was made to seem that the lady was sawed in half. The everyday images which flood our experience have this advantage over the tricks of magic; even after we have been taken behind the scenes, we can still enjoy the pleasures of deception. Paradoxically, too, the more we know about the tricks of image building, about the calculation, ingenuity and effort that have gone into a particular image, the more satisfaction we have from the image itself. The elaborate contrivance proves to us that we are really justified (and not stupid either) in being taken in. (Boorstin 1961:194–195)

Thus, Boorstin is not simply an enlightening teacher criticizing the prevalence of the *pseudo-event* and calling for a return to a real world. Rather, he is a skilled doctor diagnosing the twisted nature of people's reception of media in the contemporary age. As shown by the case of magic, people sometimes want to be elaborately deceived: the audience is often pleased to be involved in a mechanism in which the bridge between the expected goal and the present situation is unclear. People's imagination is stimulated to look for ways to bridge the gap, driving their eyes to concentrate on the event. Here, an attractive blank space to induce people's attention is differently proposed: it can be devised even in the unclear process toward reaching a goal set up outside our common sense.

Contemporary studies on advertising have further pursued the function of elaborate ambiguity. Edward McQuarrie and David Mick (1996:427) attested that consumers paid more attention to figurative than to nonfigurative advertising language. Figurative advertising language was proved to promote consumers' sense of joy in decoding advertising messages and to be more memorable for them. Natalia Yannopoulou and Richard Elliott (2008) adopted the term "open-text advertisements," which are open to alternative and multiple interpretations, to understand the efficacy of contemporary ads that contain complex layers of rhetoric. Although open-text advertisements contain a single expression, they can send multiple messages to recipients.

Working within the framework of active audience theory, David Morley (1993) maintained that both audience interpretations and media content are always polysemic. Wan-Hsiu Sunny Tsai's (2012) argument on niche-targeted marketing, particularly gay window advertising, pivots on the term "purposeful polysemy." What we can identify in these explorations in the field of contemporary advertising is that various positions in a single interpretive space can be compatible, or, such a mechanism gives a more positive reputation to a specific piece of advertising.

In considering this combination of ambiguity and strategy, Eric Eisenberg (2007:8) posed a paradoxical question: "How can cohesion and coordination be promoted while at the same time maintaining sufficient individual freedom to ensure flexibility, creativity, and adaptability to environmental change?" The notion of strategic ambiguity is required in such circumstances to allow "different constituent groups [to] apply different interpretations to the symbol" (Eisenberg 2007:9). In this way, the exchange among stakeholders is expected to be "less one of consensus-making and more one of using language strategically to express values at a level of abstraction at which agreement can occur" (p. 9). The feasible and possible function of such specific ambiguity, or blank space, when embedded in an official policy has also been noted in the field of TJ studies.

Therefore, the apparent insufficiency of the various TJ episodes examined in the previous chapters could be reconsidered from the perspective of the efficacy of insufficiency, or the function of blank space. In more exact terms, a specific insufficiency in a specific context might be a key to understanding the unique function of TJ.

Koskenniemi (2002) has made an observation that is quite pertinent to this discussion. For a "wounded community" to heal itself and for future crimes to be deterred, Koskenniemi argues that a few "show trials," which are insufficient by the standards of modern justice, might well be sufficient when supported by other mechanisms (p. 11). This idea surely cannot be generalized without examining what show trials induce external support and under what conditions. However, the implications of this argument have not yet been explored in TJ studies. Leigh Payne's observation on the contextual characteristics in which the "deeper"—and thus closer to the truth—testimonies may have been elicited brings us to a more nuanced analysis of this issue:

> Debates about the past depend largely on catalysts. Fiction and lies successfully catalyse debate in part due to lurid details that unsettle audiences, in part because their audiences try to get the story right. They correct perpetrators' accounts, demanding or filling in details, challenging others, attempting to put together an accurate portrayal of the past. During the process, audiences will also struggle over official history and collective memories. (Payne 2008:226)

Errors, lies, and ambiguous stories not reflective of core experiences are all representative of a specific insufficiency or gap in the official scenario. They present imperfect information that, in an ordinary judicial setting, must be censured. However, in certain situations and under specific conditions, participants might be catalyzed by insufficiency to take action. A game of meaning-making, which may not necessarily fit an official policy script, is initiated and can enrich the complex reality and complicated relationships that attend stakeholders' experiences.

Bearing in mind these viewpoints, the episodes in the previous chapters can be read in the following manner. The meaning-making in Chapter 3 is recognized as one in which participants express oppositional or dissident ideas with regard to the official message, a deviation that can happen in the blank space created by the lack of a substantial TJ authority. The TJ program must disseminate a moralistic and prominent message, yet it lacks the presupposed legitimacy as well as the political force of ordinary governmental institutions in a stable society. This gap is interpreted as inducing the game of meaning-making.

The blank space found in the divergent movements described in Chapter 4 is the gap between the publicly raised expectations of TJ and the insufficient implementation of these expectations. Some locals clearly realize the existence of unfinished business and mold their spontaneous motivations to fill the gap.

The inadequacies of the scenarios for collective healing are a catalyst of the divergent dramas described in Chapter 5. These official scenarios are rejected by actors because they require performances that do not align with the actors' motivations and needs. Or, as in the case of Sierra Leonean "players" who may have misunderstood the rules of the court, improper rules taken from the local cultural context are adopted in composing the modified scenario.

TJ's nationalistic discourses as described in Chapter 6 can be a trigger initiating a game of meaning-making around a vague and contentious notion of "us." TJ initiatives are evaluated retrospectively as having called on social constituents to redefine their collective identity outside the official drama of the TRC. Yet this game cannot necessarily be attributed to rational dialogue among democratic players who mutually recognize each other's rights to free speech. This normative perspective has been disproved by the research data provided by the IJR. On the contrary, in a transitional society, the notion of "us," or a desirable collective identity, is not only ambiguous but also politically provocative, a sort of taboo.

However, the TJ program might be able to treat this blank space indirectly, catalyzing locals' intensive engagement in successive negotiation of a mutual relationship toward a more comprehensive framework of collective identity. Through its insufficient competence in nation building, TJ foregrounds the blank space of questioning collective identity as visible and controllable. Conversely, to cultivate an institutional setting in which people in various social positions are motivated for active engagement, such a blank space with a specific insufficiency and ambiguity may be required.

Planning a Transitional Justice Program as a Catalyst

Planning for the unplanned is a thoroughly paradoxical expression. The unplanned cannot logically be planned. It is similar to the concept of unintended consequences, which cannot be fit into the thinking of social engineering because unintended consequences can be understood only retrospectively—although a critic might object that defining unplanned content in a concrete way so as to anticipate it means that it is no longer unplanned.

This concept brings with it another difficulty. For persons in charge of policy planning and design, the concept of planning the unplanned would seem to demand that they plan for insufficient outcomes, which stem from their inadequate input. Therefore, they may be reluctant to plan for their own failure! We referred earlier to the simulation of an overly sincere bureaucrat who honestly presents a rational future blueprint that describes likely negative outcomes. Such an action could unintentionally lead to the noncooperation of related actors, thus bringing about truly negative consequences in the form of a *self-fulfilling prophecy*. There again, we see the matter that annoys that too-sincere bureaucrat. The task is to plan failure in a positive way, or to design a policy whose failure could be positively accepted by people. If given such a task, can we positively conduct our obligation in that position? Defining the term *unplanned* with a concrete expression will surely lead to a confused point with an illogical explanation.

But as Scott's understanding of the Vietnam War Memorial shows, we can explain the concept of *unplanned* in a more descriptive way—for example, in terms of an institution that "requires participation in order to complete its meaning." This expression includes various attitudes or reactions among participants while also presenting a specific pattern or grammar of behaviors.[5]

Beyond that, the phrase *planning for the unplanned* still leaves residual space for further exploration of the meaning of planning in this context. What is left is the path of "intentionally planning not to do something, or not to do any more than a certain threshold." This is the opposite of doing everything possible to make the unplanned appear. We tend to think that doing less leads to fewer outcomes or improper ones, and so we are encouraged to make our best efforts to approach an expected goal. However, there exists a dimension such that doing less in a specific threshold can produce a different and often proper outcome, as compared to doing more.

Let's return to Koskenniemi's assumption, which indicates the possible effectiveness of a show trial at eliciting external support for national reconciliation. The potential effectiveness of this image suggests a truth that is held in common with other fields. For instance, a skilled actor can convey much information through subtle eye movements rather than elaborate acting. Too much performance could result in comedy. Medicine, similarly, is effective when taken in the prescribed amounts, but taking too much can result in poisoning. These examples illuminate the TJ situation as well, by showing that the extent of the causal factor and the nature of the result are not necessarily connected by a proportional expression. In theory, as Jacques Derrida (1999) wrote when describing forgiveness in the South African context as a probable gift for a survivor, self-recovery cannot be planned by anyone, including the affected person. An individual's recovery from a traumatic experience and the collective appearance of public healing are both impossible to plan in a cause–effect scheme. Yet in a situation where people admit the significance of a specific value and feel sympathy, while harboring misgivings about the current surrounding conditions and acknowledging that freedom of expression is not guaranteed in public, an insufficient TJ program in a specific form (along with other cultural or social resources) can be a catalyst for realizing the continuation of meaning-making. The idea of planning a TJ program as a catalyst for unplanned social recovery is thus open to further exploration.

Notes

1. It thus generates what Gregory Bateson called a *double bind*, in which recipients of the message are left to question whether they should directly oppose the literal contents or need to seek a hidden motivation behind the message.

2. The term *meaning-making* has been used in a situation in which the social norms and rules that can guide social constituents' proper behavior do not function adequately, with the result that actors must create their own way of digesting the situation. Yet even in our daily lives, when one thinks of a scene where a person acts in a role play, as Goffman describes, the variations of performance have, in theory, no limit because of the possibility of minute derivations, whereas people usually

take—or cannot help but take—some distance from the roles when engaging in role playing. Some scholars also argue that *meaning-making* is interchangeable with the term *framing* (Grunwald and Rupar 2010:50–53), which has been described as indicating "persistent patterns of cognition, interpretation, and presentation, of selection, emphasis, and exclusion, by which symbol-handlers routinely organize discourse" (Gitlin 1980:7). Meaning-making surely becomes crucial in such a situation, in which these cognitive and interpretative contexts are unstable.

3. Desmond Tutu's call for forgiveness has often been misunderstood, but it is similar in character to Youk Chhang's remarks, in light of its emphasis on autonomy in taking action.

4. A still more radical critique may add the reservation that the monument may implicitly exclude those who opposed the US invasion of Vietnam and feel that this view should also be represented in the discourse on the Vietnam War.

5. Scott's explanation fits the general definition of artworks, particularly contemporary ones, so that his notion of "an institution that requires participation to complete its meaning" may be thought of being utilized for the forms of memorial or museum in terms of public representation of the past conflict and victimhood. However, other social acts such as social, political, and religious movements can also be subsumed under his explanation.

Acronyms

ADHOC	Cambodian Human Rights and Development Association
ANC	African National Congress
ASEAN	Association of Southeast Asian Nations
BEE-Com	Black Economic Empowerment Commission
CAR	Central African Republic
CAVR	Comissão de Acolhimento, Verdade e Reconciliação de Timor Leste (Commission for Reception, Truth, and Reconciliation in East Timor)
CDF	Civil Defense Forces
CEH	Comisión para el Esclarecimiento Histórico (Commission for Historical Clarification in Guatemala)
CIVICUS	Center for Cambodian Civic Education
CJR	Center for Justice and Reconciliation
CRP	Community Reconciliation Process (East Timor)
CSD	Center for Social Development (Cambodia)
CSO	civil-society organization
CVR	Comisión para Verdad y Reconciliación (Truth and Reconciliation Commission in Peru)
DC-Cam	Documentation Center of Cambodia
DDR	disarmament, demobilization, and reintegration
DED	German Development Service
DK	Democratic Kampuchea
ECCC	Extraordinary Chambers in the Courts of Cambodia (also known as KRT)
EU	European Union
FALINTIL	opposition military wing in East Timor
IBA	International Bar Association

ICC	International Criminal Court
ICTJ	International Center for Transitional Justice
ICTR	International Criminal Tribunal for Rwanda
ICTY	International Criminal Tribunal for the Former Yugoslavia
IFP	Inkhatha Freedom Party
IJR	Institute for Justice and Reconciliation
KN	*Khmer Nation*
KO	*Koh Santepheap*
KR	Khmer Rouge
KRT	Khmer Rouge Tribunal (also known as ECCC)
KS	*Khmer Scientific*
KT	*Kampuchea Thmey*
LLRC	Lessons Learnt and Reconciliation Commission
MO	*Moneaksekar Khmer*
MPTT	Missing Persons Task Team
MS	*Machas Srok Khmer*
NGO	nongovernmental organization
NP	National Party
NPA	National Prosecuting Authority
NRC	National Reconciliation Commission
OCIJ	Office of Co-Investigating Judges
PIR	Comprehensive Reparation Programme
PR	public relations
RGC	Royal Government of Cambodia
RK	*Rasmei Kampuchea*
S-21	Security Prison 21 (Torture Center in the Khmer Rouge regime, Phnom Penh)
SABC	South African Broadcasting Corporation
SAHA	South African History Archive
SFT	*Searching for the Truth* (magazine of the Documentation Center of Cambodia)
TC	truth commission
TJ	transitional justice
TJRC	Truth, Justice and Reconciliation Commission (Kenya)
TPO	Transcultural Psychosocial Organization (Cambodia)
TRC	Truth and Reconciliation Commission (South Africa)
UN	United Nations
UNTAET	United Nations Transitional Administration in East Timor
USAID	US Agency for International Development

Bibliography

Abou-El-Fadl, Reem. 2012. "Beyond Conventional Transitional Justice: Egypt's 2011 Revolution and the Absence of Political Will." *International Journal of Transitional Justice* 6:318–330.
Adhikari, Mohamed. 2005. *Not White Enough, Not Black Enough: Racial Identity in the South African Coloured Community*. Athens: Ohio University Press.
Alexander, Jeffrey C. 2011. *Performance and Power*. Cambridge: Polity Press.
Alexander, Jeffrey C., and Jason L. Mast. 2006. "Introduction: Symbolic Action in Theory and Practice: The Cultural Pragmatics of Symbolic Action." Pp. 1–28 in *Social Performance: Symbolic Action, Cultural Pragmatics, and Ritual*, edited by J. C. Alexander, B. Gissen, and J. L. Mast. Cambridge: Cambridge University Press.
Amann, Diane M. 2002. "Group Mentality, Expressivism, and Genocide." *International Criminal Law Review* 2(2):93–143.
Anders, Gehard. 2014a. "Contesting Expertise: Anthropologists at the Special Court for Sierra Leone." *Journal of the Royal Anthropological Institute* 20(3):426–444.
———. 2014b. "Transitional Justice, States of Emergency and Business as Usual in Sierra Leone." *Development and Change* 45(3):524–542.
Anderson, Benedict. 1983. *Imagined Communities. Reflections on the Origin and Spread of Nationalism*. London: Verso.
Andrieu, Kora. 2011. "An Unfinished Business: Transitional Justice and Democratization in Post-Soviet Russia." *International Journal of Transitional Justice* 5:198–220.
An-Na'im, Abdullahi Ahmed. 2013. "Editorial Note: From the Neocolonial 'Transitional' to Indigenous Formations of Justice." *International Journal of Transitional Justice* 7:197–204.
Anonymous. 2011. "Against the Grain: Pursuing a Transitional Justice Agenda in Postwar Sri Lanka." *International Journal of Transitional Justice* 5:31–51.
Aoláin, Fionnuala Ní. 2012. "Advancing Feminist Positioning in the Field of Transitional Justice." *International Journal of Transitional Justice* 6:205–228.
Apter, David E. 2006. "Politics as Theatre: An Alternative View of the Rationalities of Power." Pp. 218–256 in *Social Performance: Symbolic Action, Cultural Pragmatics, and Ritual*, edited by J. C. Alexander, B. Gissen, and J. L. Mast. Cambridge: Cambridge University Press.

Aronson, Jay D. 2011. "The Strengths and Limitations of South Africa's Search for Apartheid-Era Missing Persons." *International Journal of Transitional Justice*, 5 (2):262–281.

Arthur, Paige. 2009. "How 'Transitions' Reshaped Human Rights: A Conceptual History of Transitional Justice." *Human Rights Quarterly* 31(2):321–367.

Aston, Elaine, and George Savona. 1991. *Theatre as Sign System: A Semiotics of Text and Performance*. London: Routledge.

Autesserre, Séverine. 2014. *Peaceland: Conflict Resolution and the Everyday Politics of International Intervention*. New York: Cambridge University Press.

Baliga, Sandeep, and Tomas Sjöström. 2008. "Strategic Ambiguity and Arms Proliferation." *Journal of Political Economy* 116(6):1023–1057.

Balint, Jennifer, Julie Evansy, and Nesam McMillan. 2014. "Rethinking Transitional Justice, Redressing Indigenous Harm: A New Conceptual Approach." *International Journal of Transitional Justice* 8:194–216.

Bates, Alex. 2010. "Transitional Justice in Cambodia: Analytical Report." Atlas Project, Université Paris 1.

Bauman, Zygmunt. 2001. *Community: Seeking Safety in an Insecure World*. Cambridge and Malden: Polity Press.

Bell, Christine. 2009. "Transitional Justice, Interdisciplinarity and the State of the 'Field' or 'Non-Field.'" *International Journal of Transitional Justice* 3(1):5–27.

Boorstin, Daniel. 1961. *The Image: A Guide to Pseudo-Events in America*. New York: Vintage Books.

Boraine, Alex, and Sue Valentine, eds. 2006. *Transitional Justice and Human Security*. Cape Town: International Center for Transitional Justice.

Bosire, Lydiah Kemunto, and Gabrielle Lynch. 2014. "Kenya's Search for Truth and Justice: The Role of Civil Society." *International Journal of Transitional Justice* 8(2):256–276.

Brewer, John D. 2010. *Peace Processes: A Sociological Approach*. Cambridge: Polity Press.

Brown, Kris, and Fionnuala Ní Aoláin. 2015. "Through the Looking Glass: Transitional Justice Futures Through the Lens of Nationalism, Feminism and Transformative Change." *International Journal of Transitional Justice* 9:127–149.

Budak, Yeliz. 2015. "Dealing with the Past: Transitional Justice, Ongoing Conflict and the Kurdish Issue in Turkey." *International Journal of Transitional Justice* 9:219–238.

Bundschuh, Thomas. 2015. "Enabling Transitional Justice, Restoring Capabilities: The Imperative of Participation and Normative Integrity." *International Journal of Transitional Justice* 9:10–32.

Buss, Doris. 2011. "Performing Legal Order: Some Feminist Thoughts on International Criminal Law." *International Criminal Law Review* 11:409–423.

Campbell, Colm, and Ita Connolly. 2012. "The Sharp End: Armed Opposition Movements, Transitional Truth Processes and the Rechtsstaat." *International Journal of Transitional Justice* 6:11–39.

Carranza, Ruben. 2008. "Plunder and Pain: Should Transitional Justice Engage with Corruption and Economic Crimes?" *International Journal of Transitional Justice* 2(3):310–330.

Cassese, Antonio. 1998. "Reflections on International Criminal Justice." *Modern Law Review* 61(1):1–10.

Center for Social Development (CSD). 2007. *CSD Annual Report*. Phnom Penh: Center for Social Development.

Chhang, Youk. 2005. "Research and Healing." *Searching for the Truth*, Special English Edition, Fourth Quarter: 5.

———. 2007. "The Thief of History: Cambodia and Special Court." *International Journal of Transitional Justice* 1(1):157–172.

Chidester, David. 1999. "Stories, Fragments and Monuments." Pp. 132–141 in *Facing the Truth: South African Faith Communities and the Truth and Reconciliation Commission*, edited by J. Cochrane and J. De Gruchy. Claremont, South Africa: David Philip Publishers.

Christie, Kenneth. 2000. *The South African Truth Commission*. New York: St. Martin's.

Christie, Nils. 1977. "Conflicts as Property." *British Journal of Criminology* 17(1):1–15.

———. 1986. "The Ideal Victim." Pp. 17–30 in *From Crime Policy to Victim Policy: Reorienting the Justice System*, edited by E. A. Fattah. London: Palgrave Macmillan.

Ciorciari, John. 2009. "History and Politics Behind the Khmer Rouge Trials." Pp. 67–81 in *On Trial: The Khmer Rouge Accountability Process*, edited by J. Ciorciari and A. Heindel. Phnom Penh: Documentation Center of Cambodia.

Ciorciari, John, and Anne Heindel. 2014. *Hybrid Justice: The Extraordinary Chambers in the Courts of Cambodia*. Ann Arbor: University of Michigan Press.

Clark, Janine Natalya. 2012. "Reconciliation Through Remembrance? War Memorials and the Victims of Vukovar." *International Journal of Transitional Justice* 7:116–135.

Clark, Phil. 2010. *The Gacaca Courts, Post-Genocide Justice and Reconciliation in Rwanda: Justice Without Lawyers*. Cambridge: Cambridge University Press.

Cochran, Edwin S. 1996. "Deliberate Ambiguity: An Analysis of Israel's Nuclear Strategy." *Journal of Strategic Studies* 19(3):321–342.

Cole, Elizabeth. 2007. "Transitional Justice and the Reform of History Education." *International Journal of Transitional Justice* 1(1):115–137.

Colvin, Christopher. 2003. "Brothers and Sisters, Do Not Be Afraid of Me: Trauma, History, and the Therapeutic Imagination in the New South Africa." Pp. 153–168 in *Contested Pasts: The Politics of Memory,* edited by K. Hodgkin and S. Radstone. London: Routledge.

Commission for Reception, Truth, and Reconciliation in East Timor. 2005. *Chega! Final Report of the Commission for Reception, Truth and Reconciliation in East Timor*. http://www.etan.org/news/2006/cavr.htm.

Coser, Lewis. 1956. *The Functions of Social Conflict*. New York: Free Press.

Crocker, David. 1999. "Reckoning with Past Wrongs: A Normative Framework." *Ethics and International Affairs* 13(1):42–64.

Dacil, Keo. 2010. "The UN, Cambodia, and the Khmer Rouge: Politics Before Victims?" *Searching for the Truth,* Fourth Quarter: 4–6. http://dara-duong.blogspot.com/2010/11/un-cambodia-and-khmer-rouge-politics.html.

Dancy, Geoff. 2010. "Impact Assessment, Not Evaluation: Defining a Limited Role for Positivism in the Study of Transitional Justice." *International Journal of Transitional Justice* 4(3):355–376.

Danieli, Yael. 2004. "Victims: Essential Voices at the Court." *Victims' Rights Working Group Bulletin* 1:6.

David, Roman. 2011. *Lustration and Transitional Justice: Personnel Systems in the Czech Republic, Hungary, and Poland*. Philadelphia: University of Pennsylvania Press.

de Certeau, Michel. 1984. *The Practice of Everyday Life*. Translated by Steven Rendall. Berkeley: University of California Press.

de Greiff, Pablo. 2010. "A Normative Conception of Transitional Justice." *Politorbis* 50(3):17–29.

———. 2013. "Transitional Justice Gets Its Own Encyclopedia: Vitamins or Steroids for a Developing Field?" *International Journal of Transitional Justice* 7(3):547–553.
de Hemptinne, Jérôme. 2010. "Challenges Raised by Victims' Participation in the Proceedings of the Special Tribunal for Lebanon." *Journal of International Criminal Justice* 8(1):165–179.
Derrida, Jacques. 1999. *Sur parole*. La Tour d'Aigues: Editions de l'Aube.
Des Forges, Alison, and Timothy Longman. 2004. "Legal Responses to Genocide in Rwanda." Pp. 49–68 in *My Neighbor, My Enemy: Justice and Community in the Aftermath of Mass Atrocity*, edited by E. Stover and H. Weinstein. Cambridge: Cambridge University Press.
Dimitrijevic, Nenad. 2008. "Serbia After the Criminal Past: What Went Wrong and What Should Be Done." *International Journal of Transitional Justice* 2(1):5–22.
Dobbin, Frank. 2009. "How Durkheim's Theory of Meaning-Making Influenced Organizational Sociology." Pp. 200–222 in *Oxford Handbook of Sociology and Organization Studies: Classical Foundations*, edited by P. S. Adler. New York: Oxford University Press.
Doxtader, Erik. 2009. *With Faith in the Works of Words: The Beginnings of Reconciliation in South Africa, 1985–1995*. Claremont, South Africa: David Philip Publishers.
Drexler, Elizabeth F. 2010. "The Failure of International Justice in East Timor and Indonesia." Pp. 49–66 in *Transnational Justice: Global Mechanisms and Local Realities After Genocide and Mass Violence*, edited by A. Hinton. New Brunswick, NJ: Rutgers University Press.
———. 2013. "Fatal Knowledges: The Social and Political Legacies of Collaboration and Betrayal in Timor-Leste." *International Journal of Transitional Justice* 7(1):74–94.
Druliolle, Vincent. 2015. "Recovering Historical Memory: A Struggle Against Silence and Forgetting? The Politics of Victimhood in Spain." *International Journal of Transitional Justice* 9(2):316–335.
Drumbl, Mark A. 2007. *Atrocity, Punishment, and International Law*. Cambridge: Cambridge University Press.
Dube, Siphiwe Ignatius. 2011. "Transitional Justice Beyond the Normative: Towards a Literary Theory of Political Transitions." *International Journal of Transitional Justice* 5:177–197.
Du Bois, François, and Antje Du Bois-Pedain. 2008. "Post-Conflict Justice and the Reconciliatory Paradigm: The South African Experience" Pp. 289–311 in *Justice and Reconciliation in Post-Apartheid South Africa*, edited by F. Du Bois and A. Du Bois-Pedain. Cambridge: Cambridge University Press.
Duffy, Aoife. 2010. "A Truth Commission for Northern Ireland?" *International Journal of Transitional Justice* 4(1):26–46.
Duggan, Colleen. 2010. "Editorial Note." *International Journal of Transitional Justice* 4(3):315–328
Durkheim, Emile. 1951. *Suicide: A Study in Sociology*. Translated by John A. Spaulding and George Simpson. Glencoe, IL: Free Press of Glencoe.
———. 1960. *The Division of Labor in Society*. Translated by George Simpson. Glencoe, IL: Free Press of Glencoe.
———. 2008. *The Elementary Forms of the Religious Life*. Translated by Carol Cosman. Oxford: Oxford University Press.
Duthie, Roger. 2011. "Transitional Justice and Displacement." *International Journal of Transitional Justice* 5:241–261.

Dwyer, Clare D. 2012. "Expanding DDR: The Transformative Role of Former Prisoners in Community-Based Reintegration in Northern Ireland." *International Journal of Transitional Justice* 6:274–295.
Eisenberg, Eric. 2007. *Strategic Ambiguities: Essays on Communication, Organization, and Identity.* New York: Sage.
Elander, Maria. 2012. "The Victim's Address: Expressivism and the Victim at the Extraordinary Chambers in the Courts of Cambodia." *International Journal of Transitional Justice* 7:95–115.
Eley, Geoff. 1992. "Nations, Publics and Political Cultures: Placing Habermas in the Nineteenth Century." Pp. 289–339 in *Habermas and the Public Sphere*, edited by C. Calhoun. Cambridge: MIT Press.
Elster, Jon, 2004. *Closing the Books: Transitional Justice in Historical Perspective.* New York: Cambridge University Press.
Entman, Robert M. 2007. "Framing Bias: Media in the Distribution of Power." *Journal of Communication* 57:163–173.
Eriksson, Anna. 2009. "A Bottom-Up Approach to Transformative Justice in Northern Ireland." *International Journal of Transitional Justice* 3(3):301–320.
Eyerman, Ron. 2006. "Performing Opposition, or How Social Movements Move." Pp. 193–217 in *Social Performance: Symbolic Action, Cultural Pragmatics, and Ritual*, edited by J. C. Alexander, B. Gissen, and J. L. Mast. Cambridge: Cambridge University Press.
Fanon, Frantz. 1967. *Black Skin, White Masks.* Translated by Charles Lam Marmann. New York: Grove.
Fawthrop, Tom, and Helen Jarvis. 2004. *Getting Away with Genocide? Cambodia's Long Struggle Aagainst the Khmer Rouge.* London: Pluto Press.
Fisher, Kirsten J., and Robert Stewart, eds. 2014. *Transitional Justice and the Arab Spring.* Oxford: Routledge.
Fisher, Ronald. 2001. "Social-Psychological Process in Interactive Conflict Analysis and Reconciliation." Pp. 25–46 in *Reconciliation, Justice, and Coexistence: Theory and Practice*, edited by Mohammed Abu-Nimer. New York: Lexington Books.
Fletcher, Laurel E. 2015. "Editorial Note." *International Journal of Transitional Justice* 9:193–198.
Foster, Don, Paul Haupt, and Marésa de Beer. 2005. *The Theatre of Violence: Narratives of Protagonists in the South African Conflict.* Oxford: James Currey.
Foucault, Michel. 1982. *The Archaeology of Knowledge and the Discourse on Language.* Translated by A. M. Sheridan Smith. New York: Pantheon Books.
Fraser, Nancy. 1990. "Rethinking the Public Sphere: A Contribution to the Critique of Actually Existing Democracy." *Social Text* 25/26:56–80.
Freeman, Jo. 1979. "Resource Mobilization and Strategy: A Model for Analyzing Social Movement Organization Actions." Pp. 167–189 in *The Dynamics of Social Movements: Resource Mobilization, Social Control, and Tactics*, edited by M. N. Zald and J. D. McCarthy. Cambridge: Winthrop Publishers.
Fullard, Madeleine. 2004. "Dis-placing Race: The South African Truth and Reconciliation Commission (TRC) and Interpretations of Violence." http://www.csvr.org.za/docs/racism/displacingrace.pdf, accessed April 21, 2018.
Girard, René. 1976. *Deceit, Desire and the Novel: Self and Other in Literary Structure.* Baltimore: Johns Hopkins University Press.
———. 1977. *Violence and the Sacred.* Baltimore: Johns Hopkins University Press.
Girard, René, and Michel Treguer. 1994. *Quand ces choses commenceront. . . .* Paris: Arléa.

Gitlin, Todd. 1980. *The Whole World Is Watching: Mass Media in the Making and Unmaking of the New Left*. Berkeley: University of California Press.
Glasius, Marlies, and Tim Meijersy. 2012. "Constructions of Legitimacy: The Charles Taylor Trial." *International Journal of Transitional Justice* 6:229–252.
Goffman, Erving. 1959. *The Presentation of Self in Everyday Life*. New York: Doubleday.
Goodman, Tanya. 2006. "Performing a 'New' Nation: The Role of the TRC in South Africa." Pp. 169–192 in *Social Performance: Symbolic Action, Cultural Pragmatics, and Ritual*, edited by J. C. Alexander, B. Gissen, and J. L. Mast. Cambridge: Cambridge University Press.
Gready, Paul, and Simon Robins. 2014. "From Transitional to Transformative Justice: A New Agenda for Practice." *International Journal of Transitional Justice* 8(3):339–361.
Grodsky, Brian K. 2011. *Costs of Justice: How New Leaders Respond to Previous Rights Abuses*. Notre Dame, IN: University of Notre Dame Press.
Grunwald, Ebbe, and Verica Rupar. 2009. "Journalism Curiosity and Story Telling Frame: A Comparative Study of Australian and Danish Newspapers." *Journalism Practice* 3(4):392–403.
———. 2010. "Capturing Meaning-Making in Journalism." *Journalistica* 2:48–78.
Gutmann, Amy, and Dennis Thompson. 2000. "The Moral Foundations of Truth Commissions." Pp. 22–44 in *Truth v. Justice: The Morality of Truth Commissions*, edited by R. I. Rotberg and D. Thompson. Princeton: Princeton University Press.
———. 2004. *Why Deliberative Democracy?* Princeton: Princeton University Press.
Hamber, Brandon. 2009. *Transforming Societies After Political Violence: Truth, Reconciliation, and Mental Health*. New York: Springer-Verlag.
Hamber, Brandon, and Gráinne Kelly. 2005 "The Challenge of Reconciliation in Post-Conflict Societies: Definitions, Problems and Proposals." Pp. 188–203 in *Power Sharing: New Challenges for Divided Societies*, edited by I. O'Flynn and D. Russell. London: Pluto Press.
Harris, Bronwyn. 2004. "Arranging Prejudice: Exploring Hate Crime in Post-Apartheid South Africa." Centre for the Study of Violence and Reconciliation. http://www.csvr.org.za/docs/racism/arrangingprejudice.pdf.
Hasegawa, Kōichi, and Takashi Machimura. 2004. "Social Movements and Social Movement Theories Today" (in Japanese). Pp. 1–24 in *Social Movements as Public Spaces*, edited by K. Soranaka, K. Hasegawa, T. Machimura, and N. Higuchi. Tokyo: Seibundoh.
Haslam, Emily. 2011. "Subjects and Objects: International Criminal Law and the Institutionalization of Civil Society." *International Journal of Transitional Justice* 5(2):221–240.
Hayner, Priscilla B. 2001. *Unspeakable Truths: Confronting State Terror and Atrocity*. New York: Routledge.
———. 2010. *Unspeakable Truths: Transitional Justice and the Challenge of Truth Commissions*. New York: Routledge.
Heder, Steve. 2011. "A Review of the Negotiations Leading to the Establishment of the Personal Jurisdiction of the Extraordinary Chambers in the Courts of Cambodia." August 11. http://www.cambodiatribunal.org/sites/default/files/A%20Review%20of%20the%20Negotiations%20Leading%20to%20the%20Establishment%20of%20the%20Personal%20Jurisdiction%20of%20the%20ECCC.pdf.
Heder, Stephen, and Brian Tittemore. 2004. *Seven Candidates for Prosecution: Accountability for the Crimes of the Khmer Rouge*. Phnom Penh: Documentation Center of Cambodia.

Hinton, Alexander Laban. 2005. *Why Did They Kill? Cambodia in the Shadow of Genocide*. Los Angeles: University of California Press.
———. 2010a. "Introduction: Toward an Anthropology of Transitional Justice." Pp. 1–24 in *Transitional Justice: Global Mechanisms and Local Realities After Genocide and Mass Violence*, edited by A. Hinton. New Brunswick, NJ: Rutgers University Press.
———, ed. 2010b. *Transitional Justice: Global Mechanisms and Local Realities After Genocide and Mass Violence*. New Brunswick, NJ: Rutgers University Press.
Hobsbawm, Eric. 1983. "Introduction: Inventing Traditions." Pp. 1–14 in *The Invention of Tradition*, edited by E. Hobsbawm and T. Ranger. New York: Cambridge University Press.
Holness, Toni, and Jaya Ramji-Nogales. 2011. "Participation as Reparations: The ECCC and Healing in Cambodia." Pp. 172–190 in *Cambodia's Hidden Scars: Trauma Psychology in the Wake of the Khmer Rouge*, edited by B. V. Schaack, D. Reicherter, and Y. Chhang. Phnom Penh: Documentation Center Cambodia.
Hopgood, Stephen. 2013. *The Endtimes of Human Rights*. Ithaca: Cornell University Press.
Humphrey, Michael. 2003. "From Victim to Victimhood: Truth Commissions and Trials as Rituals of Political Transition and Individual Healing." *Australian Journal of Anthropology* 14(2):171–187.
Ignatieff, Michael. 1996. "Articles of Faith." *Index on Censorship* 25:110–122.
Iliff, Andrew R. 2012. "Root and Branch: Discourses of 'Tradition' in Grassroots Transitional Justice." *International Journal of Transitional Justice* 6:253–273.
Institute for Justice and Reconciliation. 2001. "Truth and Reconciliation Survey 2001." Cape Town, South Africa: Institute for Justice and Reconciliation (CD-ROM).
———. 2009. "SA Reconciliation Barometer: Ninth Round Media Briefing." Cape Town, South Africa: Institute for Justice and Reconciliation. http://sabarometerblog.files.wordpress.com/2009/12/sarb_report_final_draft1.pdf, accessed February 3, 2011.
International Bar Association (IBA). 2011. "Safeguarding Judicial Independence in Mixed Tribunals: Lessons from the ECCC and Best Practices for the Future." http://www.cambodiatribunal.org/sites/default/files/reports/Cambodia%20report%20%28Sept%202011%29.pdf, accessed April 22, 2018.
International Criminal Court (ICC). 2006. Strategic Plan for Outreach of the International Criminal Court, ICC-ASP/5/12 (September 29, 2006).
January, Sativa. 2009. "Tribunal Verité: Documenting Transitional Justice in Sierra Leone." *International Journal of Transitional Justice* 3(2):207–228.
Jeffery, Anthea. 1999. *The Truth About the Truth Commission*. Johannesburg: South African Institute of Race Relations.
Jones, Briony. 2012. "Exploring the Politics of Reconciliation Through Education Reform: The Case of Brčko District, Bosnia and Herzegovina." *International Journal of Transitional Justice* 6:126–148.
Kaldor, Mary. 2006. *New and Old Wars: Organized Violence in a Global Era*. Cambridge: Polity Press.
Kelman, Herbert C. 2008. "Reconciliation from a Social-Psychological Perspective." Pp. 15–32 in *The Social Psychology of Intergroup Reconciliation*, edited by A. Nadler, T. E. Malloy, and J. D. Fisher. New York: Oxford University Press.
Kelsall, Tim. 2013. *Culture Under Cross-Examination: International Justice and the Special Court for Sierra Leone*. Cambridge: Cambridge University Press.
Kent, Lia. 2012. *The Dynamics of Transitional Justice: International Models and Local Realities in East Timor*. Oxford: Routledge.

Kesselring, Rita. 2017. *Bodies of Truth: Law, Memory, and Emancipation in Post-Apartheid South Africa*. Redwood City, CA: Stanford University Press.
Kiousis Spiro. 2011. "Agenda-Setting and Attitudes." *Journalism Studies* 12(3):359–374.
Koc-Menard, Nathalie. 2014. "Notes from the Field: Exhuming the Past After the Peruvian Internal Conflict." *International Journal of Transitional Justice* 8:277–288.
Koskenniemi, Martti. 2002. "Between Impunity and Show Trials." *Max Planck Yearbook of United Nations Law* 6:1–35.
Kriesberg, Lois. 2001. "Changing Forms of Coexistence." Pp. 47–64 in *Reconciliation, Justice, and Coexistence: Theory and Practice*, edited by M. Abu-Nimer. New York: Lexington Books.
Kriesi, Hanspeter, Ruud Koopmans, Jan Willem Duyvendak, and Marco G. Giugni. 1995. *New Social Movements in Western Europe: A Comparative Analysis*. Minneapolis: University of Minnesota Press.
Kritz, Neil. 1995. *Transitional Justice: How Emerging Democracies Reckon with Former Regimes*. Washington, DC: US Institute of Peace Press.
Krog, Antjie. 1998. *Country of My Skull*. New York: Three Rivers Press.
———. 2003. "The Choice for Amnesty: Did Political Necessity Trump Moral Duty?" Pp. 115–120 in *The Provocations of Amnesty: Memory, Justice and Impunity*, edited by C. Villa-Vicencio and E. Doxtader. Claremont, South Africa: David Philip Publishers.
Kymlicka, Will. 2010. "Transitional Justice, Federalism, and the Accommodation of Minority Nationalism." Pp. 303–333 in *Identities in Transition: Challenges for Transitional Justice in Divided Societies,* edited by Paige Arthur. Cambridge: Cambridge University Press.
Laplante, Lisa J., and Kelly Phenicie. 2010. "Media, Trials and Truth Commissions: 'Mediating' Reconciliation in Peru's Transitional Justice Process." *International Journal of Transitional Justice* 4:207–229.
Lederach, John Paul. 1997. *Building Peace: Sustainable Reconciliation in Divided Societies*. Washington, DC: US Institute of Peace Press.
Levitt, Peggy, and Sally Merry. 2009. "Vernacularization on the Ground: Local Uses of Global Women's Rights in Peru, China, India and the United States." *Global Networks* 9(4):441–461.
Löytömäki, Stiina. 2013. "The Law and Collective Memory of Colonialism: France and the Case of 'Belated' Transitional Justice." *International Journal of Transitional Justice* 7:205–223.
Luhabe, Wendy. 2007. "The Moral Bases of Stakeholder Society." Pp. 18–27 in *Visions of Black Economic Empowerment*, edited by X. Mangcu, G. Marcus, K. Shubane, and A. Hadland. Auckland Park, South Africa: Jacana Media.
Ma, Shu-yun. 1992. "Nationalism: State-Building or State-Destroying?" *Social Science Journal* 29(3):293–305.
Mafuna, Eric. 2007. "From Politics to Business." Pp. 31–37 in *Visions of Black Economic Empowerment,* edited by X. Mangcu, G. Marcus, K. Shubane, and A. Hadland. Auckland Park, South Africa: Jacana Media.
Mamdani, Mahmood. 2009. "Response by Mahmood Mamdani." *International Journal of Transitional Justice* 3(3):472–473.
Mandela, Nelson. 2010. *Conversation with Myself*. London: Macmillan.
Mani, Rama. 2007. "Looking Back and Moving Forward: The Nexus Between Development and Transitional Justice." Paper presented at the Building a Future on Peace and Justice Congress, June 25–27, 2007, Nuremburg, Germany.
Mannheim, Karl. 1940. *Man and Society in an Age of Reconstruction*. Translated by Edward Shils. London: Routledge.

Manning, Peter. 2014. *Justice, Reconciliation and Memorial Politics in Cambodia*. PhD thesis, London School of Economics.

Mbembe, Achille. 2001. *On the Postcolony*. Berkeley: University of California Press.

McAdam, Doug. 1982. *Political Process and the Development of Black Insurgency, 1930–1970*. Chicago: University of Chicago Press.

———. 1996. "Conceptual Origins, Current Problems, Future Directions." Pp. 23–40 in *Comparative Perspectives on Social Movements: Political Opportunities, Mobilizing Structures, and Cultural Framings*, edited by D. McAdam, J. D. McCarthy, and M. N. Zald. Cambridge: Cambridge University Press.

McAdam, Doug, John D. McCarthy, and Mayer N. Zald. 1996. "Introduction: Opportunities, Mobilizing Structures, and Framing Processes—Toward a Synthetic, Comparative Perspective on Social Movements." Pp. 1–20 in *Comparative Perspectives on Social Movements: Political Opportunities, Mobilizing Structures, and Cultural Framings*, edited by D. McAdam, J. D. McCarthy, and M. N. Zald. Cambridge: Cambridge University Press.

McAdams, A. James. 2011. "Transitional Justice: The Issue That Won't Go Away." *International Journal of Transitional Justice* 5(2):304–312.

McCargo, Duncan. 2010. "Thailand's National Reconciliation Commission: A Flawed Response to the Southern Conflict." *Global Change, Peace, and Security* 22(1):75–91.

McCarthy, John D., and Mayer N. Zald. 1977. "Resource Mobilization and Social Movements: A Partial Theory." *American Journal of Sociology* 82(6):1212–1241.

McDowell, Sara. 2007. "Who Are the Victims? Debates, Concepts and Contestation in 'Post-Conflict' Northern Ireland." http://cain.ulst.ac.uk/victims/introduction/smcd07whoarethevictims.html.

McEvoy, Kieran. 2008. "Letting Go of Legalism: Developing a 'Thicker' Version of Transitional Justice.'" Pp. 15–47 in *Transitional Justice from Below: Grassroots Activism and the Struggle for Change*, edited by K. McEvoy and L. McGregor. Portland, OR: Hart Publishing.

McGregor, Lorna. 2013. "Transitional Justice and the Prevention of Torture." *International Journal of Transitional Justice* 7:29–51.

McQuarrie, Edward F., and David G. Mick. 1996. "Figures of Rhetoric in Advertising Language." *Journal of Consumer Research* 22:424–438.

Melucci, Alberto. 1996. *Challenging Codes: Collective Action in the Information Age*. Cambridge: Cambridge University Press.

Merry, Sally. 2006. "Anthropology and International Law." *Annual Review of Anthropology* 35:99–116.

Merton, Robert K. 1957. *Social Theory and Social Structure*. Revised and enlarged edition. Glencoe, IL: Free Press.

Mills, C. Wright. 1940. "Situated Actions and Vocabularies of Motive." *American Sociological Review* 5(6):904–913.

Minow, Martha. 1999. *Between Vengeance and Forgiveness: Facing History After Genocide and Mass Violence*. Boston: Beacon Press.

Misztal, Barbara A. 2010. "Collective Memory in a Global Age: Learning How and What to Remember." *Current Sociology* 58(1):24–44.

Moffett, Luke. 2014. "Navigating Complex Identities of Victim-Perpetrators in Reparation Mechanisms." *Queen's University Belfast Law Research Paper* 13. http://papers.ssrn.com/sol3/papers.cfm?abstract_id=2494759.

Mohan, Mahdev, and Sangeetha Yogendran. 2017. "Victims' Rights, Reparations and Rituals at the ECCC." Manuscript submitted for publication.

Moon, Claire. 2008. *Narrating Political Reconciliation: South Africa's Truth and Reconciliation Commission*. London: Lexington Books.

———. 2009. "Healing Past Violence: Traumatic Assumptions and Therapeutic Interventions in War and Reconciliation." *Journal of Human Rights* 8(1):71–91.
Morley, David. 1993. "Active Audience Theory: Pendulums and Pitfalls." *Journal of Communication* 43(4):13–19.
Morrissey, Mike, and Marie Smyth. 2002. *Northern Ireland After the Good Friday Agreement: Victims, Grievance and Blame*. London: Pluto Press.
Mouffe, Chantal. 2005. *On the Political*. London: Routledge.
Moyo, Khanyisela. 2015. "Mimicry, Transitional Justice and the Land Question in Racially Divided Former Settler Colonies." *International Journal of Transitional Justice* 9:70–89.
Musila, Godfrey. 2010. *Rethinking International Criminal Law: Restorative Justice and the Rights of Victims in the International Criminal Court*. Saarbrücken, Germany: Lambert Academic Publishing.
Mutua, Makau. 2015. "Editorial: What Is the Future of Transitional Justice?" *International Journal of Transitional Justice* 9:1–9.
Nadler, Arie, and Nurit Shnabel. 2008. "Instrumental and Socioemotional Paths to Intergroup Reconciliation and the Needs-Based Model of Socioemotional Reconciliation." Pp. 37–56 in *The Social Psychology of Intergroup Reconciliation*, edited by A. Nadler, T. E. Malloy, and J. D. Fisher. New York: Oxford University Press.
Nagy, Rosemary. 2008. "Transitional Justice as Global Project: Critical Reflections." *Third World Quarterly* 29(2):275–289.
———. 2013. "The Scope and Bounds of Transitional Justice and the Canadian Truth and Reconciliation Commission." *International Journal of Transitional Justice* 7:52–73.
National Reconciliation Commission. 2006. *Overcoming Violence Through the Power of Reconciliation* (Report of National Reconciliation Commission). Bangkok: NRC.
Ndahinda, Felix Mukwiza. 2013. "The Bemba-Banyamulenge Case Before the ICC: From Individual to Collective Criminal Responsibility." *International Journal of Transitional Justice* 7(3):476–496.
Norval, Aletta J. 2007. *Aversive Democracy: Inheritance and Originality of the Democratic Tradition*. Cambridge: Cambridge University Press.
Nutall, Sarah. 2009. *Entanglement: Literary and Cultural Reflections on Post Apartheid*. Johannesburg: University of the Witwatersrand Press.
Obradović-Wochnik, Jelena. 2013. "The 'Silent Dilemma' of Transitional Justice: Silencing and Coming to Terms with the Past in Serbia." *International Journal of Transitional Justice* 7:328–347.
Ohlin, Jens David. 2007. "On the Very Idea of Transitional Justice." *Whitehead Journal of Diplomacy and International Relations* 8(1):51–68.
Oliver, Pamela E., and Gerald Marwell. 1992. "Mobilizing Technologies for Collective Action." Pp. 251–272 in *Frontiers in Social Movement Theory*, edited by A. Morris and C. Mueller. New Haven: Yale University Press.
Orentlicher, Diane F. 2013. "From Viability to Impact: Evolving Metrics for Assessing the International Criminal Tribunal for the Former Yugoslavia." *International Journal of Transitional Justice* 7(3):536–546.
Osiel, Mark. 1997. *Mass Atrocity, Collective Memory, and the Law*. New Brunswick, NJ: Transaction Publishers.
Palmer, Nicola. 2015. *Courts in Conflict: Interpreting the Layers of Justice in Post-Genocide Rwanda*. Oxford: Oxford University Press.
Park, Crystal L. 2010. "Making Sense of the Meaning Literature: An Integrative Review of Meaning Making and Its Effects on Adjustment to Stressful Life Events." *Psychological Bulletin* 136(2):257–301.

Parry, Benita. 2004. *Postcolonial Studies: A Materialist Critique*. New York: Routledge.
Parsons, Talcott. 1951. *The Social System*. London: Routledge.
———. 1968. "Social Interaction." Pp. 429–441 in *International Encyclopedia of the Social Sciences*, edited by D. Sills. New York: Macmillan and Free Press.
Parsons, Talcott, and Edward Shils, eds. 1951. *Toward a General Theory of Action*. Cambridge, MA: Harvard University Press.
Payne, Leigh. 2000. *Uncivil Movements: The Armed Right Wing and Democracy in Latin America*. Baltimore: Johns Hopkins University Press.
———. 2008. *Unsettling Accounts: Neither Truth nor Reconciliation in Confessions of State Violence*. Durham: Duke University Press.
Pena, Mariana, and Gaelle Carayony. 2013. "Is the ICC Making the Most of Victim Participation?" *International Journal of Transitional Justice* 7:518–535.
Peskin, Victor, and Mieczysław P. Boduszyńskiy. 2011. "Balancing International Justice in the Balkans: Surrogate Enforcers, Uncertain Transitions and the Road to Europe." *International Journal of Transitional Justice* 5:52–74.
Philips, Tessa. 2011. "Race, Place, and Self in the Experience of a Bystander." *International Journal of Psychoanalytic Self Psychology* 6(3):405–426.
Pillay, Navanethem. 2007. "Editorial Note." *International Journal of Transitional Justice* 1(3):315–317.
Posner, Eric A., and Adrian Vermeule. 2004. "Transitional Justice as Ordinary Justice." *Harvard Law Review* 117(3):761–825.
Prieto, Juan Diego. 2012. "Together After War While the War Goes On: Victims, Ex-Combatants and Communities in Three Colombian Cities." *International Journal of Transitional Justice* 6:525–546.
Putnam, Robert D. 1993. *Making Democracy Work: Civic Traditions in Modern Italy*. Princeton: Princeton University Press.
———. 2000. *Bowling Alone: The Collapse and Revival of American Community*. New York: Simon and Schuster.
Rasmussen, J. Lewis. 2001. "Negotiating a Revolution: Toward Integrating Relationship Building and Reconciliation into Official Peace Negotiations." Pp. 101–128 in *Reconciliation, Justice, and Coexistence: Theory and Practice*, edited by M. Abu-Nimer. New York: Lexington Books.
Renan, Ernest. 1990. "What Is a Nation?" Pp. 7–19 in *Nation and Narration*, edited by H. K. Bhabha. Translated by Martin Thom. London: Routledge.
Renner, Judith. 2013. *Discourse, Normative Change and the Quest for Reconciliation in Global Politics*. Manchester, England: Manchester University Press.
Riek, Blake M., Samuel L. Gaertner, John F. Dovidio, Marilynn B. Brewer, Eric W. Mania, and Marika J. Lamoreaux. 2008. "A Social-Psychological Approach to Postconflict Reconciliation." Pp. 255–274 in *The Social Psychology of Intergroup Reconciliation*, edited by A. Nadler, T. E. Malloy, and J. D. Fisher. New York: Oxford University Press.
Rigby, Andrew. 2001. *Justice and Reconciliation: After the Violence*. London: Lynne Rienner Publishers.
Rill, Leslie A., and Corey B. Davis. 2008. "Testing the Second Level of Agenda Setting: Effects of News Frames on Reader-Assigned Attributes of Hezbollah and Israel in the 2006 War in Lebanon." *Journalism and Mass Communication Quarterly* 85(3):609–624.
Risse, Thomas, Stephen C. Ropp, and Kathryn Sikkink, eds. 1999. *The Power of Human Rights: International Norms and Domestic Change*. Cambridge: Cambridge University Press.

Robins, Simon. 2011. "Towards Victim-Centred Transitional Justice: Understanding the Needs of Families of the Disappeared in Postconflict Nepal." *International Journal of Transitional Justice* 5:75–98.

———. 2012. "Challenging the Therapeutic Ethic: A Victim-Centred Evaluation of Transitional Justice Process in Timor-Leste." *International Journal of Transitional Justice* 6:83–105.

———. 2015. "Mapping a Future for Transitional Justice by Learning from Its Past." *International Journal of Transitional Justice* 9:181–190.

Robinson, Isabel. 2015. "Truth Commissions and Anti-Corruption: Towards a Complementary Framework?" *International Journal of Transitional Justice* 9:33–50.

Ross, Fiona. 2003. *Bearing Witness: Women and the Truth and Reconciliation Commission in South Africa*. London: Pluto Press.

Rowen, Jamie. 2012. "Mobilizing Truth: Agenda Setting in a Transnational Social Movement." *Law and Social Inquiry* 37(3):686–718.

Saunders, Rebecca. 2011. "Questionable Associations: The Role of Forgiveness in Transitional Justice." *International Journal of Transitional Justice* 5:119–141.

Schaap, Andrew. 2005. *Political Reconciliation*. New York: Routledge.

Scheufele, Dietram A., and David Tewksbury. 2007. "Framing, Agenda Setting, and Priming: The Evolution of Three Media Effects Models." *Journal of Communication* 57:9–20.

Schiff, Benjamin. 2008. *Building the International Criminal Court*. New York: Cambridge University Press.

Scott, James. 1998. *Seeing like a State: How Certain Schemes to Improve the Human Condition Have Failed*. New Haven: Yale University Press.

Sharp, Dustin. 2015. "Emancipating Transitional Justice from the Bonds of the Paradigmatic Transition." *International Journal of Transitional Justice* 9(1):150–169.

Shaw, Rosalind, and Lars Waldorf. 2010. "Introduction: Localizing Transitional Justice." Pp. 3–26 in *Localizing Transitional Justice Interventions and Priorities After Mass Violence*, edited by R. Shaw, L. Waldorf, and P. Hazan. Stanford: Stanford University Press.

Shaw, Rosalind, Lars Waldorf, and Pierre Hazan, eds. 2010. *Localizing Transitional Justice Interventions and Priorities After Mass Violence*. Stanford: Stanford University Press.

Siani-Davies, Peter, and Stefanos Katsikas. 2009. "National Reconciliation After Civil War: The Case of Greece." *Journal of Peace Research* 46(4):559–575.

Simić, Olivera, and Kathleen Daly. 2011. "'One Pair of Shoes, One Life': Steps Towards Accountability for Genocide in Srebrenica." *International Journal of Transitional Justice* 5(3):477–491.

Sivac-Bryant, Sebina. 2015. "The Omarska Memorial Project as an Example of How Transitional Justice Interventions Can Produce Hidden Harms." *International Journal of Transitional Justice* 9:170–180.

Sloane, Robert D. 2012. "The International Tribunal for Rwanda." Pp. 261–282 in *The Rules, Practice, and Jurisprudence of International Courts and Tribunals*, edited by C. Giorgetti. Leiden: Brill.

Smyth, Marie. 1998. "Remembering in Northern Ireland: Victims, Perpetrators and Hierarchies of Pain and Responsibility," Pp. 31–49 in *Past Imperfect: Dealing with the Past in Northern Ireland and South Africa*, edited by B. Hamber. Derry: Incore.

Sperfeldt, Christoph. 2012. "Cambodian Civil Society and the Khmer Rouge Tribunal." *International Journal of Transitional Justice* 6:149–160.

Stan, Lavinia, and Nadya Nedelsky, eds. 2013. *Encyclopedia of Transitional Justice*. 3 vols. Cambridge: Cambridge University Press.

Steinberg, Rosen. 2013. "Transitional Justice in the Age of the French Revolution." *International Journal of Transitional Justice* 7:267–285.
Stepakoff, Shanee, G. Shawn Reynolds, Simon Charters, and Nicola Henry. 2014. "Why Testify? Witnesses' Motivations for Giving Evidence in a War Crimes Tribunal in Sierra Leone." *International Journal of Transitional Justice* 8:426–451.
Subotić, Jelena. 2009. *Hijacked Justice: Dealing with the Past in the Balkans.* Ithaca: Cornell University Press.
———. 2012. "The Transformation of International Transitional Justice Advocacy." *International Journal of Transitional Justice* 6:106–125.
Suhrke, Astri. 2001. "Peacekeepers as Nation-Builders: Dilemmas of the UN in East Timor." *International Peacekeeping* 8(4):1–20.
Tarrow, Sydney. 1994. *Power in Movement: Social Movements and Contentious Politics.* New York: Cambridge University Press.
Teitel, Ruti G. 2003. "Transitional Justice Genealogy." *Harvard Human Rights Journal* 16:69–94.
Theidon, Kimberly. 2013. *Intimate Enemies: Violence and Reconciliation in Peru.* Philadelphia: University of Pennsylvania Press.
Thoms, Oskar, James Ron, and Roland Paris. 2010. "State-Level Effects of Transitional Justice: What Do We Know?" *International Journal of Transitional Justice* 4(3):329–354.
Thomson, Susan, and Rosemary Nagy. 2011. "Law, Power and Justice: What Legalism Fails to Address in the Functioning of Rwanda's Gacaca Courts." *International Journal of Transitional Justice* 5:11–30.
Tilly, Charles. 1978. *From Mobilization to Revolution.* N.p., NJ: Longman Higher Education.
———. 1986. *The Contentious French: Four Centuries of Popular Struggle.* Cambridge: Belknap Press.
Transparency International. 2017. "Corruption Perceptions Index 2016." https://www.transparency.org/news/feature/corruption_perceptions_index_2016; accessed on December 15, 2017.
Truth and Reconciliation Commission. 1998a. *Truth and Reconciliation Commission of South Africa Report.* Vol. 1. Cape Town: Juta.
———. 1998b. *Truth and Reconciliation Commission of South Africa Report.* Vol. 4. Cape Town: Juta.
Tsai, Wan-Hsiu Sunny. 2012. "Political Issues in Advertising Polysemy: The Case of Gay Window Advertising." *Consumption Markets and Culture* 15(1):41–62.
United Nations Secretary General (UNSG). 2002. *Report of the Secretary General on the United Nations Transitional Administration in East Timor,* UN Doc S /2002/432, 14 April. New York: United Nations.
Valji, Nahla. 2003. *Creating the Nation: The Rise of Violent Xenophobia in the New South Africa.* Master's thesis, York University. http://www.sahistory.org.za/sites/default/files/file%20uploads%20/riseofviolent.pdf, accessed April 21, 2018.
———. 2004. "Race and Reconciliation in a Post-TRC South Africa." Paper presented at a conference entitled "Ten Years of Democracy in Southern Africa," organized by the Southern African Research Centre, Queens University, Canada, May 2004.
van der Merwe, H. 2003. "National and Community Reconciliation: Competing Agendas in the South African Truth and Reconciliation Commission." Pp. 101–124 in *Burying the Past: Making Peace and Doing Justice After Civil Conflict,* edited by N. Biggar. Washington, DC: Georgetown University Press.
van der Merwe, H., and Audrey R. Chapman. 2008. "Did the TRC Deliver?" Pp. 241–279 in *Truth and Reconciliation in South Africa: Did the TRC Deliver?*

edited by A. R. Chapman and H. van der Merwe. Philadelphia: University of Pennsylvania Press.

van der Merwe, Hugo, and Laurel E. Fletcher. 2014. "Editorial Note." *International Journal of Transitional Justice* 8:1–5.

van der Merwe, Hugo, Victoria Baxter, and Audrey R. Chapman. 2009. "Introduction." Pp. 1–11 in *Assessing the Impact of Transitional Justice: Challenges for Empirical Research*, edited by H. van der Merwe, V. Baxter, and A. R. Chapman. Washington, DC: US Institute of Peace Press.

van Wijk, Joris. 2013. "Who Is the 'Little Old Lady' of International Crimes? Nils Christie's Concept of the Ideal Victim Reinterpreted." *International Review of Victimology* 19(2):159–179.

Victims' Rights Working Group. 2010. "The Impact of the Rome Statute System on Victims and Affected Communities." http://www.refworld.org/docid/4bf3ad682.html.

Villa-Vicencio, Charles. 2002. "Reconciliation as a Metaphor." Pp. 224–244 in *Theology in Dialogue: The Impact of the Arts, Humanities, and Science on Contemporary Religious Thought*, edited by L. Holness and R. K. Wustenburg. Claremont, South Africa: David Philip Publishers.

———. 2003. "Restorative Justice: Ambiguities and Limitations of Theory." Pp. 30–50 in *The Provocations of Amnesty: Memory, Justice and Impunity*, edited by C. Villa-Vicencio and E. Doxtader. Cape Town: David Philip Publishers.

Vinck, Patrick, and Phuong Pham. 2010. "Outreach Evaluation: The International Criminal Court in the Central African Republic." *International Journal of Transitional Justice* 4(3):421–442.

Wagstaff, Jeremy. 2010. "Southeast Asian Media: Patterns of Production and Consumption. A Survey of National Media in Ten Countries." Open Society Foundation. https://www.opensocietyfoundations.org/reports/southeast-asian-media-patterns-production-and-consumption.

Wale, K. 2013. "Confronting Exclusion: Time for Radical Reconciliation." South African Reconciliation Barometer Survey 2013 Report. Cape Town: Institute for Justice and Reconciliation. http://reconciliationbarometer.org/wp-content/uploads/2013/12/IJR-Barometer-Report-2013-22Nov1635.pdf.

———. 2014. "Reflecting on Reconciliation: Lessons from the Past, Prospects for the Future." South African Reconciliation Barometer Survey 2014 Report. Cape Town: Institute for Justice and Reconciliation. http://reconciliationbarometer.org/wp-content/uploads/2014/12/IJR-SA-Reconciliation-Barometer-Report-2014.pdf.

Walgravel, Stefaan, and Peter Van Aelst. 2006. "The Contingency of the Mass Media's Political Agenda Setting Power: Toward a Preliminary Theory." *Journal of Communication* 56(1):88–109.

War Crimes Research Office. 2007. "Victim Participation Before the International Criminal Court." https://www.wcl.american.edu/impact/initiatives-programs/warcrimes/our-projects/icc-legal-analysis-and-education-project/reports/report-1-victim-participation-before-the-international-criminal-court/, accessed April 21, 2018.

Weah, Aaron. 2012. "Hopes and Uncertainties: Liberia's Journey to End Impunity." *International Journal of Transitional Justice* 6:331–343.

Weaver, David H. 2007. "Thoughts on Agenda Setting, Framing, and Priming." *Journal of Communication* 57:142–147.

Weber, Max. 1922. *Wirtschaft und Gesellschaft*. Tubingen: J. C. B. Mohr (P. Siebeck).

———. 1930. *The Protestant Ethic and the Spirit of Capitalism*. Translated by Talcott Parsons. London: George Allen and Unwin.

Weinstein, Harvey M. 2011. "The Myth of Closure, the Illusion of Reconciliation: Final Thoughts on Five Years as Co-Editor-in-Chief." *International Journal of Transitional Justice* 5:1–10.

White, Michael, and David Epston. 1990. *Narrative Means to Therapeutic Ends*. New York: W. W. Norton.
Willis, Paul. 1977. *Learning to Labour: How Working Class Kids Get Working Class Jobs.* Farnborough: Saxon House.
Wilson, Richard A. 2001. *The Politics of Truth and Reconciliation in South Africa: Legitimizing the Post-Apartheid State*. Cambridge: Cambridge University Press.
Winter, Stephen. 2013. "Towards a Unified Theory of Transitional Justice." *International Journal of Transitional Justice* 7:224–244.
World Bank. 2008. *Defining Heroes: Key Lessons from the Creation of Veterans Policy in Timor-Leste.* Washington, DC: World Bank.
Yannopoulou, Natalie, and Elliott Richard. 2008. "Open Versus Closed Advertising Texts and Interpretive Communities." *International Journal of Advertising* 11(1):9–36.
Yusuf, Hakeem O. 2007. "Travails of Truth: Achieving Justice for Victims of Impunity in Nigeria." *International Journal of Transitional Justice* 1(2):268–286.
Zartman, William I., and Viktor Kremenyuk, eds. 2005. *Peace Versus Justice: Negotiating Forward- and Backward-Looking Outcomes.* Lanham, MD: Rowman and Littlefield.
Žižek, Slavoj. 2000. *The Fragile Absolute: Or, Why Is the Christian Legacy Worth Fighting For?* London: Verso.
Zunino, Marcos. 2011. "Releasing Transitional Justice from the Technical Asylum: Judicial Reform in Guatemala Seen Through *Technē* and *Phronēsis*." *International Journal of Transitional Justice* 5:99–118.

Index

acceptance of transitional justice projects, 72–74
accountability: effective operation of processes, 102–103; elements of a contemporary institutionalized TJ program, 36; positive deviants, 54(n4); responsibility of Western powers for conflict situations, 60
active audience theory, 204
activists of memory, 134
Adams, Brad, 87
adversary, conflict and, 177–178
advertising, effective, 203–204
affirmative action in South Africa, 185–190
African National Congress (ANC), 116; black-on-black violence, 77; critical evaluation of the TRC, 41; media coverage of the TRC reports, 2; racial identity politics, 188
Agiza, Ahmad, 60
agonism, 179–184, 191(n8)
Alexander, Jeffrey, 140–141
ambiguous expression, 202–203
American Nazi Party, 12–13
Anderson, Benedict, 35–36, 173–174
apologies for harm done, 11
Arendt, Hannah, 191(n8)
Argentina: civilization without law, 54(n2); manipulation of official drama, 143
artworks, 208(n5)

assessments: criticisms of past TJ programs, 40–43; five-strand reconciliation model, 52; negative media evaluations of Cambodia's ECCC, 86–88; positive comments by participants, 127–128.97–99; relationship between Kenya's TJRC and civil society organizations, 108–109
Association of Southeast Asian Nations (ASEAN), 121
Autesserre, Séverine, 5–7, 20
authoritarian regimes: censorship of dissident ideas, 90–91; limits of divergent social movements, 126–127
authority of delimitation, 75–76
aversive democracy, 179

Bemba, Jean-Pierre, 103
beneficiaries, 41
Benzien, Jeffrey, 150–152
bias: allegations of discrimination in South Africa's TRC, 77–78; biased ideal for Serbia's program, 63–64; discourse analysis applied to goodwill and ideals announcements, 76–77; excluding specific political positions from TJ mobilization, 107–108; ideal image of victims, 78–79; importance of a neutral TJ, 74–75; the question of media neutrality in TJ perception, 82–83; ruptures in official drama,

138–139; South Africa's Mamelodi Four case, 116–118
Biko, Steve, 93
Bisho Massacre (South Africa), 148
Black Economic Empowerment Commission (BEE-Com; South Africa), 185–187, 191(n14)
"blackness" in South Africa, 185–190, 191(n14)
black-on-black violence, South Africa's, 77
Blunk, Siegfried, 84–85
Boorstin, Daniel, 2, 203
Botha, P.W, 2
brand policy, 32
Brasilia: planned scientific city, 7–8
budget: for the CDS, 123; complications of long examinations, 101–102; ECCC, 130(n5); industrialization of TJ, 31–32; proof of positive outcomes justifying funding, 100; TJ documentation, 35–36; TJ implementation, 22–23
by-products of transitional justice, 18–19

Calvin, John, 45, 57(n20)
Cambodia: Center for Social Development, 68–72, 122–127; common elements with South Africa's TRC, 5; complaints of delayed justice, 101; DC-Cam, 119–122, 126–127, 163, 200–201; divergence of local social movements, 118–127; as global norm adopters, 64; hybrid tribunal, 56(n12); involvement of the victims in the process, 57–58(n24); Khmer Rouge Tribunal, 2–3; lack of improvement in the justice system, 3–4; local distrust of international actors, 23–24; local social movements, 118–127; locals' recovery through meaning-making, 200; media ambivalence in TJ portrayal, 83–84; moralistic public messages, 89; politics of victimhood, 79–80; public forums exploring locals' perceptions of, 69–72; responsibility of Western powers for conflict, 61. *See also* Extraordinary Chambers in the Courts of Cambodia; Khmer Rouge Tribunal

Cambodian Genocide Program (Yale University), 119
Cambodian Human Rights and Development Association (ADHOC), 163
Canadian Truth and Reconciliation Commission, 13
capitalism resulting from unintended consequences, 28–29, 54(n6)
Cartwright, Silvia, 138
catalyst, transitional justice programs as, 206–207
Cayley, Andrew, 84, 121
Center for Cambodian Civic Education (CIVICUS), 124–125
Center for Justice and Reconciliation (CJR; Cambodia), 124–125
Center for Social Development (CSD; Cambodia), 68–69, 122–127
Cham people (Cambodia), 120–122
Chea Leang, 84
Chhang, Youk, 86–87, 119–122, 126, 131(n15), 200–201, 208(n3)
Chum Mey, 138
Ciskei Defence Force (South Africa), 149–150
citizenization, 176
Civil Defense Forces (CDF) trial (Sierra Leone), 153–156
civil servants, educating about Cambodia's transitional justice, 121
civil society organizations (CSO): expanding the transitional justice field to include, 12; Guatemala's failed judicial reform, 42; Kenya's TJ attempts, 108–109; relationship between Kenya's TJRC and, 108–109; transcending South Africa's TRC agenda, 9; as true believers, 64
Clark, Phil, 24–25, 27–28, 95, 144, 161–162, 172–173, 198
collective action, 47–48, 55(n7), 58(n25), 105
collective identity: basic requirements for TJ design, 21–22; defining through collective behavior, 53; redefining outside the official TRC drama, 205–206; requirements for preventing recurrence of violence, 51–52. *See also* nationalism
colonialism, 175–176

Colored people, South Africa's, 187–188
Comisión para el Esclarecimiento Histórico (Guatemala), 176
Comissão de Acolhimento, Verdade e Reconciliação de Timor Leste (CAVR; East Timor), 72, 145–146, 198
Commission of Truth and Friendship in Indonesia and East Timor, 13
Commission to Counteract Attempts at Falsifying History to Damage the Interests of Russia, 33–34
commonalities in transitional justice systems, 5–6
communication: DC-Cam activities creating space, 119–120; fear and distrust between victims and perpetrators, 25; meaning-making, 199–200; sequential model of institutionalized TJ, 56(n15); Sierra Leoneans' struggles with the court, 197–198; South Africa's Reconciliation Barometer Survey, 114–115. *See also* media; official drama; public message
compulsory mobilization, 95–97, 127
conflict: defining, 177–178; defining transitional justice, 11–12; politics of victimhood exacerbating, 81–82
conflict resolution: development of institutional TJ, 39–40
conscription, mobilization as, 96
consultation process: discourse analysis, 75–77; East Timor, 72–74; importance of neutrality, 74–75; limitations of, 77–78; local access to, 16; South Africa, 73–74. *See also* official drama; witness testimony
contemporary institutionalized transitional justice, defining, 34–40
contentious coexistence, 18, 53, 109, 170, 177
corruption: Cambodia's court system, 23–24; critical evaluation of South Africa's TRC, 41; DC-Cam's stance on court officials, 120; leading to dysfunctional legal norms, 25–26; media covering questioning Cambodia's ECCC's legitimacy, 86–88
Corruptions Perceptions Index, 54(n1)
Coser, Lewis, 177–178, 189
coup d'état: Thailand, 33

court examinations. *See* official drama; witness testimony
Court Watch Project (Cambodia), 123
criticisms of transitional justice programs, 40–43
cultural initiatives: Sierra Leone's Fambul Tok, 115–116
cultural norms, official drama and, 164–165
cycle of a transitional justice (transitional justice) system, 5–6

DC-Cam, 119–122, 126–127, 163, 200–201
de Certeau, Michel, 45–46
de Greiff, Pablo, 100
de Klerk, F.W., 77–78
deliberative democracy, 177–178
demobilization and reintegration (DDR), 12
democracy and democratization: Cambodia's social movements promoting, 126–127; civilization without law, 54(n2); dynamic equilibrium, 177–178; governance indicators, 54(n1); local perception of ECCC and the rule of law, 70–72; requirements for preventing recurrence of violence, 51–52; social conditions that shape a transitional society, 23; substate nationalism, 18, 53, 170, 176–178, 189
democratic reciprocity, 179, 181–182
derivative work in official drama, 146–150
desire. *See* mimetic desire
deviant perception of the public message, 44–46, 56–57(n19)
deviations and derivatives from expected steps, 43–44
diaspora population: Cambodia's local social movements, 118–119, 126–127
didactic materials for schools, 11
Dindīć, Zoran, 64–65
disappeared individuals: South Africa's Mamelodi Four case, 116–118
disarmament, 12
discourse analysis, 75–77
dissent: challengers to South Africa's TRC, 77–78; conflicts inside Cambodia's ECCC, 84–86; by local victims, 90; media ambivalence in TJ portrayal, 83–84
distrust of transitional justice projects, 13–14; of arrogant judges, 138–139;

fear between perpetrators and victims, 24–25; leading to dysfunctional legal norms, 25–26; localization of institutional transitional justice, 21
divergent mobilization: blank space in, 205; meaning-making within TJ programs, 197–198; official drama, 142; from official mobilization, 46–48; propagated repertoires, 133; South Africa's Missing Persons Task Team, 116–117. *See also* Center for Social Development; DC-Cam; unintended consequences
Documentation Center of Cambodia (DC-Cam), 68
domestic politics: conflicts within Cambodia's ECCC, 84–86; excluding specific political positions from TJ mobilization, 107–108; international manipulation of justice discourse, 64–68; party challengers to South Africa's TRC, 77–78; representation of testimony in the public sphere, 74–75; strategic use of TJ discourse to influence Sierra Leone's, 67–68
donors: expectations leading to failure in peace and justice initiatives, 7; external pressures on TJ outcomes, 100–101; funding Cambodia's CSD, 123; importance of mobilization in demonstrating influence, 94; official expectations of external actors, 14. *See also* international community
Dorfman, Ariel, 125
double bind, 207(n1)
double contingency, 58(n28), 141–142
Doxtader, Erik, 179–180
drama. *See* official drama
Drexler, Elizabeth, 26
Duggan, Colleen, 20
Durkheim, Emile, 17, 55(n7), 134
Duthie, Roger, 27
dynamic equilibrium, 18, 177–178
dynamic nature of transitional justice, 10–11, 28
dysfunction in transitional justice, 29–30, 48, 136–137

East Timor, 145–146; accessibility of CAVR reports and testimony, 174; consultation process, 72; emulating elements of South Africa's TRC, 37; external pressures on TJ completion, 100; focus on positive deviants, 28; gender issues associated with witness testimony, 106; grammar of nationalism, 170–172; hierarchy of suffering, 82; legacy of mistrust, 24; mobilization and outreach, 16; obligatory participation in TJ, 95–96; unintended consequences of omitting military participation, 26–27; victims' pursuit of personal agendas, 145–146
education: Cambodia's CIVICUS, 124–125; DC-Cam's history text, 120–121; developing a TJ program, 11; school as social space, 57(n21); social mobilization, 45; TJ as pedagogic medium, 59
effectiveness of transitional justice projects: ECCC's hybrid structure, 63; ruptures in official drama, 139–140; South Africa's TRC, 52. *See also* assessments
Egypt: antipathy to the international goodwill approach to TJ, 60–61; moralistic public messages, 89
elements of transitional justice design, 21–22, 51–53, 193–194. *See also* mobilization; outreach
emergent design approach, 115–116
empathy: reaching a settled condition with TJ, 39–40
empowerment of participants: "blackness" in South Africa, 187–188; constructing a contemporary institutionalized TJ project, 35–36; critical evaluation of TJ programs, 42; layers of unintended consequences, 27; politics of victimhood, 90; requirements for preventing recurrence of violence, 51–52; South Africa's government divergence from TJ, 116–118. *See also* victim participation and empowerment
Encyclopedia of Transitional Justice, 32
Eskom lawsuit (South Africa), 187, 191(n15)
ethnic politics, 176
eufunction, 29
European Union (EU) influencing Serbia's domestic politics, 64–66
expectations of transitional justice programs. *See* goodwill and ideals

Index   231

expressivism, 17, 134
external actors, local distrust of TJ and, 23
Extraordinary Chambers in the Courts of Cambodia (ECCC), 3–4; balancing domestic and international laws with ECCC, 61–63; budget outcomes, 130(n5); creating ruptures in official drama, 138; critical newspaper coverage, 84–89; CSD criticism, 123–124; CSD forum questions, 70(table); establishment of, 91(n7); inadequate resources for implementation, 102; layers of meaning in official drama, 162–165; local ownership, 15; negative media evaluations, 86–88; principles of institutionalized TJ, 38–39; public forums exploring locals' perceptions, 68–72; Seng's resignation as a civil party, 125–126; Victims Unit, 118–119

fact-finding forums, 11
failure of transitional justice systems, 5–7; by-products of TJ, 18–19; criticisms of past TJ programs, 40–43; deviations and derivatives from expected steps, 43–44; incorporating obstacles in a TJ design, 194–195; macro level failure of social-engineering projects, 7–8; TJ ideals and actual outcomes, 193–194; translating surface failure into local circumstances, 15. *See also* unintended consequences
fairness, 45
fake transitional justice, 32–34, 36, 67–68
false confessions, 143–145
Fambul Tok (Sierra Leone), 115–116, 197
fear between victims and perpetrators, 24–25
feminist movement, 58(n25)
Fofana, Moinina, 158, 160
Ford Motor Company, 11–112
foreign donors. *See* donors
forgiveness: the ideals and realities of TJ, 24
Foucault, Michel, 15, 59, 75–76
founding myth of nation building, 173–174
framing analysis, 47. *See also* meaning-making in the transitional justice process
Fullard, Madeleine, 117
functionalism, 29

gacaca court (Rwanda), 13, 25; defining, 54(n3); false testimony by perpetrators, 144–145; focus on unintended consequences, 27–28; layers of meaning in official drama, 162; locals' meaning-making, 199–200; overly controlled mobilization, 95–96; religious perceptions framing confessions, 161–162; spontaneous divergence from the TJ program, 198
Geisel, Ernesto, 143
Gellner, Ernest, 173
gender-sensitive issues: model of TJ as a social movement, 106; South Africa's TRC, 36
General Motors, 111
genocide: false confessions, 145; fear and distrust between victims and perpetrators, 24–25
German Development Service (DED), 68
Girard, René, 170, 181–184, 189, 191(n13)
global human-rights regime, 31
global liberalism, 31
global norms: international bias in TJ projects, 63–64
goals of transitional justice projects: constructing a contemporary institutionalized TJ project, 35; crucial elements for prevention recurrence of violence, 51–53; formal failures and successful unplanned practices, 7–9; official expectations of donors, 14; positive data trends, 102–103; TRC's report failing to include, 52. *See also* goodwill and ideals
Gobodo-Madikizela, Pumla, 113
Goffman, Erving, 17, 50, 136, 207(n2)
goodwill and ideals: disagreement surrounding TJ targets, 78–82; discourse analysis, 76–77; divergence of events from the official plans, 193–194; goals of institutional TJ programs, 59–60; limitations of the consultation mechanism, 77–78; locals challenging, 68; moral legitimacy of TJ projects, 89–91; shifting locals' suspicions of TJ, 93–94
Gqozo, Oupa, 148–150
grammar of nationalism, 170–171
Greensboro Truth and Reconciliation Commission, 12–13

Guatemala: accommodating substate nationalism, 176; failure of judicial reform, 42
Gutmann, Amy, 179

Hamber, Brandon, 52
Hanan, Mack, 203
Hasegawa, Kōichi, 105
Hayner, Priscilla, 109
healing as objective for transitional justice, 204–205
hedging discourse, 154–156
A Hero's Journey (Gusmao), 171
hierarchy of suffering, 79–82, 90, 106
high-modern state projects, 7
Hinton, Alexander, 163–164
Historical Truth Commission (Russia), 33–34
Hobsbawm, Eric, 170
human rights: Cambodia's Center for Social Development, 122–126; political exploitation of TJ programs, 14; use of media to promote, 82–83
Human Rights Watch, 87
Hun Sen, 61, 87, 91(n7)
hybrid court system, 3, 56(n12), 62–63, 200–201. *See also* Extraordinary Chambers in the Courts of Cambodia; Khmer Rouge Tribunal

ideal victims, 78, 135, 154–156, 170
ideals. *See* goodwill and ideals
identity: "blackness" in South Africa, 185–190, 191(n14); reaching a settled condition with TJ, 39–40; South Africans' post-conflict racial rivalries, 18; South Africa's Reconciliation Barometer Survey, 113–114; substate nationalism, 18, 53, 170, 176–178, 189. *See also* collective identity
Ieng Sary, 62, 85
Ieng Thirith, 87
The Image: A Guide to Pseudo-Events in America (Boorstin), 203
image of a transitional justice entity, 15
image-making, 203
imagined community, nationalism and, 173–174
implementation of transitional justice: ambiguities as obstructions for, 26; roles and resources, 101–102; success of the public slogan, 51–52. *See also* unintended consequences
indigenous populations, 176; "blackness" in South Africa, 185–190, 191(n14); Canadian Truth and Reconciliation Commission, 13
industrialization of transitional justice, 31–32
ineffective peace building, 6–7
Inkhatha Freedom Party (IFP): black-on-black violence, 77
Institute for Justice and Reconciliation (IJR; South Africa), 113–115
institutional conditions: collective activities and events in a TJ program, 14; defining transitional justice, 12; expectations leading to failure in peace and justice initiatives, 7
institutional transitional justice bodies: construction of contemporary transitional justice programs, 34–40; practical objectives, 37–40; purpose in establishing, 17–18; social conditions that shape a transitional society, 22–27; theoretical framework for unintended consequences, 29–30. *See also specific courts and tribunals*
instrumental norm adopters, 64
instrumentalist approach to nationalism, 173
integration during nation building, 174–175
interdisciplinarity in transitional justice, 11–12
International Bar Association (IBA), 62
International Center for Transitional Justice (ICTJ), 11
international community: external pressures on TJ outcomes, 100–101; foreign viewpoints in Cambodia's ECCC, 87; influencing Serbia's domestic politics, 64–68; local investment and Western intervention, 100; political pressure causing bias for TJ projects, 63–64. *See also* donors
International Criminal Court (ICC), 13; assessment of outcomes, 103; constructing a contemporary institutionalized TJ program, 37–40; importance of outreach and participation, 100; Kenyan indictment case, 109; new justice innovations, 38

International Criminal Tribunal for Rwanda (ICTR), 94, 174
International Criminal Tribunal for the Former Yugoslavia (ICTY): audience challenges to TJ activities, 15; including local society, 37–38; international manipulation of domestic politics, 64–66; local ownership, 46; unanticipated effects, 54(n5)
international tribunals, 12–13; Cambodia's negotiation for, 61–63; local ownership of tribunals, 3

Javanović, Čedomir, 65
judicial reform, failure of Guatemala's, 42

Kaing Guek Eav, 39
Karugarama, Tharcisse, 103
Kelsall, Tim, 153–156, 158, 167(n10), 197
Kenya: relationship between TJRC and civil society organizations, 108–109
ketteyuos (reputation and honor), 163, 165
Khieu Samphan, 62
Khmer Courage Curriculum, 125
Khmer Rouge: politics of victimhood, 79–80
Khmer Rouge Tribunal (Cambodia), 3, 7–8, 61–63, 121. *See also* Extraordinary Chambers in the Courts of Cambodia
Khoisan people, South Africa's, 188–189
Khulumani et al. v. Barclays National Bank et al., 111
Khulumani Support Group, 110–112, 196–198
kick-starting a transitional justice project, 34–35
kinetic social institution, 27, 43
knowledge production, 75–77, 173
Kondewa, Allieu, 158, 160
Koskenniemi, Martti, 134, 204, 207
Kranh, Tony, 39
Ku Klux Klan, 12–13
Kymlicka, Will, 18, 53, 170, 176–178, 189

latent functions, 29, 199
Learning to Labour (Willis), 45
legitimacy: arrogant judges casting doubts on the court's, 138–139; expectation of a self-fulfilling prophecy, 103; fake TJ, 32–34; media covering questioning Cambodia's ECCC's, 86–88; the politics of victimhood, 80–81; propagation of repertoires, 48; ruptures in official drama, 138; Sierra Leoneans' struggles with the court, 197–198; TJ as an authentic and ethical mass medium, 59
Lemonde, Marcel, 85
Lessons Learnt and Reconciliation Commission (LLRC), 34
liberalist justice regime, 100
litigation for symbolic and financial reparations, 111
local context, 7, 22
local government, 100; negative reactions towards TJ, 90–91; public message, 60; transcending South Africa's TRC agenda, 9
localization, 46–48, 72–74; authenticity of positive comments on TJ, 97–99; expanding the transitional justice field to include, 12–13; importance for TJ success, 21–22; local perception of TJ at an NGO forum, 68–69; media influence on TJ perception, 82–89; pastoral mode of power in society, 59; South African consultation process, 73–74; steps in localization of institutionalized TJ, 40
Loromunu (Westerners of East Timor), 82
Lorosa'e (Easterners of East Timor), 82
luck, 45

Ma, Shu-Yun, 175–176
Machimura, Takashi, 105
Madikizela-Mandela, Winnie, 130–131(n10)
Maduna, Penuell, 111
Mamasela, Joe, 143
Mamdani, Mahmood, 77
Mamelodi Four (South Africa), 116–118
Mandela, Nelson, 2, 77–78, 172, 181, 182(fig.), 185
manifest functions, 29
Mannheim, Karl, 130(n2)
mass graves: DC-Cam data gathering, 119; Kosovo Albanians, 67
mass medium, transitional justice as, 59
Mau Buti, 171
Mbeki, Thabo, 77, 111, 116, 185

Index

Mead, George Herbert, 20
meaning-making in the transitional justice process, 207(n2); strategic ambiguity, 202–206; as unintended consequence, 44, 196–202
meaning-supplied processes, 199–200
media: ambivalence between pro-government and political opposition portrayals of TJ, 83–84; critical newspaper coverage of the ECCC, 84–89; declining coverage of Cambodia's justice system, 3–4; influence on transitional justice, 82–89; institutionalization of Cambodia's DC-Cam movement, 122; polysemic nature of, 204; reporting the truth of TJ in a transitional society, 88–89; spin as political propaganda, 195
Medvedev, Dmitry, 33–34
memory politics, transitional justice as, 76–77
Merton, Robert, 29, 103
message. *See* public message
messiness of transitional justice, 8, 13, 22, 48
military: unintended consequences of omitting military in TJ implementation, 26–27
Mills, C. Wright, 16, 97–98, 130(n2)
Milošević, Slobodan, 64–65
mimetic desire, 53, 170, 181–185, 189, 191(n13)
Missing Persons Task Team (MPTT; South Africa), 116–118
mobilization: authenticity of positive comments on TJ, 97–99; basic requirements for TJ design, 21–22; Cambodia's local social movements, 118–119; constructing a contemporary institutionalized TJ project, 35; divergent and official mobilization, 46–48; excluding specific political positions from, 107–108; fake TJ lacking process for, 32–33; increasing significance and importance of, 127–130; local entities' response to official mobilization, 16; locals' vocabulary regarding participation, 99–102; overcontrol of Rwanda's gacaca mobilization, 95–97; propagation of social movement repertoire, 109–110; questioning the model of TJ as social movement, 105–108; Sierra Leone's Fambul Tok, 115–116; as social movement, 103–109; South African History Archive, 112–113; South Africa's Institute for Justice and Reconciliation, 113–115; South Africa's Khulumani Support Group, 110–112; spontaneous participation, 104–105. *See also* divergent mobilization; outreach
Moon, Claire, 77
moral entrepreneurs, 134
moral legitimacy, 89–91, 99
moral repair, 39–40
Mothers of the Plaza de Mayo, 12, 143
motive, vocabularies of, 16, 130(n2)
mourning, 161–162
multiculturalism, South Africa's, 185

narrative therapy, 135–136
nation building: disagreement and sustainable relationships, 181–185; dynamic equilibrium and contentious coexistence, 177; the emerging definition of reconciliation, 179–181; formal goals of TJ, 189; institutional TJ as project for, 170–175; selective remembrance, 171–173; sociology of nationalism, 173–175
National Party (NP), 77
national reconciliation. *See* reconciliation
National Reconciliation Commission (NRC; Thailand), 33, 55(n11)
nationalism: DC-Cam's increasing sense of, 122; grammar of, 170–171; meaning-making around we-them, 205–206; nation and state in a post-conflict setting, 175–177; sociology of, 173–175; substate, 18, 53, 170, 176–178, 189. *See also* collective identity
nation-states in post-conflict settings, 175–177
neoliberalism, 100–102
Nepal: distrust of the judiciary, 24
Neth Pheaktra, 88
niche-targeted advertising, 204
Nigeria: criticism of the TJ process, 42
Nil Nonn, 138

nongovernmental organizations (NGO): applying a hierarchy of victimhood, 80; Cambodia's civil party participation, 163; Cambodia's Khmer Rouge Tribunal, 3; Cambodia's local social movements, 118–119; importance of TJ cooperation with, 108–109; Kenya's TJ attempts, 108–109; public forums in Cambodia, 68–69; South Africa's Institute for Justice and Reconciliation, 113–115

noninstitutional activities defining transitional justice, 12

non-state-level activities defining transitional justice, 12

norm resisters, 64

normalized transitional justice, 13; constructing a contemporary institutionalized TJ program, 35–40; emergence of unintended consequences, 30–32

Norman, Hinga, 158, 160

Norodom Ranariddh, 61

Northern Ireland: public image of ideal victims, 79

Ntsebeza, Dumisa, 113

objectives of institutionalized transitional justice, 37–40

O'Brien, Patricia, 85

Office of Co-Investigating Judges (OCIJ; Cambodia), 85

official drama: actors' miscommunication, 153–1546; basic requirements for TJ design, 21–22; cautious cooperation, 156–157; challenging an official script, 150–153; dual meaning and different roles, 165–167; false confessions, 143–145; multilayered covert performances of invisible scripts, 162–165; performative failures, 147–150; psychological need for, 134–136; pursuit of a personal agenda, 145–146; reasons for producing fictional information, 157–160; reasons for rupture, 137–142; religious experience, 161–162; role expectation and performance, 136–137; roles and events following public announcement, 48–50; strategies and tactics for manipulating, 142–144; truth commissions, tribunals and courts, 133–134; venues and scripts, 16–18; victims creating personal views of collective history, 146–147; victims' pursuit of personal agendas, 145–146

official mobilization, 46–48

open-text advertisements, 204

outreach, 16; basic requirements for TJ design, 21–22; Cambodia's local social movements, 118–119; DC-Cam, 119–120; East Timor's lack of outreach, 72; increasing local support for TJ, 99–100; increasing significance and importance of, 127–130; methods of disseminating information, 94–95; public mediation between courts and individuals, 47; shifting locals' suspicions of TJ, 93–94. *See also* mobilization

Palmer, Nicola, 174

Paris Peace Agreement (1991), 61

Parliamentary Watch Project (Cambodia), 123

Parsons, Talcott, 58(n28), 141–142

pastoral mode of power, 59

Pavković, Nebojša, 65–66

Payne, Leigh, 142–144, 170, 177, 189, 204–205

Peaceland (Autesserre), 6–7

perpetrators: challenging preconstructed scripts, 150–153; critical evaluation of South Africa's TRC, 41; false confessions, 143–145; fear and distrust between victims and, 24–25; government control of witness testimony, 96; politics of victimhood, 79–80; unintended consequences in official drama, 148–150

Peru: emulating elements of South Africa's TRC, 37; the politics of victimhood complicating reparations, 80–81

Pestman, Michiel, 159–160

Petit, Robert, 85, 91(n21)

planning for the unplanned, 10, 207

pluricultural approach to nationhood, 176

political context: Cambodia's negotiation for an international tribunal, 61–63; constraints on local social movements, 118–119

political manipulation: failure of TJ programs, 42–43; fake TJ, 32–34; Rwandan government's control over witness testimony, 96
political opportunity structure theory, 47, 58(n26)
political theater, 136. *See also* official drama
political-opportunity structure, 202
politicization of social movements: DC-Cam, 121
politics of victimhood, 79–82, 90
polysemy in audience interpretations and media content, 204
positive data trends, 102–103
positive deviants, 27–28, 43, 54(n4)
post-colonial governments, 175–176
post-conflict contexts: defining transitional justice, 11–12; emergence of unintended consequences, 30–31; social conditions that shape a transitional society, 22–23
postmodern society: theatrical analysis of official drama, 140–141; unstable authority, 105
The Practice of Everyday Life (Certeau), 46
Preah Vihear, Cambodia, 122
primordial ethos, 173
propagation of movement repertoires, 47–48, 118
protest: Seng's protests against the ECCC, 125–126
The Protestant Ethic and the Spirit of Capitalism (Weber), 28–29, 45, 54(n6)
pseudo-events, 202–203
pseudo-social movement, transitional justice as, 108
pseudo-transitional justice projects, 32–34, 36
psychological need for official drama, 134–136
public message: application of spin, 195; constructing a contemporary institutionalized TJ project, 34–37; deviant perception of, 44–46, 56–57(n19); East Timor's lack of outreach, 72; international community calling for social change, 60–63; messiness of scenarios following, 48–50; moral legitimacy of the senders, 89–91; shifting locals' suspicions of TJ following, 93–94; TRC's failure to reach citizens, 52
public relations (PR), 3; Cambodia's ECCC, 68; East Timor's inadequate consultation and local ownership, 72; impact on foreign donors, 93; mapping out a new TJ program, 35; mobilization of locals, 47; South African consultation process, 73–74; South Africa's consultation process, 74. *See also* outreach
Putnam, Robert, 184

racial issues: "blackness" in South Africa, 185–188, 191(n14); policy design and implementation, 197; victim statements collected from each population group by the South Africa's TRC, 106(table)
rainbow nation, South Africa as, 185
reconciliation, 18; disagreement and sustainable relationships, 181–185; the emerging definition in post-conflict states, 179–181; institutional TJ's official goal, 169–170; interpreting, 56(n14); interracial relationships in post-TRC South Africa, 185–186; requirements for achieving, 51–53; selective remembrance, 171–173; Sierra Leone's Fambul Tok, 115–116; South Africa's affirmative action policies, 189–190; South Africa's Reconciliation Barometer Survey, 113–114
Reconciliation Barometer Survey (South Africa), 113–114
redistribution policy (South Africa), 188
reference individuals, 191(n12)
regime change: responsibility of Western powers for conflict, 60–61
religious perceptions framing confessions, 161–162
Renan, Ernest, 170
reparations: the politics of victimhood complicating, 80–81; South Africa's symbolic and financial reparations, 111
resilience of community, 184–185
resource management, 14; East Timor's lack of, 72; mobilization as social

movement, 104–105; politics of victimhood, 81. *See also* donors
resource mobilization theory, 47, 58(n25)
responsibility for past abuses, 60–61, 79
restorative justice, 55(n9)
restructuring, redefinition, and transformation of identity, 40
retributive justice defining transitional justice, 11
role-playing, 50
Royal Government of Cambodia (RGC), 101
Ruby World Cup (1995), 172
rule of law. *See* democracy and democratization
Russia: political utilization of TJ, 33–34
Rwanda: focus on unintended consequences, 27–28; the ideals and realities of TJ, 24; mobilization and outreach, 16; mutual fear between victims and perpetrators, 24–25; overly controlled mobilization, 95–97; vocabularies of motive in victim interviews, 98

sanctions for nonparticipation of locals, 95–97
scenarios, 48–50
Scott, James, 7–9, 20, 202, 208(n5)
security sector reform (SSR) and disarmament, 12
Seeing like a State (Scott), 7–9, 202
self, sense of, 25
self-fulfilling prophecy, 103, 206–207
self-recovery, 9, 13, 29–30, 44, 194, 197, 207
Sendero Luminoso (Shining Path), 80–81
Seng, Theary, 119, 122–126
sequential model of institutionalized transitional justice, 40, 56(n15)
Serbia: audience challenges to TJ activities, 15; the biased TJ ideal, 63–64; critical evaluation of TJ programs, 42; enlightenment campaign, 107–108; international manipulation of justice discourse, 64–66; moralistic public messages, 89. *See also* International Criminal Tribunal for the Former Yugoslavia
Serious Crimes Process, 72
short-term official projects, 28

Sierra Leone: cautious cooperation in official drama, 156–157; critical evaluation of the special tribunals, 41; divergent dramas, 205; emulating elements of South Africa's TRC, 37; Fambul Tok, 115–116, 197; hedging discourse in official drama, 153–156; motives for witness testimony, 98–99; strategic use of TJ discourse, 67–68
Simmel, Georg, 177
simplification of an object, 8
skepticism, 15, 25–26
Sleuk Rith Institute, 121
Smith, Anthony, 173
social cohesiveness, 18; Durkheim's work on suicide and crime, 55(n7); dynamic equilibrium, 177; ECCC ceremony following TJ completion, 38–39
social conditions shaping a transitional society, 22–27
social control: overly controlled mobilization, 95–97
social integration and reintegration, 35–36, 51–53
social mobility, 45
social movements, 58(n25); Cambodia's Center for Social Development, 122–126; DC-Cam, 119–122; defining, 105; divergence in Cambodian TJ, 118–127; invariable elements of, 105; limits of divergent movements, 126–127; politicization and institutionalization of DC-Cam, 120–122; positive divergences of TJ plan, 202–203; propagation of movement repertoire, 109–118; questioning the model of TJ as, 105–108; spontaneous participation as central agenda, 104–105; TJ mobilization as, 103–109
social norms, 58(n28); international goodwill approach to TJ, 60–63; international political pressure causing bias for TJ projects, 63–64; representation in public space, 5353; role expectation in official drama, 136–137; ruptures in official drama, 141
social phenomenon, TRC as, 196–197
social psychology: development of institutional TJ, 39–40
social recovery, 19, 193–194
social system theory, 141–142

social-engineering projects, 7–10
social-movement theory, 47–48
sociological theory, 15, 19–20
sociopolitical movements defining transitional justice, 12
Sok An, 85
Sonn, Franklin, 187
South Africa: "blackness" in, 185–188, 191(n14); consultation process, 73–74; democratic reciprocity in deliberative democracy, 179; distrust of judicial legitimacy, 24; dynamic equilibrium in interactions of conflict, 18; elements of a contemporary institutionalized TJ program, 36; exclusionist nature of TRC nationalism, 172–173; government divergence from a TJ program, 116–117; Institute for Justice and Reconciliation, 113–115; Khulumani Support Group, 110–112, 196; locals' meaning-making of TJ processes, 200; media influence on TJ, 82–83; as a rainbow nation, 185; South African History Archive, 112–113; spontaneous engagement of locals, 110; unplanned derivatives of the TRC, 196. *See also* Truth and Reconciliation Commission
South Africa Broadcasting Corporation (SABC), 82–83, 113
South African History Archive (SAHA), 112–113, 196–197
sovereign mode of power, 59
Speak Truth to Power: Voices from Beyond the Dark (Dorfman), 125
spectaclization in the media, 88–89
spin, 195
spontaneous engagement of locals, 109–110
Sprizzo, John, 111
Sri Lanka: criticism of the TJ process, 42–43; political utilization of TJ, 34
state-level activities defining transitional justice, 12
Stepakoff, Shanee, 98
strategic action plan, 196
Studzinski, Silke, 138
Subotić, Yelena, 63–64, 66–67
substate nationalism, 18, 53, 170, 176–178, 189

success: incorporating obstacles in a TJ design, 194–195; Weber's view of, 54(n6)
successive inquiry process, 200–201
suicide, Durkheim's work on, 55(n7)
symbols, national building and, 170

Tarrow, Sidney, 104
technical proficiency: ineffectiveness and failure in peace building, 6–7
Teitel, Ruti, 30–31
Thailand, fake TJ and, 33, 55(n11)
Thaksin Shinawatra, 33
theatre of renewal, 134
therapeutic ethics, 170
Thompson, Dennis, 179
Tilly, Charles, 109
Transcultural Psychosocial Organization (TPO Cambodia), 68, 163
transitional justice (TJ), defining, 10–13
"Transitional Justice in a New Era" (Teitel), 30–31
transitional society, social conditions shaping, 22–27
transitional state, defining, 10–11
trauma: self-recovery of locals, 44; sensitivity stemming from distrust and mutual fear, 25. *See also* official drama; victim participation and empowerment
traumatized subjectivity, 25
true believers, 64
truth: assessment of South Africa's TRC, 52; assumption about the effectiveness of truth-telling, 56(n16); discourse analysis, 75–77; hedging discourse, 154–156; media reporting of TJ, 88–89; producing fictional information in official drama, 157–160. *See also* official drama
Truth, Justice and Reconciliation Commission (TJRC; Kenya), 108–109
Truth and Reconciliation Commission (CVR; Peru), 37, 80–81
Truth and Reconciliation Commission (TRC; East Timor), 72, 145–146, 198
Truth and Reconciliation Commission (TRC; South Africa), 182(fig.); archive of the TRC as social phenomenon, 112–113; assumption about the effectiveness of truth-

telling, 56(n16); building public support before implementation, 89; challenging an official script in testimony, 150–153; common elements with Cambodia's KR Tribunal, 5; converting criticisms into local initiatives, 9–10; critical evaluations, 41; declining interest in and effectiveness of, 1–3; defining transitional justice, 10–11; disagreement and sustainable relationships, 181–185; dissidents challenging the goodwill and ideals, 77–78; elements of a contemporary institutionalized TJ program, 36–37; emerging definition of reconciliation, 179–180; five-strand reconciliation model for evaluating, 52; gender issues associated with witness testimony, 106; grammar of nationalism, 171; Khulumani Support Group, 110–112; manipulation of the official drama, 143–145; media influence on TJ perception, 82–83; performative failures in official drama, 148–150; ruptures in official drama, 140; social rebuilding actions, 9; victim statements collected from each population group, 106(table); victims creating personal views of collective history, 146–147; xenophobic exclusionism, 172–173
Truth and Reconciliation Special Report (television broadcast), 83, 113
truth commissions, 13; accessibility of reports and testimony, 174; fake TJ, 33–34; Kenya, 108–109; Peru, 37, 80–81. *See also* East Timor; *entries beginning with Truth and Reconciliation;* Sierra Leone; South Africa
Tutu, Desmond, 2, 78, 161, 181, 182(fig.), 208(n3)

Ubuntu, 186
UN Development Programme, 109, 156–157
unanticipated effects, 27, 54(n5)
unintended consequences, 15; ambiguities as obstructions for TJ implementation, 26; cautious cooperation in official drama, 156–157; fake TJ, 32–34; interpreting impacts on a local society, 21–22; locals' meaning-making as, 198–202; normalization of TJ, 30–32; omitting the military from East Timor's TJ, 26–27; performative failures in official drama, 147–150; resulting from the politics of reconciliation, 179–180; self-recovery of locals, 44; Sierra Leone's Fambul Tok, 115–116, 197; South Africa's Khulumani Support Group, 110–112, 196; theoretical backgrounds and contexts, 27–30; three layers, 27; Weber on capitalism, 54(n6)
United Nations: Cambodia's local distrust of international actors, 23–24; conflicts within Cambodia's ECCC, 85; defining transitional justice, 10–11; ECCC establishment, 62–63; Khmer Rouge representation, 61
United Nations High Commissioner for Human Rights, 100
United Nations Transitional Administration in East Timor (UNTAET), 100, 135. *See also* East Timor
United States influencing Serbia's domestic politics, 65
unplanned derivatives, 196–197
Unsettling Accounts: Neither Truth nor Reconciliation in Confessions of State Violence (Payne), 142–144
US Agency for International Development (USAID), 124

values, expressing in official drama, 151–152
Vann Nath, 88
vernacularization, 28
Vi Houi, 124
victim participation and empowerment: adopting institutional TJ, 21; assessment of outcomes, 103; Cambodia's victims' involvement, 57–58(n24); court and truth commissions, 16–17; critical evaluation of TJ programs, 42; disagreement over goodwill and ideals, 78–82; as emblematic agents for reconciliation, 170; as heroes of war, 171–172; ideal victim, 78; ideal

victims, 78, 135, 154–156, 170; medical treatment of accused Cambodians, 86–87; politics of victimhood, 79–82, 90; responsiveness of TJ to victims, 56(n17). *See also* official drama; witness testimony
Vieira de Mello, Sérgio, 135
Vietnam War Memorial, Washington, DC, 143, 202, 206–207, 208(n4)
vision of a TJ program, 195
vocabularies of motive, 16, 97–98
voluntary surrender, 32

Weber, Max, 28–29, 45, 54(n6), 130(n2)
we-them grouping, 40; evaluating the effectiveness of TJ programs, 52–53; exclusionary discourse of nationalism, 189; language as unifying factor, 175; meaning-making around the concept of "us," 205–206
"Why Testify? Witnesses' Motivations for Giving Evidence in a War Crimes Tribunal in Sierra Leone" (Stepakoff et al.), 98–99
Wildschut, Glenda, 113
Willis, Paul, 45
Wilson, Richard, 165, 180

wise women (South Africa), 36, 106
witness testimony: complications of long examinations, 101–102; constructing a contemporary institutionalized TJ project, 35; discourse analysis, 75; fake TJ lacking, 33; gender issues associated with, 106; locals' vocabulary regarding participation, 99–102; motives for testifying, 97–99; as path to forgiveness, 120; representation in the public sphere, 74–75; Rwandan government's control over, 96; South Africa's Mamelodi Four case, 116–118. *See also* consultation process; official drama; victim participation
World Bank: Guatemala's failed judicial reform, 42

xenophobic exclusionism of South Africa's TRC, 172–173

Yale University, 119
You Bunleng, 84
Youth Leadership Challenge (television program), 124

Zuma, Jacob, 188

About the Book

Though transitional justice has been hailed by many as the best path toward reconciliation and stability in post-conflict and democratizing societies, criticisms of the approach also abound, with a significant number of TJ programs labeled failures.

What accounts for this difference of opinion? How is success measured? Have the societies that sought to implement a plan for TJ followed the trajectory laid out in the policy design phase? And if not, was success sometimes achieved despite this variation—or perhaps because of it? Toshihiro Abe addresses these questions through an exploration of TJ projects at the local level in Africa, Asia, and Europe.

Highlighting the tension between national goals and local realities, and finding unexpected positive outcomes within the context of official failure, Abe provides an important new understanding of the diverse outcomes of TJ policy.

Toshihiro Abe is professor of sociology at Otani University.